What Mad Pursuits!

What Mad Pursuits!

MORE MEMORIES OF A YALE LIBRARIAN

Donald C. Gallup

"What mad pursuit?"

KEATS, *Ode on a Grecian Urn*

NEW HAVEN

The Beinecke Rare Book & Manuscript Library

YALE UNIVERSITY

Library of Congress Cataloging-in-Publication Data

Gallup, Donald Clifford, 1913–
    What mad pursuits! : more memories of a Yale librarian / Donald C. Gallup.
    p. cm.
    Sequel to: Pigeons on the granite.
    Includes bibliographical references and index.
    ISBN 0-8457-3132-7
  1. Gallup, Donald Clifford, 1913–   .
  2. Librarians—Connecticut—New Haven—Biography.
  3. Beinecke Rare Book and Manuscript Library—History.
  4. Libraries—Connecticut—New Haven—Special collections—American literature.
  5. Libraries—Connecticut—New Haven—Special collections—Manuscripts.
  6. Rare book libraries—Connecticut—New Haven—History—20th century.
  I. Gallup, Donald Clifford, 1913–   Pigeons on the granite.
  II. Title.
    Z720.G19A3   1998
    020'.92—dc21
    [B]   98-19324
                                                                      CIP

Acknowledgments appear on pages 298–300.

Contents

Pursuing O'Neill in Elm City and Manhattan

Pursuing Eliot in New Haven, Cambridge, and New York

Illustrations

James Fosburgh, '33. James T. Babb (1953). *Oil on canvas, 50 x 41 inches. Beinecke Library, gift of the Yale Library Associates.*

Pigeons Was People

1924–1988

IF MY *Pigeons on the Granite,* published by the Beinecke Rare Book and Manuscript Library in 1988, had an idiosyncratic title the blame was entirely mine. Christa Sammons and Ralph Franklin, whose concern for the book's production went far beyond that dictated by their official responsibility for it, tried to dissuade me. Christa repeated James Laughlin's opinion, born of long years of experience in publishing at New Directions, that title must always convey subject, preferably in the very first word. But all to no avail: *Pigeons on the Granite* it was from the start, although we did agree to use the subtitle ("Memories of a Yale Librarian") as running head; equating *Pigeons* on the left with T. S. Eliot, Gertrude Stein, and Georgia O'Keeffe on the right offended too violently the Sammons-Franklin sensibilities. I shall leave it, even now, for the reader to discover the explanation for my title. But columbophiles are hereby advised that the Beinecke did *not* sponsor a treatise on pigeons: the book was primarily about people, inevitably of course including me.

Surely Donald Gallup appeared all too often in its 353-plus pages; but there is a figure whose importance to me and to the Yale Library was far greater than is spelt out in my book: James T. Babb. He was university librarian during the first half of my thirty-three-year tenure as curator of the Collection of American Literature, having first become acting librarian in 1942 and then librarian in 1945. He proved himself to be the ideal person for the job at a golden time for Yale.

A whole generation earlier, in 1924, planning for the new Sterling Memorial building and the call to action of Professor Chauncey B. Tinker in his famous Alumni Day speech on *The University Library* had provided a vigorous impulse. Tink made two particular points that are still striking after more than seventy years: "that, for all the millions appropriated for the erection of a new library, no cent [could] be [used] ... for either books, binding, or service to readers";

and "what could be more delightful, what more worthy of a Yale man, than to make himself personally responsible for discovering one of the weaker sections in the [collections of the] Library and filling it?" (And he pointed out that it was not necessary to be a J. P. Morgan to do this.) Under the direct inspiration of the Tinker appeal, an alumni committee on the library was formed, headed by the distinguished business executive Frank Altschul, of the Class of 1908. Its fourteen-man membership was a veritable roster of Yale alumni known to be actively interested in collecting books and manuscripts. Then or in the years soon following, members of that committee gave significant collections and substantial funds designated specifically for the use of the library.

Andrew Keogh, the librarian, had good reason to appreciate that the university, to be worthy of receiving gifts, must furnish proper accommodations for special collections that, from their very nature, had to be protected and used under controlled conditions. And so the plans for the new building provided handsome quarters for the Babylonian Collection, the Coin Collection, the Penniman Library on Education, the Speck Collection of Goethe and Goetheana, the Dickson Collection of Henry Fielding, the Yale Collection of American Literature, the James Fenimore Cooper Collection, and others. Provision was made also for the 1742 Yale Library and the considerable accumulation of rare materials that already existed (Elihu Yale gave us our first illuminated manuscript in 1724).

By a happy coincidence, at just this time funds became available to subsidize the publication of the *Yale University Library Gazette*. Its first issue, in June 1926, was devoted to the Melk Abbey copy of the Gutenberg Bible, just given by Mrs. Edward S. Harkness. The actual opening of the Sterling Library in the fall of 1930 (my freshman year at Yale) was followed in December by the formal reorganization of the alumni committee on the library as the Yale Library Associates, modelled roughly on two already extant similar groups, Les Amis du Louvre in Paris, and the Friends of the Bodleian at Oxford.

Although for several years after Sterling opened, the Yale Collection of American Literature and other special rooms were available to readers only at certain limited hours, their curators having other duties to perform, the Rare Book Room, from the day it first began to serve the public, 23 February 1931, operated on a full-time basis. It was supervised by Professor Tinker, the newly appointed—and unpaid—Keeper of Rare Books, and his able assistant, Miss Emily Hardy Hall. Even though during my undergraduate years I ventured only rarely beyond the nave of the vast Sterling cathedral, I still retain a vivid picture of Miss Hall as she advanced upon the public catalogue, clutching the just-received list of a book dealer, and can hear her cry of triumph as she discovered some new treasure in the open stacks. That is how she and Tink began to fill the Rare Book Room shelves.

The long process of identifying items for transfer to special collections continued—and continues to this day—and some major funds, like those given by Albert H. and Starling W. Childs, were received in the late 1920s and in the 1930s, but the impetus provided by the new building and its inviting empty spaces was hard put to survive the lean years of the Great Depression and the Second World War. By 1945 when Jim Babb became librarian, alumni had returned from the armed forces—and the OSS—and could begin to think once more about books and manuscripts.

Jim was himself a collector (he owned fine collections—of William Beckford, nineteenth-century American fiction, William McFee, Vardis Fisher, and Ernest Hemingway—and of course gave all of them to Yale), and he was especially interested in rare books and manuscripts. He and Tink knew very well that most of the available library funds had to be used for bread-and-butter purposes—salaries; purchase of the current books and periodicals in all the fields of knowledge that a large university library must cover in order to attract faculty and teach students; and the not inconsiderable cost of binding. Both men knew that it would not be just the number but, even more importantly, the quality of its books and manuscripts that would establish Yale among the great libraries of the world. And that quality could be enormously improved by taking advantage of the expertise of friends who were forming major collections and would be willing to give them to Yale if they could be assured that their gifts would be cared for and used with the proper respect. And so Jim emphasized all through his librarianship the vital importance of the Library Associates, doing his best to interest other alumni and book collectors in Yale. Paul Mellon, John Hay Whitney, David Wagstaff, Louis M. Rabinowitz, Dr. Arthur E. Neergaard, William Robertson Coe, Henry Taylor, James Osborn, Thomas E. Marston, the Rosenblooms, the Beineckes—these are only a few of the individuals who, encouraged by Jim Babb's enthusiasm and interest, gave collections to Yale. He played a major role in the decision of members of the Beinecke family to give funds for the building that bears their name—which, in turn, provided impetus for a new avalanche of gifts when it opened in 1963.

Jim was fortunate in finding talented people to help him: Fritz Liebert and Marjorie Wynne to carry on after Chauncey Tinker and Emily Hall in the Rare Book Room; Alec Vietor in the Map Collection; Archibald Hanna, Jr., in Western Americana; Tom Marston in classics; Dick Gimbel in aeronautics; and Jim Osborn and Curt von Faber du Faur for their own collections. Jim Babb was properly concerned as well for the hundreds of thousands of books on the open shelves, tended by Gordon Kenefick in circulation; Donald Wing in accessions; Henry M. Fuller for a tragically brief stint as head reference librarian, and Dorothy F. Livingston as chief of the catalogue department.

Having found qualified persons he could trust, Jim Babb had the expert administrator's gift of being able to delegate authority, while at the same time, in an unobjectionable, not too obtrusive way, keeping himself well informed as to what was going on. If a subordinate like me had little talent for fund raising, Jim was willing to take on responsibility for this difficult but essential part of a curator's job. Although a surprising number of outstanding collections did come to Yale as gifts and bequests, especially in the years just after World War II, still some acquisitions cost what were at the time very considerable amounts of hard cash. I remember particularly the campaign that Jim masterminded in 1954 for the purchase of eight spectacular medieval illuminated manuscripts, six of them once in the collection of Sir Thomas Phillipps, probably the most famous manuscript collector of all time. The Art Gallery, the Library of the School of Music, alumni, friends, faculty members, and library staff all joined in. Several of them contributed to the descriptive report, printed in the *Gazette*,★ of what they called "one of the most important additions to the Yale University Library in its history":

> Yale has had no collection in this field that could be regarded as adequate; but such is the excellence of the present acquisition that this defect hardly exists any longer. More material of the same sort may come to us in the future; but the superb quality of what we now have is not likely ever to be surpassed. ... the very level of the Library has been raised.

Jim's eagerness to add to our resources for research was contagiously persuasive. The apparent ease with which he secured necessary funding was deceptive, and I did not in *Pigeons* give him sufficient credit for making possible some key additions to the Collection of American Literature during my curatorship—the William Carlos Williams and Edmund Wilson papers, for example.

Jim could be, now and then, a stern taskmaster. The few occasions on which this aspect was revealed were so remarkable that I may perhaps be forgiven for mentioning two of them even though it was not I but Marjorie Wynne who was most directly concerned. The first involved the *Mellon Chansonnier*, a unique collection of late fifteenth-century French songs, one of Yale's treasures, given in 1940 by Paul Mellon. The manuscript was published in facsimile in 1979, but up to that year was required viewing by students in various courses in the School of Music. The day before a group was scheduled to visit the Rare Book Room (in the pre-Fritz Liebert period), Marjorie, who had the responsibility of producing the manuscript, discovered to her consternation that it was no longer in its proper place. She herself examined every item in the manuscript vault in an effort to locate the missing volume, but in vain. In desperation, she began to consider the terrible eventuality that it might have been stolen, and decided that she must report the disappearance to her boss. His reaction was characteristic: he reassured her that of course the manuscript had not been stolen, it must be somewhere in the

---

★"Eight Medieval Manuscripts," by several members of the faculty and the library staff. *Yale University Library Gazette* (Jan. 1955), [99]–112, with 5 plates.

Rare Book Room; and then, in his blunt and seemingly not very sympathetic fashion, he gave Marjorie an ultimatum: she must find the *Mellon Chansonnier* in time to produce it for the Music School class even if she had to spend the entire twenty-four hours looking for it.

She returned to the Rare Book Room on the verge of tears, crushed by the enormity of the problem confronting her (the collection even then contained some 130,000 volumes). When the curator of American literature happened to drop by, he was welcomed effusively as a friend in distress and was told of the crisis. The manuscript, when last seen, had been contained in a cloth folding-box, the height of which was given on the catalogue card as 22.5 centimeters. Armed with a measuring stick of exactly that length, he started at the beginning of the book vault, removing from the shelf and examining every item contained in a case of the given height. Within five minutes, not far along in the section devoted to English literature, he found the *Chansonnier* box with the manuscript in place inside it, shelved as a first edition of George Meredith. (In the Rare Book Room, call-number labels were not pasted to books or even to cases; instead the number was typed on a slip laid into the book with the number protruding. Somehow the tag belonging to the Meredith first edition had fallen from the book and was mistakenly inserted, by some bursary assistant whose mind was not on what he was doing, in the box containing the *Chansonnier*.) When the YCAL curator came up from the book vault, waving the volume, and asked whether anyone had been looking for it, both were given an incredulous but warm welcome by a much relieved rare book librarian. I'm sure that the Music School class when it arrived the next day had no inkling of how close it had come to not being able to see the famous manuscript.

The second occasion during which long-suffering Marjorie Wynne encountered the harshness of James T. Babb grew out of the unauthorized printing of some material housed in the manuscript division of the New York Public Library. Selected correspondence addressed to the lawyer-collector and friend of authors, John Quinn, had, by the provisions of his will, been transcribed under the supervision of his secretary, Jeanne Robert Foster. The transcripts were bound into thirteen volumes and deposited in the library in 1938 for use by scholars—but under certain rigidly enforced restrictions designed to safeguard, for a period of fifty years, the property rights and privacy of the authors concerned. Important letters of J. M. Synge, James Joyce, A. E. Housman, T. S. Eliot, and other Irish, British, and American writers became a gold mine for scholars seeking information to give added interest and significance to doctoral dissertations and learned books.

One individual who was allowed access to the Quinn transcripts and who signed the required agreement not to copy or publish any of the letters was Peter Kavanagh, brother of the Irish poet, Patrick Kavanagh. He decided that, in spite of the embargo on publication, some passages were so important that they must be publicized, because John Quinn, in his words, "deserved better than the obscurity of the Manuscript Room of the New York Public Library." Possessed of an apparently photographic memory, he read a volume of the correspondence in three one-hour sessions each day over a period of thirteen work days. After each session, he left the building, retired to Bryant Park, and there wrote out on scratchpads the quotations that he had memorized. In this way he accumulated one hundred and sixty excerpts. These he proceeded to put into type on a handpress that he had built himself and set up in his two-room flat on East 29th Street. By dint of long, hard work, he managed eventually to print one hundred twenty-nine copies of a pamphlet of fifty-two pages, entitled *The John Quinn Letters: A Pandect*, binding them himself in wrappers. He gave a few copies to close friends, sent one to the British Museum, and announced that he would offer the remainder to libraries and "recognized" collectors at thirty-five dollars a copy.

Of course the New York Public Library was quick to react, as it was bound to do under the terms governing the deposit of the letters in its manuscript division, suing for an injunction to prevent Kavanagh's proposed distribution of his pamphlet. On Sunday, 17 January 1960, the affair was featured on the front page of the *New York Times*.

I, as both collector and bibliographer of T. S. Eliot, was extremely eager to acquire a copy of the pirated pamphlet and, early the next morning, I telephoned John Kohn of the Seven Gables Bookshop in New York to see what could be done. John actually talked with Kavanagh, but was told that, pending the resolution of the lawsuit, no additional copies would be released. I was in New York only a few days later for a meeting of the Bibliographical Society of America held at the Grolier Club, and decided that nothing could be lost and something might possibly be gained from talking to Kavanagh myself—of course in a strictly private capacity and not as a representative of Yale. I found him at home in his third-floor walk-up, where he showed me his printing press and, stacked in a corner, the copies of the Quinn pamphlet. We talked at some length. I explained that, as bibliographer of Eliot, I was eager to record details of the publication, containing, as it had been reported to do, selections from Eliot's letters; and as a collector of Eliot first editions, I'd very much like, if at all possible, to secure a copy. He did allow me to set down some of the data I needed; but I failed to persuade him to let me have a copy of the booklet, and was obliged to leave empty-handed.

That evening, at the Grolier Club, Jim Babb was summoned to the telephone to answer a reporter from the *New York Times*, checking Kavanagh's gleeful announcement to the paper that a representative of the Yale Library had, that very afternoon, bestowed its blessing on the crime that the New York Public Library was trying to prosecute. Unfortunately, Marjorie Wynne, also in town for the BSA meeting, had visited the NYPL that afternoon and, in the Berg Collection, had discussed the Kavanagh affair with her friend Lola Szladits. Quite undeservedly, Marjorie became branded with the awful stigma of having given Yale's endorsement to the piracy. Jim let her know that he did not approve, and she was once again very much upset. The following morning, in New Haven, he discovered that it was I who had been the culprit, and he summoned me to his office. Because I had made it quite clear to Kavanagh that, although employed by Yale, I was speaking with him solely as a private individual, I did not share completely Jim's feeling that I had been guilty of acting against the best interest of continued friendly relations with our sister institution in Manhattan.

(The New York Supreme Court eventually required Kavanagh to destroy all but twelve copies of the Quinn pamphlet. Counsel had checked the excerpts as printed against the library's typed copies and found them to be "almost verbatim," thus paying tribute to a truly remarkable feat of memory. In 1966, one of the surviving copies was accepted as a gift by the Library of Congress. Two years later, B. L. Reid's biography, *The Man from New York: John Quinn and His Friends*, published in both New York and London by Oxford University Press, quoted extensively from the letters, of which the originals had been given earlier in 1968 to the New York Public Library by Quinn's niece, Mrs. Thomas Conroy. Reid's book and the attendant publicity concerning the manuscript of *The Waste Land*, given by Eliot to Quinn, bequeathed by him to his sister, then by her to her daughter, Mrs. Conroy, and subsequently purchased from her by the Berg Collection, effectively rescued Quinn from the obscurity that Peter Kavanagh had feared might be his fate.)

Most of my activities as collector and bibliographer have not been so controversial. They led to a long and much valued friendship with Frances Steloff, who died at the age of 101 in 1989. (A film on her activities as bookseller was nominated in the preceding year for a Motion Picture Academy Award.) When I began to collect first editions, Frances was the foremost American dealer in the "moderns," and her Gotham Book Mart, first on 49th and then on 47th Street in New York, was a mecca for young people interested in Eliot, James Joyce, Henry Miller, Ezra Pound, Gertrude Stein, and other contemporary writers. It was in November 1936 that Frances wrote me about a copy of Eliot's third book of poems, *Ara Vus Prec* (1919), number 48 of the 220 unsigned copies, this one for some reason signed by Wyndham Lewis. She had laid into the copy to sell with it a holograph postcard from Eliot to John Rodker, printer and publisher of the book. This read in its entirety:

18 Crawford Mansions
Crawford St. [London] W. 1

3. 10. 19

It has just occurred to me that the title *ARA VUS PREC* would do, for it is noncommittal about the newness of the contents, and unintelligible to most people.

T. S. Eliot

Frances felt that twenty-five dollars for the two items was a reasonable price, and I certainly agreed that it was by no means exorbitant, for the postcard was the origin of an error in the title. It should have been *Ara Vos Prec*, as the Provençal phrase is quoted in the *Divine Comedy,* but Eliot had been using an edition of Dante of which the editor, like him, did not know that in Provençal there is no such word as "*vus.*" I ordered the book and postcard by return mail, but, alas! another collector had called at the shop, seen the book, and purchased it—from a clerk who was not aware that Frances had already offered it to me. So far as I know, that copy and postcard have still not surfaced, although the text of the card was printed, from my typed copy, in the first volume of the Eliot *Letters* in 1988.

Frances at one time owned another prize that I also failed to acquire. This was the broadside, designed by E. McKnight Kauffer and posted at the New York World's Fair in 1940 in a show of pictures of the bombing of London. It printed Eliot's "Lines Written to Accompany This Exhibition of Photographs"—later included in his *Collected Poems* as "Defence of the Islands." Frances added a postscript to a letter to me early in 1941: "When you come in again remind us to show you an Eliot item not for sale." On my next visit to the shop she showed me the broadside, explaining that she was not at liberty to sell it because Ted Kauffer had given it to her personally. (It was he who had devised the sign that hung above the door of her shop, illustrating its motto, "Wise Men Fish Here.") I took down the details that I needed for the *Bibliography,* and accepted without question her statement that she could not let me have the item.

It is extremely rare: only a very few copies were printed and those on poor paper. Some years later, after Kauffer's death, still having seen only one other copy—that owned by the artist himself—I ventured to try to persuade Frances to change her mind. To my surprise she said that she would have been glad to let me have the broadside but, unfortunately, in the move of the shop from 49th to 47th Street, it had been misplaced; if it ever turned up she would see that it was offered first to me. I continued to remind her about it whenever I visited the shop. On one of those occasions, she commented that when she had first shown the broadside to me, I should have put it under my arm and walked off. Of course, in 1941, I'd never have dared risk displeasing her in that way.

Her copy of the rare sheet never did turn up, so far as I know, but another one is now in the Yale Collection of American Literature in the Beinecke Library. In the early 1960s Marion Dorn, Ted Kauffer's widow, gave the copy that Eliot had inscribed for her to the Pierpont Morgan Library, along with the autograph draft of the poem itself. (The library had acquired Eliot's letters to the Kauffers in 1956.) Because the broadside "did not really belong in the Morgan Library," the director, Fred Adams (Yale '32), and the trustees waited until Marion Dorn was dead and then gave the item to Yale "In honor of Donald Gallup's bibliographical studies of the work of T. S. Eliot." It was most gratefully received.

In *Pigeons on the Granite* I wrote briefly about a *New Haven* bookseller, Robert J. Barry, Sr., and the firm of C. A. Stonehill. The shop, at first on the ground floor and then upstairs in the J. Press building on York Street, was important to me in the early years of my book collecting. Indeed, I was even for a brief time a Stonehill employee, and worked, while I was in the graduate school, on the preparation of one of the firm's catalogues. (Among many attractive items we listed were some Joyce manuscripts that had been originally the property of Sylvia Beach, the first publisher of *Ulysses*. They were sold, I am happy to say, to John Slocum, and eventually came to the Yale Library as part of the Eileen and John J. Slocum Collection of James Joyce.)

After I had left New Haven and had begun to teach English at Southern Methodist University in Dallas, I acquired through Bob Barry a copy of Ezra Pound's rare first book, *A Lume Spento* (Venice,

LINES WRITTEN BY T. S. ELIOT

TO ACCOMPANY
THIS EXHIBITION OF PHOTOGRAPHS

Let these memorials of built stone—music's
enduring instrument, of many centuries of
patient cultivation of the earth, of English
verse

be joined with the memory of this defence of
the islands

and the memory of those appointed to the grey
ships—battleship, merchantman, trawler—
contributing their share to the ages' pavement
of British bone on the sea floor

and of those who, in man's newest form of gamble
with death, fight the power of darkness in air
and fire

and of those who have followed their forebears
to Flanders and France, those undefeated in defeat, unalterable in triumph, changing nothing
of their ancestors' ways but the weapons

and those again for whom the paths of glory are
the lanes and the streets of Britain:

to say, to the past and the future generations
of our kin and of our speech, that we took up
our positions, in obedience to instructions.

T. S. Eliot

T. S. ELIOT

9th June, 1940

Marion v. Dönis Copy.

1908). But my commitment then to collecting Pound was not absolutely one hundred percent, and when Bob later offered me presentation copies of three early first editions of Eliot, inscribed to the critic Edgar Jepson and his wife Susan, I could afford them only by returning the *A Lume Spento* for credit. (Years later, through George Kirgo, who was also for a short but memorable period a New Haven bookseller, I acquired a second copy of *A Lume Spento*, this one with a presentation inscription to a fellow student at the University of Pennsylvania. I thus gained the distinction of being probably the only private collector who has owned two copies of Pound's first book. I gave that copy to Yale in 1986.)

An expensive Eliot item, also offered by Bob Barry, that I was not, alas! able to purchase was the famous first portrait by Wyndham Lewis. The painting had gained a good deal of notoreity because, when a committee of the Royal Academy in London refused to permit it to be hung in an exhibition of contemporary British painting, a fellow artist, Augustus John, then much better known than Lewis, resigned from the academy in protest. In Dallas, Texas, in 1938, I had read some of the news stories of the fracas caused by John's resignation, and was astonished to receive a telegram from Bob Barry, relaying Charles Stonehill's offer of the picture. Because the price was the exact equivalent of my entire year's salary at SMU, I was obliged to decline, albeit reluctantly. The painting was subsequently sold to the museum at Durban, South Africa, and has been widely exhibited. Forty years later, in 1978, when a handsome drawing for the portrait was to be sold at auction in London, I asked Anthony Rota to try to buy it for me. I had the slight satisfaction of being the underbidder, but the drawing went to join the painting in Durban.

Although the fact that Bob Barry, Jr. specialized in material of earlier periods than the twentieth century meant that I had little dealing as a collector with the Stonehill bookshop after his father ceased being active, my relationship with the firm flourished again for an all-too-brief period when Henry W. Wenning was a partner. Henry revived the firm's interest in contemporary books and manuscripts, and for a few years he and his learned catalogues added a great deal to my life both as collector and librarian. Henry had earlier under-

T. S. ELIOT

&

EZRA POUND

COLLABORATORS IN LETTERS

by

DONALD GALLUP

HENRY W. WENNING / C. A. STONEHILL, INC.

NEW HAVEN

1970

taken also a publication program, and issued in 1966 a limited first edition of *The Blowing of the Seed*, by the West-Coast poet William Everson (formerly Brother Antoninus). When an article I had written about the Eliot-Pound friendship appeared in the *Atlantic Monthly* for January 1970, the magazine's policy made it impossible to include the two hundred sixty-eight footnotes with which my account was perhaps somewhat *over*-documented. In November, the firm of Henry W. Wenning/C. A. Stonehill reprinted the article in pamphlet form accompanied by every one of the notes. Henry's departure from New Haven to re-enter the world of finance was a great loss to the trade in contemporary books and manuscripts. His death in 1987 was much regretted by all those who had had the good fortune to enjoy his friendship.

I could go on almost indefinitely with anecdotes of my experiences as librarian, collector, editor, and bibliographer. Some of those given here were actually deleted from *Pigeons on the Granite* by those coldhearted editors Ralph Franklin and Christa Sammons. I hope that any reader who happens to run across the book will find it worth the time spent in looking at or even—dare I hope?—reading it.

Albert Sterner. Owen F. Aldis (1908). *Conté and black crayon on paper, 20 x 15 inches. Beinecke Library, gift of Mrs. Aldis.*

YCAL, the *BAL*, and Jacob Blanck

1911–1991

I

ON 23 FEBRUARY 1910, Owen Franklin Aldis, a graduate of Yale in the Class of 1874 and a distinguished Chicago lawyer and realtor, wrote the Reverend Anson Phelps Stokes, secretary of the university:

I beg to acknowledge with thanks the copy of [P.K.] Foley's Bibliography [*American Authors, 1795–1895* (1897)] duly checked. ... After a hasty glance at it I should say the Yale Library contains a large number of the commoner books but few of the rare ones; also, I suppose, few if any presentation copies. ... My idea of the best arrangement if satisfactory to you and Mr. Schwab [*the librarian*] is as follows.—As soon as I have completed my catalogue and have had all books of any consequence covered properly with wrappers of various colored cloth, to give the whole collection to the University. ... I do not however wish it to be mixed with so-called Americana, Indians, and all that kind of matter. What I am undertaking is simply a collection of American literature in first editions, and the word literature being used in the restrictive sense. It would not for instance, bar Daniel Webster's speeches, or some of Jonathan Edwards Sermons. But it would leave out the Mathers, the frightful funeral elegies of our forefathers and many other books of the kind. In other words let it be an alcove devoted to Belles-Lettres only or attempts at Belles-Lettres.

I am willing to follow on a trail of this kind to the end and spend all the money I can afford to make it as perfect as possible. ...

The Yale Library reminds me of a Natural History Museum of which I was once trustee. It had a white rhinoceros skull but no specimens of the common earthworm. Now your collection of Russian and Japanese books is fine. But you need first editions of all the little, poor, crawling American authors put up and preserved for future generations in as perfect a form as possible.

The gift of some six thousand volumes of first and important editions followed in November 1911 and was duly shelved in a separate alcove in the Old Library (now Dwight Hall). Of course Aldis had

had to rely upon dealers to supply him with books and manuscripts. From 1903 until 1909 he seems to have bought principally from Foley himself, who had begun business in Boston in 1896. Although the first large purchases for Aldis were in the sales of C. F. Libbie & Co. in that city, Foley relied as a rule not so much upon auctions as on scouts, advertisements (particularly in country newspapers), and the descendants of authors and their publishers. He wrote to Aldis on 12 July 1909:

I have already compiled new lists of the books still wanted, and have forwarded them to trusty hands. Wholesale advertising has not proved successful, and the communication forwarded direct to him whom we look upon as likely to supply our wants is far more effective than such information, should it reach him in a more general way, and as if *he* were only one of many. ...

I have used such means as I thought most effective to reach survivors of ... old-time publishing houses, but am met by the information that very little importance was attached to an author's work, soon as it passed through the printer's hands. ... However, I still have some hope of reaching members of the families—members who were not connected with the *business,* and therefore all the more likely to appreciate letters etc.

Occasionally, Foley's advice to Aldis was, from our modern point of view, reprehensible. These passages are from letters of 1906:

[William Allen] Butler's "Parnassus," as you will perceive, is water-stained, but the paper is good and will bear cleansing, so as to leave it as clean as issued; I do not recommend cleansing as a rule, but this little thing has proved such a will-o'-the-wisp that I thought it better to secure the copy ... .

[Lydia Huntley] Sigourney's "Whisper [to a Bride]" came in second-edition form and, considering its fine condition, I thought it perhaps better to attach it; should an unsatisfactory copy of the first appear, the binding will be worth having. "Richard Hurdis" ([William Gilmore] Simms) was in rather unsatisfactory state, so I sent an odd Volume I which I happened to have, that your binder may substitute the concluding leaves for those which are stained in the other.

And this from 1908:

Longfellow's "Evangeline" is a third edition, but if I remember rightly your first was not quite satisfactory, and the text of the third being the same as the first, except the advertisements, perhaps the cover etc. of that which I send may be of great aid.

But I am being unfair to both men in pointing out these few survivals of nineteenth-century collecting methods. Only one of Foley's suggestions was actually carried out by Aldis, and the exhaustive campaign which both collector and bookseller waged for the improvement of copies resulted in a relatively high standard of condition for the period during which the collection was assembled; the number of books in original boards or wrappers is considerable, and the dozens of unique and out-of-the-way items that Foley supplied are extremely impressive.

Although his bibliography contained errors, it continued for years to be a very useful tool. And Foley's letters to Aldis (fortunately preserved in YCAL) contain occasional corrections of his work. On 12 July 1909, he wrote:

Regarding the "wants," you may cancel "William Guthrie," 1798, by [William] Dunlap ... . I thought the crime of placing the little load on Dunlap's shoulders was mine—but on examination find that Sabin's Dictionary was at fault, and that I merely borrowed the fault therefrom. You can also strike out Julia Ward Howe's "Golden Eagle," 1876, which was written by J. *B.* Howe, and her "Hyppolytus," 1858, which is believed to have been acted *from manuscript* and never printed. Halpine's two Dublin titles, 1870, also take rank among the books which were projected, but never assumed tangible shape.

I have done considerable prowling after some of these waifs and strays and believe, in time, I shall assume the form of a point of interrogation! Besides wrestling with references in American libraries, colleges, etc., I have sprinkled similar enquiries through sources of information in England, Ireland and Scotland—and some of my correspondents begin to show signs of weariness. If I could divorce myself from the grind for a whole year, and go into the thing regardless of cost (time, labor, currency, etc.), I think much might be accomplished in gleaning hidden facts—but that is a task which I dream of, rather than expect to accomplish.

A letter from Aldis which made a complimentary reference to the bibliography occasioned a revealing reply from Foley. It is dated 28 August 1909:

I thank you, sincerely and gratefully, for your kind words, whilst feeling conscious—there is none more so—that neither my performance nor self merit them. The twelve years which have passed since the appearance of that magnum opus (bless the mark!) have convinced me of how ill prepared I was for the task. But travelling a road unexplored, except by travellers whose suggestions were so often worse than useless, because mislead-

ing, and with no real guide save instinct one only wonders that the performance was not even worse ... .

Yes—first editions must, I suppose, be acknowledged dull, but not
entirely separated from the glow of romance ... .

If the two men had had another five years in which to work on
the collection, one wonders what the result might have been. As
early as 8 June 1909, before Aldis's extensive purchases at major auction sales later that year, Foley (who, next to its owner, probably
knew the collection best) could write:

Yale College Library will possess the best representative collection of
American literature, in its first published form, in the land—this is no
figure or flower of speech, either. Many of the items are not duplicated
elsewhere, without mentioning the unique feature which is formed by the
addition of letters and manuscripts relating to the authors' works, and in so
many cases to the volume which shelters the manuscript or the letter itself.
It will, indeed, form a princely gift, and in what form could one prefer to
be remembered than in connection with a gift which will endear him to
generation and generation!

Aldis was from the first insistent that the collection at Yale not be
called by his own name in order that others might be more willing
to add to it, and the conditions which he laid down were those
under which he believed its growth might be most rapid. A separate
room with accommodations for students was to be provided; a special custodian was to be appointed; and no stamp or mark or writing
of any kind was to be made in or upon any of the books.

Being pretty well acquainted with the peculiarities of book collectors
[he wrote to Professor Emeritus T. R. Lounsbury on 27 November 1911], it ...
seemed to me important to impress upon their minds that the collection
would be carefully cased, guarded and preserved, in a scrupulously clean
and perfect condition; and therefore, I inserted certain conditions about
such matters into the gift, so that the University Library could get all the
collectors and book worms on its side!

He outlined even more concrete plans for the growth of the collection in a letter to Librarian J. C. Schwab on 28 December:

My intention was ... to try to make this collection bibliographically complete, and one containing not only the rare books but all books,—that is,
first editions and collected editions, so as to make it useful ... and perhaps
indispensable to bibliographers, biographers, historians and students of

American literature; to protect it thoroughly, and to so shelve it that it might be used with the utmost possible convenience. ...

An earlier letter, of 20 December, had pointed out that

many of these books are not expensive or rare and yet I think they ought to be in this collection. In a word I should be glad to see the Library add ... whatever proper material it has in good condition of American Belles Lettres of first editions from the earliest period down to and including the Authors living and writing in the year 1900. The fact that such books may be cheap or not valuable from a money point of view has little or nothing to do with their value for the scholarly study of American Literature.

Aldis therefore proposed first that all books not already protected be put into cloth wrappers *at his expense* and the whole collection arranged under author, chronologically; then, that an exact list be made of all titles, including such as could be added from the Yale Library. When this work was completed, he would send to Yale "a reasonably intelligent person of some bibliographical experience" who would go over the principal authors with the latest and best bibliographies, and make careful lists of all gaps to be filled. With such lists, proper advertising, and the aid of Foley and other booksellers, Aldis expected to continue the work of collecting even though he could (because of eye trouble) give the matter very little personal attention. "It seems to me foolish," he wrote to Schwab,

to go on without a clear and definite plan in the expenditure of money at random on rare books. I never have collected in this way and do not wish to begin now. ... We shall doubtless lose some ... books by this delay, but in the end will more than make up ... by having a systematic plan for buying and filling gaps in an orderly way.

It was in the matter of the proposed transfer of books from the stacks that the plans came to grief. The library simply did not have sufficient funds to replace volumes transferred and did not feel that they could be withdrawn from circulation—particularly in the undergraduate library. But Aldis became insistent on this point, and eventually refused to continue buying for Yale until a list of books transferred was sent him. This was never done, and as a result several hundred titles which were being held by Foley and other dealers pending the consolidation of the collection were never purchased. One of these was William Cullen Bryant's rare first publication, *The Embargo* (1808), which Foley had turned up and offered for the collection at $2500.* Although Aldis was tempted, he felt that he did not wish to make even an offer to Foley until his preliminary conditions were met by Yale. Had not the First World War intervened, they might have been, but from 1918 until he died in Paris in 1925, Aldis spent most of his time in France and was no longer actively in touch with the collection.

Even when I became curator in 1947, more than thirty-six years after the arrival of the Aldis books at Yale (although the collection of which they are the nucleus had been increased approximately fourfold), they had not been completely catalogued—a situation which had resulted in Yale's holdings not being adequately known among book people and scholars generally. The donor's plan for a collection that would be bibliographically complete was still very far from realization. But although the general development had not been so rapid as he had hoped it would be, additions to the first editions and manuscripts of individual authors, like Clemens, Cooper, and Whitman—to mention only three of the most important—had caused those sections to take their place among the most distinguished in the world.

In 1947 I wrote of "the impossible goal of bibliographical completeness," but pointed out that

the most difficult part of the task of collecting had already been finished in 1911. The collection is in effect a memorial not only to its founder but also to the Boston bookseller who contributed so substantially to its accumulation. ... It is fitting that future bibliographers, biographers, and historians, coming to appreciate the resources of this collection of books and manuscript material, should apply not only to Aldis but to Foley himself those words from his letter already quoted: "... in what form could one prefer to be remembered than in connection with a gift which will endear him to generation and generation!"

---

*We were fortunately able to purchase a copy of the Bryant pamphlet, in the very first year of my YCAL curatorship, at a price considerably less than $2500.

II

As the field of "American literature" continued inexorably to expand with the advance of the United States into the twentieth century, the need for a bibliographical guide to continue, correct, and expand Foley's *American Authors* became ever more apparent. In 1925 Merle Johnson published the first of his one-volume compilations of *American First Editions,* which, after his death, continued to be "revised and enlarged" by Jacob Blanck. Lyle Wright, limiting himself to *American Fiction* in first edition, began (1939) with the period 1774 to 1850. Although Johnson attempted to indicate "points" of state and issue, neither he nor Wright gave much more information about each book than author, title, publisher, date, and pagination.

In the very early 1940s, Blanck, admitting that "no bibliographical work compiled by a solitary worker could be better than reasonably adequate," proposed that the Bibliographical Society of America supervise his compilation of a much more detailed and comprehensive American bibliography. When the Lilly Endowment, Inc., of Indianapolis, agreed to fund the project, the society appointed a committee to serve in the supervisory role. One of the foremost collectors of American literary first editions, Carroll A. Wilson, was made chairman, and the other members were James T. Babb (Yale), Clarence S. Brigham (American Antiquarian Society), William A. Jackson (Harvard), and David A. Randall (then head of Scribner's rare book department in New York, subsequently librarian of the Lilly Library, Bloomington, Indiana). When Wilson died in 1947, Frederick B. Adams, Jr., director of the Pierpont Morgan Library, New York, succeeded him as chairman. Adams's successors were, in 1969, William H. Bond and, in 1982, Roger E. Stoddard, both librarians of the Houghton Library at Harvard.

At a conference sponsored by the Bibliographical Society of America held at the Houghton Library on 2 May 1992, the successful completion of the fifty-year project was celebrated. In his talk on "Jacob Blanck and *BAL,*" Bill Bond gave a graphic account of some initial complications that had involved Yale:

Jacob Blanck at work on the BAL. *Photograph by Sol. M. Malkin.*

As soon as *BAL* was announced as a soundly funded enterprise, others tried to get in on the act. One of them, Gilbert M. Troxell, curator of the Yale Collection of American Literature, did his best to unseat Jacob Blanck as compiler of the bibliography. Troxell claimed to have a very similar work in process of compilation, supposedly a revision of Foley, though later no convincing evidence of it was forthcoming. ... Pending the resolution of this problem, Troxell appeared on the letterhead with the title of "Consultant."

In the early days, the committee met as frequently as busy men could manage, with both Jake and Troxell in attendance. Jake was asked to compile a sample list in approximately the form eventually adopted for *BAL*. Bret Harte was the chosen author; there was no reliable bibliography of Harte, and plenty of material was to be found in New York, New Haven, Worcester, and Cambridge. Jake consulted them all, and produced a typescript of just over sixty single-spaced pages circulated to the committee just before a decisive meeting was to be held in Worcester on 17 June 1944.

He had ample reason to suspect that an attempt would be made to oust him, and he took precautions. ...

Troxell, who had been expected to attend the meeting, bowed out at the last minute but gave a small sheaf of notes to his superior officer, Jim Babb. When a certain book came up for discussion, Babb referred to the notes and pointed out that Jake had failed to list several distinct printings; but Jake referred the committee back to his preface, where the matter had indeed been noted as a problem to be settled on the basis of further investigation. When they came to *Gabriel Conroy* (1876; now *BAL* 7285), Babb again spoke up: Jake had failed to note a variant at Yale with yellow endpapers, which Babb had brought along for all to see. Jake had indeed examined the copy in New Haven, and without looking at it again he asked the committee to inspect the lower left corner of the front inside cover, where traces of the original endpaper could still be seen: the yellow endpapers were a later substitution. Shortly afterward, the Yale copy of another title was displayed with a presentation inscription dated some weeks earlier than the publication date Jake had recorded. Again, without taking the book in his hands, Jake was able to say, "Oh, yes, I know that copy; the inscription is honest enough, but it has been inserted from another book. Just look at the watermark, which is wrong for this book." Dave Randall held the leaf up to the light and exclaimed, "This book is a goddam fake." Babb was embarrassed and furious at having been deceived by one of his own staff. Shortly after this episode, which Carroll Wilson later referred to as "the Battle of Worcester," Troxell disappeared from the letterhead of *BAL,* and Jake was allowed to proceed without further hindrance.

In his preface to the first volume, Jacob Blanck summarized the various procedures by which were established (1) a list of the 281 authors (dead before the end of 1930) whose works were to be described; (2) the material by these writers that was to be included; and (3) an acceptable form of description. One of these procedures requires special comment. This involved Blanck's assignment to his associates of

the task of reading the principal American and British book-trade journals, to gather material relating to the publications of our authors. The information was recorded and was most important in establishing publication dates. This activity also produced information relating to certain forgotten publications by some of our authors. Fifty book-trade periodicals were read ... ; thirty-five were American, the remaining fifteen British. ... (p.xii)

Theoretically this made it possible to answer one of the most bothersome questions concerning the first editions of American writers, especially during the period when copyright regulations were in dispute: when a work was published in both England and the United States in the same year, which came first? Already a two-volume bibliography, by I. R. Brussel, had been devoted to the problem, *Anglo-American First Editions* (1935–36). Volume one, *East to West,* described first editions of English authors whose books were published in America before their publication in England, from 1826 to 1900; volume two, *West to East,* covered the period 1786 to 1930 for American authors whose books were published in England before their publication in America.

The vast amount of Jacob Blanck's preliminary work involved also the compilation of checklists of the separate publications of the authors, based on works devoted either wholly or in part to them, and on the catalogues of most of the major American libraries, including the American Antiquarian Society, Brown, Harvard, the Huntington, the Library of Congress, the New York Public, the University of California at Los Angeles, the University of Southern California, and Yale. The principal private libraries consulted were those of C. Waller Barrett and Carroll A. Wilson. These collections provided the great mass of basic material.

His strained relationship with Gilbert Troxell made use of the Yale Collection of American Literature difficult for Jake Blanck during the first years of his work on the *BAL*. A few months after I had taken over the curatorship, he visited the library and wrote me on 28 October 1947:

Let me again thank you for a most pleasant day. You can only guess how much it means to me to be able to go to the Aldis room under the new regime. I prefer not to elaborate on this.

With the *BAL* in mind, we had from the start made some effort to shape the collection to provide maximum support. In 1939, Mrs. George Buell Alvord had given to the library in memory of her husband, a member of the Yale Class of 1895, the sum of $25,000, the income to be used for the purchase of books and manuscripts in the field of American literature. As Aldis had pointed out in 1911, many of the books we needed were inexpensive, and a surprising number were acquired over the years on the Alvord Fund.

But by far the richest source for YCAL acquisitions was gifts and bequests of entire libraries, especially from Yale alumni like Leonard Bacon, Francis Hyde Bangs, William Rose Benét, Henry Seidel Canby, Frederick Mortimer Clapp, Sinclair Lewis, Eugene O'Neill, Norman Holmes Pearson, Cole Porter, and Bradford Swan—to mention only a few of those that came to Yale during the period of my curatorship. These contained many books by American writers, often in first edition, and frequently titles that were either lacking in YCAL or varying from our copies.

(The Yale Library had reason to be indebted to the librarian of the Yale Club of New York for one important collection. This had been offered to the club by Mr. and Mrs. Robert Blum, he a graduate in the Class of 1916. It consisted of books and manuscripts collected with remarkable astuteness by Mrs. Blum's brother, Godfrey Frank Singer, author of *The Epistolary Novel* (1933). Recognizing that the collection was not appropriate for the Yale Club's library, intended primarily for browsing, the librarian suggested to the Blums that it ought to go to the university. They did present it to Yale in memory of their son, W. Robert Blum, Jr., who had died of leukemia at the age of twenty-five. It contained books and manuscripts of English, Irish, and American authors. Their quality may be indicated by just three of the American titles:

the first printing of Hawthorne's *The Marble Faun* (1860); Melville's *Moby Dick* (1851), in a rare variant binding; and 114 pages of the original manuscript of *The Gilded Age,* by Samuel Clemens and Charles Dudley Warner.)

To get the maximum benefit from such gifts and bequests, it was of course necessary to devote a good deal of time to the comparison of copies. Publishers of the major American writers frequently had editions of their books bound in cloths of different colors. Sometimes the color has no bibliographical significance; but when a work sold well and there were numerous printings, the color of the cloth occasionally indicates a new binding-up of first-edition sheets. Possible different printings may be indicated also by publishers' advertisements, ranging from a single leaf, either integral or inserted, to substantial catalogues added by the binder, often with varying dates, and sometimes listing a variant number of titles. A page-by-page search for textual differences was seldom feasible (unless some author bibliography had already recorded them), but even quick comparison often yielded results. While YCAL was housed in the Sterling Memorial Library, physical circumstances made this detailed comparison difficult. Libraries received had to be stored temporarily in such basement space as happened to be available, where lighting was almost always inadequate. (During the long period when Donald Wing was head of accessions, his phenomenally detailed knowledge of the entire library's holdings meant that books which seemed likely candidates for YCAL or other special collections were routinely referred to the proper curator. After his untimely death, we all did the best we could in the limited amount of space and time available.)

Even when copies in variant bindings were, otherwise, apparent duplicates, I added them to the collection,★ expecting that if indeed the *BAL* failed to discover different states or issues among them, then some successor-curator could make the decision to discard.

★To avoid the charge of increasing frivolously the costs of cataloguing, I adopted the practice of adding copies only to the YCAL main and shelf cards. Readers, having found a book listed in the Sterling catalogue, on coming to consult it in YCAL, often had the pleasant surprise of finding multiple copies. And for my own benefit as well as that of a few privileged informed persons, I made a record on the verso of the YCAL main card of the history of those extra copies.

With purchases, and acquisitions through gift and bequest, we were able to make Jacob Blanck's visits to New Haven more worthwhile. And at last, after thirty-six years, it became possible to transfer from the open stacks first editions that were either lacking in the Collection of American Literature or represented there by less desirable copies. An Aldis copy that had been recased or otherwise "improved" was quite acceptable for everyday use in the open stacks, and the curator of YCAL was thus able to reduce the risk of being charged with "decimating" the circulating collections.★

The available funds were insufficient to enable us to replace Aldis copies of the most important—and expensive—books when these had been "cleansed" or repaired in a way that robbed them of much of their value for bibliographical research. Fortunately, untampered-with copies of a good many of these rarities came to us over the years, especially in the Willard S. Morse Clemens collection given by Walter Francis and Mary E. Dillingham Frear, the James Fenimore Cooper collection given by the Cooper family, and the Walt Whitman collection given by Adrian Van Sinderen. (A set of the three volumes of Melville's *The Whale*—the rare first edition of *Moby Dick,* lacking in the Aldis collection, issued in England a month before its American publication—came as a gift only a few years after we had finally managed to purchase a copy— which the seller was happy to take back at the price we had paid.)

A book we never replaced was the Aldis copy of Hawthorne's first publication, *Fanshawe* (1828), issued anonymously only three years after its author had graduated from Bowdoin. He later destroyed any copies he could get his hands on, having come to regret a certain juvenile extravagance in its language. (One passage has remained in my mind from my first reading of the novel some sixty years ago. Fanshawe's friend, Edward Walcott, standing beside a forest stream, catches sight of a trout "of noble size" hiding in a recess caused by the current.

'Now would I give the world,' he exclaimed, with great interest, 'for a hook and line,—a fish spear, or any piscatorial instrument of death!')

★A charge actually made against me in 1948 by the head reference librarian, Anne S. Pratt.

The Aldis copy of this opus had been "cleansed" and provided with new endpapers. Although we never acquired a more satisfactory copy, I did find an original free front endpaper for the book. In the shop of the late Charles Hamilton, then one of the principal New York dealers in manuscripts, I was permitted to go through the stock of miscellaneous single letters and autographs and came across a leaf bearing an inscription:

This story was written by Hawthorne. His wish that it should never be reproduced in print (expressed to me in a letter [of 12 Jan. 1851]) should be respected.

J. T. F.

May, 1864.

The lines had been written in his copy of *Fanshawe* by James T. Fields. (The novel *was* reprinted only twelve years later, in 1876, as *Fanshawe and Other Pieces,* and by Fields's former partner, James R. Osgood.)

Approving of our policy of accumulating binding and other variants, Jake Blanck wrote me on 27 April 1948 to suggest an elaboration of it:

Sudden thought department...

Every so often (quite often, in fact) I find it necessary to buy known reprints of books in order to establish primacy for some of the books to be described in the bibliography. ...

Now for the sudden thought: at the moment I have three copies of the 1869 editions of "Little Women" that I'm using in my study of the first edition. I hate to throw them away...so...would Aldis want to have them? It seems to me that it would be ideal to have on your shelves a copy of the first edition together with the two or three known reprints. ... Do you think that as bibliographical studies they would have any value in Aldis?

If you feel as I do in this I'll send the "LW"'s down and will, in future, send along other reprints together with explanatory notes. ... I think that tomorrow's bibliographers will bless Aldis for such a collection. And, too, the doubting Thomases can be referred to the collection.

What do you think?

In those fortunate times of far better service from the United States post office, I could answer Jake on the following day:

I'm all for making the collection ... of the greatest possible value to bibliographers and agree with you that there's a place here for any and all reprints which can easily be mistaken for the first edition, particularly in the case of the more important books. *Little Women* is certainly one of those, and we'd be delighted to have the three copies.

A binding variant was the subject of another exchange in February 1949. Jake reported that the edition of Washington Irving's *Journal* (*1823–1824*) prepared by my old graduate-school professor Stanley T. Williams and published by the Harvard University Press in 1931 occurs not only in maroon cloth with sides blindstamped and top edges gilt, but also in blue cloth with sides unstamped and top edges plain.

The suspicion is that the maroon preceded the blue. Do you know? Or would you ask Prof. Williams? Further suspicion: Copies bound in Harvard's maroon had the extra features & were for the exclusive use of the lads in Cambridge. The copies in Yale blue, lack the extra features, & (in Harvard's opinion) are good enough for those people in New Haven.

I replied on 11 February:

Stanley Williams has never seen the Irving *Journal* in blue cloth! But he says that he is quite sure that the book was remaindered by the Harvard University Press and, if so, this blue cloth is almost certainly a remainder binding. In any case, I think there can be little doubt that it is much later than the maroon. The copy in YCAL has a presentation inscription from STW to C. B. Tinker dated 20 Mar 1931 and is in the maroon cloth. Another copy, in the stacks, came to the Library from the Yale University Press in 1931 and is also in maroon cloth ... . So I'm afraid we must (reluctantly) abandon your theory of Harvard's sentimentally sending blue and not crimson copies to Yale!

When the first volume of the *Bibliography* was being printed by Yale University Press, in 1955, the committee, through Jim Babb and Fred Adams, sent me a set of galleys and asked for my suggestions. I responded at some length. Not being fully aware of the great amount of work that had already been done for all 281 authors, and feeling strongly that the *BAL* must not be cluttered up with unimportant or negative information which would add materially to the cost and decrease the usability of the volumes, I made some sweeping recommendations:

1) that entries ... for all volumes not containing material by the subject author printed for the first time be omitted. ...

2) that all entries for sheet-music editions be deleted excepting only such entries as represent the first appearance in print of a particular poem by the subject author. ...

3) that unimportant statements, testimonials, etc., be disregarded. ...

4) that letters and reports signed with others be disregarded unless it can be established that the material was of necessity written by the subject author concerned. ...

5) that bibliographical notes be pared down to essentials. ...

6) that entries be deleted for items established to be not by the subject author, or items in the preparation of which subject author merely cooperated.

7) that an author's contributions to newspapers and periodicals [with occasional exceptions] not be listed as main entries. ...

8) that first separate editions (containing no new material by the subject author) be mentioned only in the notes to the entry for the volume from which they were reprinted ... .

9) that later editions (containing no important new material by the subject author) be mentioned only in notes to the earlier edition ... .

And I urged that an index be issued with each volume.

But Fred Adams felt that it was much too late to make such drastic changes in policies. I replied on 12 April:

From what Jim [Babb] told me of the meeting [of the committee], I gather that the general opinion was that although some of the material in volume one might be not absolutely necessary, Jake had done the work, the information might be useful to somebody, and therefore it might as well be printed. My point was of course that, once committed in volume one to a policy of presentation, you will be stuck with it for the remaining seven volumes. And Jake's work could be enormously speeded up and printing costs substantially reduced by the omission of many entries which no one would expect to find in a large-scale bibliography of this kind.

I still feel very strongly that the policy on the sheet-music entries adopted by the Committee is ill-advised. ... I cannot see that sheet-music reprints of poems already collected by the author have any place in this type of bibliography ... . Since Jake is obviously not going to live long enough to be sure of locating and listing all such items, it seems to me that the only solution is to agree that they not be represented. ...

Fred elaborated on policies on the 22nd:

In general, the Committee feels that where a great deal of work has been done, let us say on reprints and sheet music, there is no reason to withhold the information from the purchaser of the Bibliography, and with this I thoroughly agree. It would not speed up Jake's work very much at this stage to omit such material from the printed volumes. ...

Believe me, I appreciate very greatly the time and interest you have devoted to the Bibliography. I only regret that you were not a member of the Supervisory Committee from the start, but neither was I.

I had written to Jake Blanck about the galleys on 6 April:

I am sorry that we did not have longer last Monday to go over the galleys in detail, but now that the major policies have been confirmed there's little point to most of my queries. I offer one or two observations for what they are worth: ...

Of my five "observations"—largely concerning inconsistencies and the treatment of later editions and reprints—Jake reported on the 6th that he had already caught two, agreed with two others, and did not agree with the fifth. He ended his letter with a comment on sheet music:

Sheet music. PLEASE!!! I'd rather tell you about this than write about it. I tried my dmdst to have the Committee rule out this sort of material but without success. ... It's a separate study, or should be, and I've said so time and again; and say so in my preface.

Well, now to get back to the galleys. ...

Proofing is a *lousy* way to spend your life. Don't do it.

I continued to go over the galleys as they came from the press, and in the course of my work as curator was constantly checking entries in the published volumes. One point that invariably rankled was the failure of *BAL* to give Yale credit for its copies of important books. Jake explained the policy to me on 3 April 1959 (and on several other occasions):

As for locating certain of the entries in Y. The field rules forbid this in many cases. Unless we've actually examined the book, *and collated it in full,* it (the location, that is) doesn't go in. And after we've seen and fully collated two copies of a book then all other copies that swim into our ken are given the shortest sort of examination and checking *vs* the entry. Hence, many of the books in Y (and in AAS, etc.) aren't located in *BAL*... which isn't a census. Such an undertaking would be endless.

William A. Jackson, as librarian of the Houghton Library at Harvard and a member of the supervisory committee, had been supportive of the *BAL* project from the start, and he was responsible for the establishment of its headquarters in the Houghton Library. His untimely death in October 1964 was an occasion for deep regret. Jake wrote me on the 21st:

We're all shocked by Bill's death. It seems impossible and will continue to seem so for some time to come. I simply can't believe it. It's a tragedy …and a tremendous loss to bibliography and to scholarship. And I know I've lost a friend…and that's something no one can afford or take lightly. Perhaps I'll see you later today at the services. …

Houghton Library is in a pall of deep gloom. I have the feeling that even the readers sense it.

I simply can't believe it.

I answered the next day:

Yes, the loss to bibliography and scholarship in Bill's death will never be repaired and the gap will be there for a long time to come.

I had to choose between going to New York for the Grolier Club and, especially, Norman [Pearson]'s talk (which was extremely well received) and coming up for the funeral. I was sorry not to be present.

The collecting standards followed now and then by Foley and occasionally seconded by Aldis were often deplored by both Jake and me. This is from a letter of 18 November 1964 about Sidney Lanier's *Florida:*

The <1875> copy, I suspect, is a Foley (sometimes called blue plate) special. Nothing much wrong with it, tho…outside of the following: it's been recased and resewn and the endpapers are almost surely not the originals; the final leaf is lacking; the inscription (genuine enough) has been inserted…perhaps from another book; and just to make the thing really interesting you'd better date it 1881… Outside of that it's a lovely copy.

But the disappointments were outweighed by the pleasant surprises. Jake had written to me in July 1966 about a broadside listed as by Francis Scott Key, of which the only copy located was Yale's— *Supplement to the Boston Gazette, for . . . April 28, 1808 . . . Mr. Key's Speech . . . :*

The query is this: Is this really by our man? Or some other gent named Key? The Harvard file of the paper lacks the supplement, but we've checked the paper for an editorial note; negative.

Any thoughts on the matter?

I was obliged to give Jake at first a completely negative report:

In re your inquiry as to our unique Francis Scott Key item, there is no record apparently now in any catalogue that we ever had this. … It is definitely not in our file of the *Boston Gazette,* at least not in its presumably proper place (after the issue for 28 April 1808), and it is not among our octavo or quarto Key books. I haven't checked among our folios but shall before I mail this. I'm afraid I can't do anything about answering your question until I find the item. I gather you are absolutely certain that you saw it at Yale?

And I signed myself: "Puzzled." Fortunately, I was able to add a postscript before the letter went off:

Well, it was in the YCAL folios. I think your use of it must have caused someone to suspect that the cataloguing was wrong and now there's apparently no cataloguing at all. The broadside states that the speech is taken from the *Washington Federalist*. Unfortunately, we have just one issue of that paper for 1808 and I am sure it wouldn't be the right one. Possibly you could check Harvard's set and see if the *Federalist* didn't identify Mr. Key as Philip Barton Key (1757–1815). I think the speech must certainly have been by him and not by Francis Scott Key. P. B. Key was apparently representative of the 3rd Md. congressional district at the time and opposed the Embargo (see *DAB*).

So—over to you, Sir!

Jake responded promptly:

I think you've supplied the KEY ... to the problem. Will check immediately...if not sooner.

Thanks and regards—

[*Signed*] Terwilliger

A happy purchase by the Beinecke of some copyright deposit copies of Jack London titles occasioned a joyous response, dated 15 December 1966:

Whyohwhyohwhy don't these dmd things turn up before we send off *ms* to the printers! But knowing how slow Y[ale] U[niversity] P[ress] is, it really doesn't matter much...and I'll certainly have plenty of time to collate those advance printings and get them into the manuscript. I doubt YUP will start to set type until next spring...if then.

In the meantime you *are* to be congratulated on getting the books. Congrats!

You may be interested in the following comments:

Martin Eden. Have collated LC's advance copy.

The Iron Heel. Ditto.

White Fang. Have collated the U[niversity of]V[irginia] copy.

Love of Life. Have not seen and so far as I know yours is the only copy. The advance printing may very well explain why the published copies have cancel title-leaf. [Merle] Johnson noted a 1906 printing; I assume that's what you have.

Before Adam. Have not seen and so far as we're concerned your copy is unique. Johnson noted a 1906 printing; I assume that's what you have.

What a loverly haul! And BAL is even more pleased than you are! Keep those books close by…I'll be down to work on them.

Occasionally, Jake would steer our way items that he knew would be of particular interest. This happened in October 1967 with a book by Joseph Holt Ingraham. Benjamin Tighe, a dealer in Athol, Massachusetts, had sent to Blanck to be collated for the *BAL* a copy of the first edition of Ingraham's *Eleanor Sherwood*. In returning the copy to Tighe on 21 October, Jake wrote him:

Since Yale has the only other copy known to BAL, an imperfect example; and since your copy is imperfect as well, why not give Yale first refusal? In that way the two can be mated and a complete copy (of sorts) made. I doubt that Yale (if it gets your copy) will attempt surgery; but your copy and Yale's should be on the same shelf.

Let me urge you, then, to write to Donald C. Gallup, The Beinecke Library, Yale University, about this thing.

I was able to report to Jake on 8 November:

Mr. Tighe's *Eleanor Sherwood* is now safely here and we are buying it. As you suspected, we shall be keeping both copies for we can't bring ourselves to remove the wrappers from Tighe's copy and attach them to our, trimmed copy. Unfortunately, a piece of the text missing from our copy is also missing from the Tighe copy, but only a few words are involved and I daresay the world will get along without them for at least a few more years until another copy turns up.

I had, only a week earlier, written to Jake about another title by Ingraham:

Lyle Wright seemed to agree with me about Ingraham's *Mark Manly*. If you agree with us that Wright I. 1317 precedes 1316 and that therefore it should be enshrined in the revised *BAL* as the true first edition of that deathless book, won't you write a little note on it for the YUL GAZETTE and we'll reproduce the cover-title as an illustration? This would please Ed Ingraham (who gave it to us) and everybody would be happy. If you could scribble off the note and get it to me within the next ten days or so, I would be particularly pleased for I could put it into the January GAZETTE, on which I am now beginning to think about preparing to start to work.

And I added to my letter of 8 November:

Now that *Eleanor Sherwood* is our gal, perhaps you would consider including a note on her with your note on *Mark* for the GAZETTE? …

Jake replied on the 10th:

There's no doubt at all that you're correct *in re* Ingraham's *Mark Manly;* and we will cancel *BAL* No. 9956 and insert a description of the 31-page job. What a difference the light of your reasoning...to say nothing of the presence of the unique wrapper on the Yale copy...does make. Have you told Lyle [Wright] that he'll have to reverse his numbers, now that we know the 31-pager was issued under date 1843?

As for giving the *Gazette* our corrected entries for *Mark Manly* and *Eleanor Sherwood.* I have no objection to doing so, but in the past such additions and corrections appeared in *P[apers of the]B[ibliographical]S[ociety of] A[merica].* Yet, these corrections are the result of Yale purchases and the *Gazette* should make them public.

I'm writing to Fred Adams to get his okay...I doubt that he'll tell us nay.

He enclosed a draft of his proposed note. It was headed "*BAL* Addenda," and I hastened to write him on the 16th:

Many thanks for your note and enclosure. I think Fred Adams might very well have some reservations about allowing your note of "BAL Addenda" in its more or less official form to be printed except in the *BSA Papers.* I had thought of something not quite so official. To save time I have redrafted the note and am sending a copy to Fred as well as to you. Please change it as you will, but this is the kind of thing I had in mind. *[I enclosed a revised draft of his note—retitled* "Two Revisions in the Bibliography of Joseph Holt Ingraham."]

Although I expressed to Jake our appreciation of his generosity now and then in rather exaggerated terms, he knew that our gratitude was sincere. One of my notes to him was dated 5 May 1971:

The copy of the first printing of the first revised edition of Mr. [John Ames] Mitchell's *The Last American* ([1902]) has just arrived safely and a beautiful thing to look at it is indeed. Mine eyes dazzle! We're delighted to have it and shall begin once more to hold our heads high, no longer weighted down with shame at the knowledge that the Yale copy is of the second printing and imperfect. Many thanks.

Occasionally I couched in light terms a serious criticism, as happened on 11 September 1972 in reference to the galleys for volume six and Jake's description of form A of Joaquin Miller's *Forty-nine* [and] *Danites* (1882):

Referring to a gathering of 4 leaves as a "4to gathering," my dear Jacob, is sloppy bibliographical practice quite unworthy of you. The gathering is bibliographically 8vo, I suppose, but in 4s.

But Jake ignored my reprimand and persisted in his error, for "4to gathering" is the reading in the volume as published.

III

Although the burden of our correspondence was heavily earnest, both Jacob Blanck and I at times endeavored to lighten the exchange with what we intended as humor. A sampling will give an idea of how we strove to relieve the reputed boredom of bibliographical research.

In October 1960 Jake had asked me on a postcard to indicate whether Thomas Wentworth Higginson's *Short Studies* (1880) had a triple or a double rule at the top and bottom of its spine. When I questioned him about the significance of this point, he reassured me that the surviving copyright deposit copy had stamping in black, gold, and blind, and must therefore be the true first binding, but he didn't answer my query about the rule. I wrote him on the 18th:

> I have spent some sleepless nights, I can tell you, tossing and turning, tormented by the thought that our copy of that key book in American Literature, T. W. Higginson's *Short Studies,* might not be "right." You can imagine, therefore, with what joyous cries of relief I received your billet doux this A.M. But still that Awful Demon Doubt rises and will not be quieted: what of the triple rule? Is all our black, our gold, our blind stamping to no avail in the presence of that added rule? Do relieve my mind at your earliest convenience by confessing that the ghost of the double rule was merely a red herring drawn hurriedly across the path to distract our attention from the true goal!

> Distractedly yours,

> Bub

And he answered—at some length—on the 20th, from "Angel's Camp":

Dear Bub:

> When I seen that you was plumb skeert I up an decided (*dee-*cided, that is) to tell orl.

> Yeers and yeers ago I seen a copy of TWHaitch's *Short Studies* in the

Noo Yawk liberry which the same was beat to all hell an gone. An to these yeer tired ol eyes thet looked like dubble rules at the top an bottom. See? An that comes ruff on us '49-ers which the same makes us our own rules and tuhell with them others.

Anyways—I started to look about and sho nuff every last dam copy hed triple rules not dubble rules. See? Up to AND incloodin the kopyright deeposit copy. ... Meanwhile, back at the hum ranch thet dmd old fool liberry in Noo Yawk hed up an rebound (*rebound,* mind) thare copy becauce it warn't in good shape. Which the same I new the fust time I laid eyes on same. Anyways—thet's the way things air in this here world. So ALL them copies I seen hev TRIPLE rules and are fixed up kinder cute in gold and black an blind—and I hope them binder fellers is gettin thare gold from us. So much fer thet. But damfool copy what's stamped black only is a ornery cuss and tohell with same. Must be a vay-rye-ant.

An speakin of two rule and three rools and the like reminds me thet I ain't hed breakfast yet and Ime sashayin over to the Widder's for a triple rool…no, I means three fingers of red eye.

Yrs

Buck Fanshawe
[*Signed with an X*]

To which I replied on the 21st:

Dear Buck,

> All is forgiven.
> Come home.

Yr

Bub

Jake had for years followed the practice of mailing double post-cards with query and postpaid reply to be checked, detached, and mailed. Such a postcard concerning the *Piccadilly Annual* (1870) elicited a query from me on 5 March 1965:

I trust that the enclosed returned postcard does not mean that all authorities heretofore have failed to recognize [Robert Henry] Newell's "Dickens" in the poem signed O.C.K. and included in the *Piccadilly Annual* (1870). Such callousness on the part of the general public would be almost too much to be borne by

Yrs. truly,
[*Signed:*] D. C. G.
Doremus Cuthbert Gabblethwop

This brought forth from Cambridge a poetic response:

Ein Lieder Ge-machtet fur der Meister von
YCAL,
Doremus Cuthbert Gabblethwop, Esq.
(Aus Ge-Written bei Hans Breitmann, Jr.)

Mit ashes und zack clot
Ge-covered am I,
Zoo teef mit de drubbles
I bust oot und gry!

Mein lieber D. Cuthbert
Ge-troppled has bin
From searching mit Newell's
Ein lieder zu fin.★

From Charles Godfrey Leland
Enough I've ge-had,
Und ven he's ge-findished
De harz moos be glad

L'Envoy (or something)

Verser ★★ poetische
Briefen vas done
Py Charles Godfrey Leland
Dot schweinhundischer vun!

★*Must be pronounced a la piscator.*—Ed.
★★*Unrelated to poesy.*—Ed.

[*Signed:*] Hans Breitmann, Jr

On an embarrassing number of occasions I called Jake's attention to omissions of titles which, he pointed out, were indeed listed, usually under "Reprints." One such note, of 14 September
1965, which I signed: "D. Clericus," related to Mary Russell
Mitford's *Stories of American Life* (3 volumes, London, 1830). Jake
merely jotted down the correct *BAL* reference numbers and
returned my letter with a note:

Bifocals @ wholesale and retail a specialty at BLANCK'S EMPORIUM—We
give S & H Green Stamps!!!★

★ E. J. and F. W. Beinecke were officers of the Sperry & Hutchinson Company, famous for
its green trading stamps.

I donned the appropriate sackcloth and ashes, and wrote him on the 20th:

How STOOPID can a guy get! Gee-WHIZ!! and to think that, as you guessed, Clericus is a member of my own department. I'd be tempted to disown him entirely if it weren't that I suspect, as you suggested, that his difficulty is his eyes. We're sending in an order to Blanck's Emporium for the bifocals and I look for a pronounced improvement in this fellow's ability to find items in *BAL* when they are listed under reprints.

When, in August 1966, I called his attention to a typographical error, "Magna Carta Stories" for "Magna Charta Stories" in *BAL* 2940, he replied on the 12th:

Dear Dr Doctor Gallup:

True to our declared policy of giving complete satisfaction we send you herewith the material lacking in your copy of BAL II, entry No. 2940. See enclosed. ...

Yours very sincerely,

[*Signed*:] Felix Gilfedder
Felix Gilfedder, Mgr.
Public Relations Department

The enclosure was a slip of paper blank save for a single typed letter *h*.

Another exchange concerned Bliss Carman's *The Vigilantes* in the already published second volume. I wrote Jake on 18 August 1966:

Far be it from me to pick flaws and fuss over details, but Browning has always been my favorite poet, Dr. Blanck, and his immortal words have never ceased to inspire me:

> "A man's reach should exceed his grasp
> Or what's a Heaven for?"

In this spirit and with no pointing finger of blame or shame, I assure you, Sir, I venture to call to your attention a very slight apparent oversight in Entry No. 2726 of your Great Work. From page 15 of that remarkable pamphlet (so aptly titled *The Vigilantes!*), you took "May 8, 1918" as a *terminus ante quem* for the item. Had you read, nay, even glanced just three pages farther, you would have come upon the date "June 26, 1918." *Verbum sap., Dr. B.*

I think we all strive in our own small and sometimes peculiar ways to extend the boundaries of knowledge however infinitesimally. It is only to serve this great and worthy cause that I have ventured, Sir, to call this small apparent oversight to your attention.

> Believe me to be
> Your humble obd't, etc.

> (Mrs.) Jaramina Quincibald Puddleston.

To which he replied on the 23rd:

Dear Miss Puddleston:

Your letter of the 18th inst. has been given most careful attention and has been filed in the Project's archives (Sec. A-16, Sub. 698/kL, Div. HB?DCG). ...

I am directed by the Editor to extend his thanks for your constant kooperation.

> [*Signed:*] F. G.

> Felix Gilfedder, Director,
> Department of Archival and Related Materials.

cc (7)

On 10 October 1966, Jake sent us for the John Kendrick Bangs collection four copies of a flier issued that same month by the Cambridge Trust Co., printing Bangs's poem "The Rooster." He addressed me by one of the pseudonyms I had used in earlier letters, and signed his own letter "Henry Wadsworth Longfellow," adding a postscript:

And if you think *I'm* going to plow through all of JKB looking for this ...in an effort to determine whether this is reprint or other...you have another think coming!

> [*Signed:*] H W L

A quick glance at Frank Bangs's biography of his father located the poem, and I wrote to Jake on the 31st:

Dear Hank,

A Happy Hallow'een to ye!

Your gift of FOUR copies of the Cambridge Trust Company's flier with John Kendrick Bangs' immortal "The Rooster" is indeed a handsome one. The poem is familiar, of course, from the equally immortal pages (p. 265, to be exact) of his son's biography, but I must confess to not being able to locate its original publication. ...

Again with many thanks, dear Hank. How are your musical settings coming along, incidentally?

Yours in the faith,

J. Cadwallader Inglepouff

Henry W. Longfellow, Esq.

His response was an antique postcard featuring the words *"HEARTIEST CONGRATULATIONS"* in beflowered letters, to which he had added a manuscript note: "—on discovery of that J.K.B. item—Mr. Dooley."

I sent off an elaborate—and lengthy!—report on 14 January 1971, again concerning a work by J. H. Ingraham:

Dear Mr. Blanck:

We, the readers and users of the *B.A.L.*, are, I think, generally agreed that it is an exemplary work, but there are still occasions when we must confess to being a trifle disappointed that the same high standards of completeness should not have been applied to—and carried through—all entries under all authors. When the author involved is so important—indeed vital—to American literature as the late Professor Ingraham, and when the work is one of his most glorious and memorable creations, *Morris Græme* (1843), then even a minor imperfection becomes almost intolerable.

I very much regret to inform you that such a blemish indeed appears to disfigure the noble profile you have drawn in *BAL* vol. 4 of the master's production. You have quite correctly—and commendably—pointed out that in copies of the first edition of *Morris Græme* a period appears after the word FEATHER on the titlepage and in other copies has disappeared. But I strongly suspect, my dear Mr. Blanck, … that in your occupation with the period—the tree, as it were—you have failed to notice the SPACING OF THE ENTIRE LINE—the forest. Furthermore, had you observed the spacing, you would probably have deduced what must be the correct order of the two states: (1) period; (2) no period; because as the line is reset in smaller type without the period, *IT IS VERY DEFINITELY OFF CENTER*. Since the Ancient Chinese remind us … that one picture is worth a thousand words, I enclose for … your edification, photographs of the two title pages taken from copies in the possession of the library of a distinguished university on the Eastern seaboard. I should … be happy to hear that though you have in this one instance perhaps strayed from the strait and narrow path of bibliographical virtue, you do acknowledge your error and are more firmly than ever resolved—in this New Year—to be satisfied with absolutely nothing short of the perfection that we, as we count the days to volume 6, have come to expect … .

Per ardua ad astra, Mr. Blanck!

One of your (only very slightly disappointed) readers.

This elicited from him the following:

Dear Sir:

I've just returned from the blackboard where I've written *Mea Culpa* 5000 times. ...
Woe! Woe! Woe!

Yours most abjectly,

[*Signed:*] Jacobus X

I V

The groans in this instance were not intended to be taken literally; but Jake, in preparing the fourth and fifth volumes of the *BAL*, had become increasingly—and more and more justifiably—infuriated with the unsatisfactory performance of the printers. He reported to me on 3 April 1959:

Still catching up on odds and ends—and expect to tackle the "final" page-proofs of *BAL* V. I do not look forward to the task...especially since John Kohn just showed me a maddening error in *BAL IV,* produced (typically) by Vail-Ballou. The reading is *correct* in first galleys, first revised galleys, first page proofs, revised (final) page-proofs—and so goddammed wrong in the book as published that I'm tempted to resign and go into something less exacting—such as murdering (by whatever means) any and all printers.

Unknown to Jake, the printing firm had become involved in an industrial dispute. The printers used the *BAL* proofs as a weapon in their conflict with management, deliberately sabotaging the type already set and proofread by Jake and his staff, with the result that proofs for volume five had to be completely reread. The manuscript for volume six was sent to a different printer!

As if difficulties with printers were not enough, Jake, almost from the start, was obliged to cope with the problem of having to replace assistants who, having reached an advanced state of training that enabled them to be of real value in the work on the *BAL*, were persuaded to accept cataloguing positions in libraries and other institutions at higher salaries than *BAL* could offer. This was particularly true because uncertainty about continuing financial support made it necessary for the project to watch its budget with great care.

Especially worrisome were the costs of resetting type when corrections—from me and others—came in after the manuscript for a particular volume had already been submitted to the Yale University Press. (By contractual agreement, costs of corrections beyond a certain percentage of the total printing bill, are the responsibility of the author.)

The volumes of the *Bibliography* as they appeared were greeted with almost universal approval—from academics, collectors, and booksellers. But, oddly enough, some of its most conspicuous achievements were responsible for adverse—and completely unwarranted—criticism from some dealers in American first editions. By giving complete signature-collations for all main entries, the *BAL* was able to indicate that first editions of many important authors had been printed first from type and then from plates cast from that same type. Technically both printings were part of the same (first) edition. To find out whether the sheets of a particular copy had been gathered in 8s or in 12s (for example), it was essential to determine how they were sewn. For a tightly bound copy, it was almost impossible to ascertain its make-up without damaging the book. Dealers protested having to ruin the pristine condition of a particularly desirable copy—and hence to decrease considerably its market value—in order to decide whether it belonged to *BAL*'s first or second printing. (On at least one occasion—a first edition of Hawthorne in the Barrett collection—even Jacob Blanck had to reserve judgment and state that, out of consideration for its "mint" condition, he could not establish definitively its status.)

In 1955 Jake had been apprehensive, I am sure, about my being allowed to see galleys of the first volume of the *BAL*. He was keenly aware that the discoveries he and his staff were making about points, states, issues, and printings would, when published, have their reverberations in the rare book market. To give the curator of the collection at Yale advance information about these findings might allow him an unfair advantage over custodians of similar collections elsewhere. Although Jake certainly never communicated to me any such concerns he may have entertained, I was resolved not to profit from information gleaned from reading the galleys. And because my proofreading of the text involved detailed checking of *BAL* entries against YCAL copies of the actual books, I was able to call his attention to occasional inconsistencies and even errors. He was characteristically kind enough to record his appreciation of my efforts in behalf of the *BAL*—efforts pursued often on my own time after library hours and on weekends—in an acknowledgment in the sixth volume (1973):

[to] Donald C. Gallup, curator of the Aldis Collection (and others) at Yale University Library, whose constant cooperation is of immeasurable value. Mr. Gallup, among other self-imposed tasks, read the galley proofs of the *Bibliography* and thereby prevented many a misstatement.

The nightmare experience with the proof for volume five and the death of his good friend and patron Josiah K. Lilly in 1966 had taken their toll on Jake. Bill Bond, who was seeing him every day at the Houghton, reported that

If the frustration resulting from volume 5 did not bring on Jake's serious health problems, one can hardly doubt that the stress and fatigue aggravated them. ... It was soon evident that Jake's health did not permit him to undertake any more of the arduous travel needed to check volume 7 against its source copies ... .

V

Jacob Blanck died on 23 December 1974, and the *BAL* was understandably slow to recover from the catastrophe of his death. In August 1975, Virginia L. Smyers took over the editing of volume seven, and worked alone for many months. She was then joined by Michael Winship, at first on a part-time basis, then full-time. When Virginia left to work on a bibliography of Dorothy Richardson in April 1982, Michael carried on.

The manuscript for volume seven, "edited and completed by Virginia L. Smyers and Michael Winship," was eventually submitted to the Yale University Press in May 1980. I was asked to read parts of it, and reported on 27 May that

the quality of the work ... is not far below that of each of the first six volumes. In detailed bibliographical work of this kind, it is unreasonable to expect that there won't be at least a few errors. For the earlier volumes I checked the galleys against the Yale copies for some of the authors in each volume; the frequency of errors in each of those volumes was roughly the same as in this sampling from volume 7.

The volume was accepted for publication in June and eventually appeared in 1983. It was appropriately dedicated: "In Memoriam Jacob Blanck 1906–1974," and a foreword detailed the complex history of the preparation of the manuscript. Roger Stoddard had become chairman of the supervisory committee in 1982, and it was he who was chiefly responsible for securing additional substantial funding by the National Endowment for the Humanities and from the foundation established in memory of Henry Weldon Barnes, Yale 1882. The manuscript for volume eight, "edited and completed by Michael Winship," was submitted to the press in June 1986 and again I was asked to read it. I reported on the 11th:

> I have checked some 300 volumes [*in YCAL*] against the entries for them in the manuscript ... and find that the high level of accuracy of the preceding volumes has been maintained. ...
> It is my opinion that the Press can proceed with confidence that the publication of the ... volume will continue to reflect great credit upon its editorial acumen and general scholarly reputation.

Plans for publication for this supposedly final volume were well advanced before it became apparent that the manuscript, largely because the Whitman and Whittier sections had taken up much more space than had been expected, would have to be divided into two. Volume eight was published in 1990, followed by volume nine the very next year. I was asked to write a comment to be used in publicity for this final·volume:

> *The Bibliography of American Literature* provides an ideal, permanent foundation for the study of the writings of our national literary authors. Its clarity, accuracy, and comprehensiveness reflect the greatest credit on the late Jacob Blanck, his assistants, and the agencies that oversaw and made possible the publication of this great work.

Edith Wharton, Litt. D., 20 June 1923. Photograph: AP/World Wide Photos.

A Backward Glance at the Edith Wharton Papers

1938–1976

I

ON 20 JUNE 1923 Yale University bestowed upon Edith Wharton the honorary degree of Doctor of Letters. She had initially declined to make the required trip to New Haven from her residence in Hyères, France, but had reconsidered when the university suggested that it was her duty to become the first woman ever to receive this honor from Yale. The citation for the degree, read by Professor William Lyon Phelps, described her as an "American novelist of international fame. Chevalier of the Legion of Honour in France," and continued:

> For nearly twenty-five years she has produced novels, some of the most notable being "The House of Mirth," "Ethan Frome," "The Age of Innocence." Her books are marked by sincerity in art, beauty in construction, distinction in style. She writes short stories and full-length works with equal skill. She is a master in the creation of original and living characters, and her powers of ironical description are exerted to salutary ends. She is a realist in the best sense of the word; revealing the inner nature of men and women without recourse to sensationalism and keeping ever within the boundaries of true art. She holds a universally recognized place in the front rank of the world's living novelists. She has elevated the level of American literature. We are proud that she is an American and especially proud to enroll her name among the daughters of Yale.

This was the first and only academic degree the novelist accepted, and when she died in 1937, it was announced that she had arranged for her manuscripts, correspondence, and other papers to be turned over to the Yale University Library.

On 7 May 1938 Mrs. Wharton's literary executor, Gaillard Lapsley, an American citizen then residing as fellow in Trinity College, Cambridge, wrote to the president of Yale, James Rowland

Angell, formally offering the papers to the university. They were to be subject to certain conditions:

The papers shall be permanently lodged in the University Library and adequately cared for and protected there.

The correspondence and other letters and papers of a biographical sort shall not be accessible until thirty years after they have been received by the University Library.

During the same period the manuscripts of Mrs. Wharton's work whether published or unpublished shall be accessible only to *bona fide* students of literature.

During the same period no unpublished work of Mrs. Wharton's whether complete or fragmentary shall be printed except by such students and then only with the consent and approval of the appropriate Professor or Professors in the Department of English.

And Lapsley added a final flourish:

May I take this opportunity, Mr. President, to put on record what I have already written to you privately, that as Mrs. Wharton's literary executor I have offered her manuscripts and papers to the University of Yale as the most suitable repository of these memorials of a great literary artist who counted her Yale doctorate among the most welcome and distinguished of the honours that she had received?

It was August before the papers were actually sent, and even then Lapsley explained that he was holding back some of them "for the use of Mr. Percy Lubbock who is engaged on a book about Mrs. Wharton." Lubbock released several items the next February as irrelevant to his research, but although he published his *Portrait of Edith Wharton* in 1947, it was seven years more before the rest of the borrowed items finally came to Yale. They included some early photographs of Edith Wharton, two of her manuscript diaries (of 1905 and 1906), a notebook of 1924–34, five postcards and six autograph letters to Henry James, written between 1911 and 1916 (a happy survival, for James destroyed most of his papers), and twenty-six autograph letters from Edith Wharton to Sara Norton, dating from 1899 to 1908. Papers that Lubbock himself had generated in writing his Wharton *Portrait* were first lent by his stepdaughter, Iris Origo, to R. W. B. Lewis for use in *his* Wharton biography, and then given, through him, to Yale.

Along with the Wharton papers, Gaillard Lapsley sent to Yale in 1938 his own long series of more than 350 letters from Mrs. Wharton. He ventured to suggest to the Yale librarian, Bernhard Knollenberg, that other of Mrs. Wharton's friends and correspondents would give her letters to Yale "if they knew that your library would be glad to receive and care for them, on terms which, for a long period, at any rate, may be described as confidential." The suggestion was acted upon promptly. Either at Yale's request or spontaneously over the years many of Edith Wharton's friends donated her letters: her sister-in-law, Mary Cadwalader Jones (112), her niece, Beatrix Farrand (72), and her cousin, Frederic R. King (250); an English friend, A. John Hugh Smith (142); and American friends like Sara Norton (217), Mrs. Winthrop Chanler (77), and Judge Robert Grant (45).

One American friend, Royal Cortissoz, the art critic, provided in his will that his twenty-four letters from Mrs. Wharton were to go to Yale to unite the two sides of their correspondence. He died on 17 October 1948 and in due course his executor, Dr. Davenport West, notified the university of the bequest. As sometimes happens at large institutions—even Yale—Dr. West's letter, received in the office of the treasurer, lay on the desk of some underling, to whom the name of Cortissoz meant nothing, for a full month before it was finally acknowledged and a copy sent to the librarian, Jim Babb. He of course responded promptly, assuring Dr. West that we'd be very happy to have the Wharton letters to add to the papers that had been given to us, and telling him that I as curator of the Yale Collection of American Literature would get in touch with him to arrange for picking them up.

I had a very pleasant visit with Dr. West (who lived at the Dakota on Central Park West) on 23 April 1949 and in the course of our conversation discovered that Cortissoz had not designated a repository for the rest of his papers. I assured Dr. West that Yale would be eager to have the entire archive. In New Haven the following morning I reported to Jim Babb, who wrote at once to confirm the library's interest.

Fortunately, the heirs agreed that all the papers could come to Yale to be kept together as the Royal Cortissoz collection. (They also donated to the Art Gallery a cabinet containing slides of paintings and of other art objects.) Cortissoz had begun his art education in employment for some fifteen years with the architectural firm of McKim, Mead, and White. In 1891, he had become art critic for the *New York Tribune* (finally, the *New York Herald Tribune*) and continued to hold that position for fifty-three years. His correspondence included letters from an imposing array of his contemporaries outstanding in various fields: Henry Adams (4), Bernard Berenson (60), Edwin H. Blashfield (24), Van Wyck Brooks (6), Joseph Duveen (27), Daniel Chester French (7), Lawrence Gilman (15), Childe Hassam (6), James G. Huneker (13), Charles Godfrey Leland (5), Clarence Mackay (about 60), Gari Melchers (15), George Moore (5), Elizabeth and Joseph Pennell (21), John Russell Pope (9), Whitelaw Reid (some 100), Theodore Roosevelt (8), Augustus Saint-Gaudens (16), Charles Scribner (29), Alfred Stieglitz (16), Booth Tarkington (9), Daniel B. Updike (7), William Winter (some 100), and Owen Wister (13, with an autograph manuscript of his poem "To Theodore Roosevelt"). Cortissoz had been a close friend—and biographer—of John La Farge, and the papers included some sixty letters from the artist, along with one of his sketchbooks, containing forty rough pencil sketches by him. There were some two hundred letters from Katherine Prescott Wormeley, and a large group of correspondence addressed to her (two letters from Henry James extend to sixteen pages).

Cortissoz had married a colleague at the *Tribune,* Ellen McKay Hutchinson, and some of the choice items in the collection were letters she had received (or "inherited") in her capacity as literary editor. These included single letters from R. D. Blackmore, Sir William Schenck Gilbert, Bret Harte, Rudyard Kipling, and Robert Louis Stevenson. There were other prizes with only indirect connection to Mr. and Mrs. Cortissoz: an autograph letter signed from Jefferson Davis to General E. S. Stedman, and one from Walt Whitman to John Hay, who had been employed as editorial writer and night editor at the *New York Tribune* in the early 1870s. Dr. West, as executor, had assembled, in original or photocopy, many of Royal Cortissoz's own letters for addition to the archive. It will be seen that these papers extended significantly the dimensions of the Yale Library's resources—and they came to New Haven in direct consequence of the bequest of twenty-four letters from Edith Wharton!

Yale *might* have had Mrs. Wharton's letters to Bernard Berenson. When his longtime friend, general assistant, and secretary, Elizabeth ("Nicky") Mariano, visited New Haven in 1963, I met her at dinner with Charles and Charlotte Seymour. Recalling B. B.'s gratitude for the Yale University Press's having published his *Studies in Medieval Painting* in 1930, Miss Mariano told us that she wanted Yale to have something from his papers and suggested as a possibility the letters he had received from Edith Wharton. We had to tell her that we felt those belonged with the Berenson archive at I Tatti; she sent us instead the surviving parts of the original manuscript of the *Studies*.

(The gift of the manuscript caused a crisis for the Italo-American postal system, happily resolved. At just this time, the Yale Library was receiving a steady stream of Italian publications under the Farmington Plan, whereby Yale was the designated American repository for these books. The packages as they came in their hundreds into the library's shipping department were gathered and stored unopened in the basement until such time as they could be properly dealt with. As luck would have it, the Berenson manuscript, mailed by Miss Mariano on 4 January 1964, had been wrapped in two packages more or less indistinguishable from those intended for the Farmington Plan. One of them, opened four months later, was correctly identified as belonging to the Collection of American Literature; but the second package was not discovered until 17 August, after Miss Mariano in Italy and I in New Haven had been fruitlessly hounding the postal authorities for several weeks.)

The first actual use of the Wharton papers was, technically, in violation of one of the conditions. The librarian was asked to search the manuscripts for unpublished critical articles by Mrs. Wharton which, according to the letter of gift, were to be "accessible only to *bona fide* students of literature" with the "consent and approval of the appropriate Professor or Professors in the Department of English."

Obviously, an exception could be made for Mrs. Wharton's literary executor gathering material for the first posthumous collection of her writings!

It so happened that the second use of the papers was also contrary to one of the conditions that Yale had been asked to accept. In 1945 Mme Louis Gillet was preparing for publication a selection of her late husband's letters. Knowing that he had corresponded with Mrs. Wharton about his translations of several of her novels, Mme Gillet appealed to Gaillard Lapsley for copies of the letters. He referred her request to the Yale librarian. Although it was no simple task to locate individual items in the correspondence (filed by Mrs. Wharton's secretary in chronological order), a few Gillet letters were eventually found. In reporting to Lapsley, the librarian reminded him of the thirty-year restriction placed on access to such papers, but added that he, as donor, certainly had the right to make an exception. Mme Gillet's request was granted and she was sent photostats of the letters.

Lapsley's and Yale's indulgence was rewarded three years later, in March 1948, when Mme Gillet wrote to inquire whether the university would like to buy "about fifty" letters and cards that Edith Wharton had written to Louis Gillet. Of course we did want the letters, and our offer for them was duly accepted. Mme Gillet entrusted delivery to an American friend who was coming to New York, where it was arranged I would pick them up on 12 January 1949. When I got to the city I found that although the letters had been left for me to collect, Mme Gillet's friend had been injured in a traffic accident and was in Roosevelt Hospital. I talked with her there and came to an agreement about method of payment (there were strict controls then over taking dollars into France). Mme Gillet had hoped that she might be able to acquire an American vacuum cleaner ("so much better than the French machines") in return for the letters. I am sorry that I have forgotten whether she eventually received her hoped-for Hoover.

II

For fifteen years, scholars wishing to use the Wharton correspondence accepted with no more than a grumble or two of protest the fact that the papers would not be available until 1968. Blake Nevius, professor of English at the University of California, Los Angeles, having spent a summer month in New Haven in 1949, working on a Wharton biography, reported to me that he had found the available material to be of little importance for a general critical study and ventured to criticize adversely the rigidity of Mr. Lapsley's conditions. He wrote in October of his feeling, shared by others he had talked with, that no writer, however important, can survive thirty years of critical neglect: if some kind of reassessment is not made promptly, it will probably never happen. The Wharton restrictions have kept many people from writing about her, because they obviously don't wish to see their work out-dated in 1968. Gaillard Lapsley had died recently and Nevius confessed to having hoped that a successor literary executor might have been willing to distinguish between papers in the Wharton archive that had biographical interest and those with little significance for the biographer but great literary importance. He would have been glad to submit what he had written for Mr. Lapsley's censorship, but the time for that had now passed.

A publisher and a scholar who shared Blake Nevius's convictions attempted, late in 1953, to do something about the situation. Harper & Row and Wayne Andrews, an architectural historian, then curator of manuscripts at the New York Historical Society, undertook a campaign to have the Wharton archive opened for their benefit. We received eloquent pleas in Andrews's behalf from both Simon Michael Bessie, a member of the firm, and Russell Lynes, managing editor of *Harper's Magazine*. Ultimately, another letter came from Mrs. Wharton's executor, Mrs. Elisina Royall Tyler, living in France. Because the problem was one that only lawyers could resolve definitively, I referred the matter for an opinion to the university's counsel, summarizing the facts as I knew them. I quoted from Mrs. Tyler's letter her wish as executor of the Wharton estate that the "correspondence and other letters and papers of a biographical sort," referred to in Mr. Lapsley's letter of 7 May 1938, be made available to Wayne Andrews for use in writing a biography of Mrs. Wharton. I added the information that

On June 11, 1938, the Yale Corporation voted "to accept with gratitude the manuscripts and papers of the late Edith Wharton, Litt. D. 1923, presented by her literary executor, Gaillard Lapsley, Esq., to the Library ... and ... to direct the Librarian in administering this collection to be bound by the terms and conditions set forth in Mr. Lapsley's letter of May 7, 1938, to the President."

and concluded:

Information is requested as to whether Mrs. Wharton's Executor has the right to require the University to break the terms of its agreement with Mr. Lapsley, and, if so, whether action to this effect by the Corporation will be required. Also, if the papers are to be opened, should the University endeavor to persuade Mrs. Tyler, in the interests of fairness and for the benefit of Yale scholars among others, to allow unrestricted access to the material in question?

Mr. Andrews's biography of Mrs. Wharton has been announced for publication by the firm of Harper's and we understand that a member of that firm was instrumental in persuading Mrs. Tyler to attempt to secure access to the restricted Wharton papers for Mr. Andrews. ...

The lawyers responded on 5 March:

It is our opinion that because of the agreement made between Yale and Mr. Lapsley it is not now legally permissible to grant the request of Mrs. Tyler ... to make available to Mr. Andrews for biographical use the correspondence and other letters and papers of a biographical sort. Since the questions of fact and law are intertwined and are a bit complicated, we have thought it might be of assistance to you to prepare a suggested draft of answer to Mrs. Tyler, which is accordingly enclosed ... .

I prepared the letter to Mrs. Tyler exactly as drafted and it went off over the librarian's signature on 8 March, with a carbon to Wayne Andrews:

This will refer to your letter of October 19, 1953, requesting us in your capacity as executor of Mrs. Edith Wharton's estate to make her correspondence available to Mr. Wayne Andrews for biographical purposes. We would wish, of course, to cooperate in meeting your request and have thoroughly discussed it among ourselves and with counsel for the

University. It unfortunately appears, however, that under the terms of the gift of Mrs. Wharton's papers to Yale, we have received this collection subject to certain limitations as to use which we are not free to alter.

As you may recall, Mrs. Wharton in Article XXIII of her French will, dated June 11, 1937, and filed at Montmorency, gave to Gaillard Lapsley all her "manuscripts, literary correspondence and documents with the request that he shall take care of the publication, sale, preservation or destruction of all such documents and manuscripts". Previously, in Article Ninth of her American will, dated December 3, 1936, with codicil of March 20, 1937, and probated in New York, Mrs. Wharton had appointed Gaillard Lapsley her literary executor and directed him "to carry out this task in accordance with instructions left by me among my papers". Thus, Mr. Lapsley appears to have obtained clear title to the correspondence now in issue, and it appears to have been Mrs. Wharton's intent that he have the power to dispose of her papers under such conditions as he might deem advisable. One of the specific conditions he did set in his gift to Yale provides that:

> "The correspondence and other letters and papers of a biographical sort shall not be accessible until thirty years after they have been received by the University Library."

The Yale Corporation, grateful to receive this valuable collection, in June, 1938 naturally acceded to and formally adopted the terms of the gift which the donor saw fit to impose—terms, I may add, which are not unusual in the light of our experience in administering literary property. Mr. Lapsley is now dead and it can only be presumed, without provision to the contrary in the wills and in his agreement with Yale, that it was not his intent, nor that of Mrs. Wharton, to vary the terms of the gift now or before the thirty-year time limit expires.

On this background I hope you will appreciate the compelling reasons why we cannot honor your request. On the other hand, of course, we will be delighted to help Mr. Andrews in whatever way we can. Please let me know if I can be of further service to you, and accept my sincere regrets that circumstances do not permit a favorable reply to your letter.

I assumed that the matter was settled, and was surprised, more than two years later, to receive from one of the Yale lawyers a carbon of his letter of 11 October 1956 to a law firm in New York:

I acknowledge receipt of your letter of October 8th. In my letter to you of April 26, 1956 I told you the conditions under which Yale University accepted a gift of the Wharton papers. Our advice to Yale is and will be that its obligation is to live up to the terms of the gift to it. I, therefore, must repeat our refusal to make the papers or any part of them available to Messrs. Harper Bros. and Wayne Andrews.

(Eventually, Andrews decided to give up the idea of writing a biography and contented himself with editing a collection of Mrs. Wharton's fiction. His *Best Short Stories of Edith Wharton* was published in 1958 and he then went on to other projects. As to Harper & Row, our story continues.)

III

In *Pigeons on the Granite* I referred briefly to what I deemed "the failure of most of the [Yale] English department faculty properly to appreciate and make use of the resources of the collection [of American literature] for research." Through the years of my curatorship unique manuscript materials by significant American writers given or bequeathed to Yale in the expectation that they would be of use to members of the Yale faculty and their students were instead being utilized chiefly by scholars from other universities. The letters of James Fenimore Cooper (Yale Class of 1806) were being edited by James Beard of Clark University, Worcester, Massachusetts; the "official" biography of Sinclair Lewis (Yale 1907) was being written by Mark Schorer of the University of California at Los Angeles; biographical works about Eugene O'Neill (Yale 1926 Hon.) were being written by Arthur and Barbara Gelb, Louis Sheaffer, and various other individuals, but no one at Yale. The list goes on and on—and continued so throughout the period of my curatorship, an especially flagrant instance coming after the death of Norman Holmes Pearson in 1975 when we could find no one at Yale interested in consummating his forty-year involvement with collecting and editing the letters of Nathaniel Hawthorne.

And so, in 1963, with the opening of the Edith Wharton papers only five years off, we were determined to make every effort to see that someone at Yale would be the first to work with this important archive. In July, in New York, Jim Babb happened to meet Armitage Watkins, whose firm, A. Watkins, Inc., were the agents for Edith Wharton's literary properties. Watkins asked about the current status of Yale's Wharton papers, and Jim advised him to write me as "the person who has all the answers." Watkins did write, proposing that we discuss the papers over lunch in New York. I thanked him for his letter and agreed that "interest in the Wharton papers seems to be building up and it would be well for us to get together." We eventually fixed upon 7 August as the date for our meeting.

Meanwhile I discussed the situation with Jim Babb and R. W. B. Lewis, professor of English and American studies, whose publications had already given him an excellent reputation in his field. He had only recently completed work on a new edition of Mrs. Wharton's *The House of Mirth,* and expressed interest in investigating her papers when they became available. We pointed out that, in accordance with standard Yale Library policy at that time, he, as a member of the Yale faculty, could be given exclusive access to the archive for a five-year period.

Of course the cooperation of the Wharton estate and its literary agent would be essential. Not only was their permission required for the publication of unpublished material by Mrs. Wharton, but Yale was not without hope that William Tyler, son and heir of Elisina Royall Tyler (who had died without having written the biography she had planned and for which she had gathered important Wharton materials), might be persuaded to deposit and perhaps eventually to give her papers for the Wharton archive at Yale.

Just before my scheduled meeting with Watkins in New York, Jim Babb received a letter from Tyler, then assistant secretary of state in Washington. He wrote, on 3 August, that he had heard that the Yale Library was thinking of opening the Edith Wharton files prior to 1968. Would Mr. Babb let him know whether the report was accurate and, if so, when the papers would be made available to the public?

I met with Watkins on the 7th of August and gave him a nine-page listing of our Wharton manuscripts and letters. He suggested that we have a further meeting in New York with the Tyler lawyer, Herbert Fierst. Back in New Haven on the 8th, I replied for Jim Babb (who was away on vacation) to William Tyler:

Mr. Babb knew that I had already planned to see Armitage Watkins yesterday in New York and asked me to let you know of any developments.

But we agreed only on a policy of continuing with caution, Mr. Watkins suggesting that possibly your lawyer, he and I might meet at some time in New York.

No, we have never had any idea of opening the Edith Wharton private papers and correspondence before the date stipulated in Yale's agreement with Gaillard Lapsley, *i.e.,* thirty years after the receipt of the papers in New Haven in the Summer of 1938. But we have hoped for a number of years that someone at Yale would wish to work with the papers when they become available … . Professor R. W. B. Lewis, who teaches in the English and American Studies departments, has expressed interest in undertaking this project. He has only just returned from six months in Italy and I have not yet had a chance to talk with him, but I am sure that his interest continues.

You may have heard from Mr. [Frederic] King that he has recently given us the Edith Wharton letters to Mrs. Jones that Mrs. Farrand did not include with those she gave us during her lifetime, and he has deposited here a similar group of Mrs. Wharton's letters to Mrs. Farrand. We very much hope that it will be possible to continue, by gift and purchase, to add to the Edith Wharton papers.

The meeting with Herbert Fierst took place at luncheon in New York on 11 September. We discussed the situation at some length. I suggested that Tyler might consider depositing his Wharton papers at Yale so that they would be available along with our papers when they were opened. The arrangements then might be similar to those with the Sinclair Lewis estate concerning the Lewis papers, with Tyler controlling access to his Wharton papers and Yale agreeing that the person authorized to use those materials would have exclusive right to consult ours. Fierst said that Tyler might like Yale to list and pack his papers, now in France, for dispatch to New Haven, and might consider the possibility of giving them over a number of years, with appropriate appraisals for income-tax purposes. He promised to discuss all this with Tyler.

I reported to Jim Babb when he returned from vacation on 27 September, and we agreed that Dick Lewis should be advised to make written application now to use the papers when they were opened in 1968, with the understanding that he would indeed be given exclusive access to them for a five-year period. Dick was, of course, eager to have matters settled so that he could make a definite commitment.

Meanwhile, Fierst reported that Mrs. William Tyler hoped to be able to list the Tyler Wharton papers during the summer in France. He thought that Tyler would then be in a better position to make provisions for their gift or deposit.

Dick Lewis decided definitely the following April to write the Wharton book, and was sufficiently confident to schedule some preliminary research on it for the summer of 1965. I communicated his decision to Herbert Fierst, adding that

I believe he plans to meet with Armitage Watkins in New York within the next few days to discuss the project. He assures me that he fully intends to write the kind of book that will be not only sound from a scholarly point of view but also appealing to such people as the Book of the Month Club judges and the general public. I hope that it will be possible eventually for you and perhaps Mr. Tyler to talk with Mr. Lewis about the book.

Fierst replied to my letter on 27 April, saying that he was pleased to learn of Professor Lewis's definite interest in writing a book on Edith Wharton. There were others who were interested, but he felt that lively competition at this stage was healthy. Armitage Watkins and he had had a long meeting in Washington just the day before with Mr. Tyler, who would soon be leaving to become United States ambassador to the Netherlands. Tyler was very much interested in the Wharton project, although he would not have time to become deeply involved in it. Fierst felt that Watkins and he would be able to reflect Mr. Tyler's views and would do all they could to cooperate.

Dick Lewis's report on the "current status of the Edith Wharton enterprise ... as background for further talks in the fall" reached me in Europe in July 1965:

I had a fairly long and amiable and reasonably well be-cocktailed lunch with Mike Watkins and his associate Peggy Caulfield in New York ... just before the rush period at college—exams, gradings, dissertations and so on ... .

It was, as I say, an amiable lunch—we moved on to first names pretty fast. Watkins said to me what you had predicted he would: that he was uneasy about a "learned, earnest, professor who couldn't breathe life into the material" and so on. He was also restive under the arrangement whereby a Yale designee would have not only first access to the Edith Wharton papers at Yale, but control over them for five years ... . I did not myself press that side of things; I acknowledged my interest in being so designated, but of course did not take any *stand* or suggest that I held any kind of whip-hand. I was, in fact, hoping to win his approval as the biographer more or less on my own credentials.

Watkins mentioned several other candidates, though none seems—in retrospect at least—very pressing. Some of them are not really equipped for the job, and of those that are, none is either interested or available. Watkins does not seem to have any favorite of his own; he has only a certain *type* in mind.

A few days after our lunch, I wrote Watkins a long letter outlining my plans, if I actually undertook the assignment. I also sent him several of the books I've written or edited. He has not answered my letter or acknowledged the books.

Meanwhile, I have written William Tyler. By a lucky coincidence, I will be in The Netherlands for five days this September, and I wrote to ask … if I might call upon him to discuss matters. No answer from that either, though there has hardly been time. But of course, if I can secure Mr. Tyler's assent, that part of the problem is settled.

As I told both Messrs. Watkins and Tyler, I am eager to get things decided very soon, since I will have a leave of absence next year— 1966–67—and it is not too early to begin planning the year. For example, I would presumably spend the summer near Hyères, examining the papers in the villa. By the way, they (the papers there) seem to have been catalogued—at least provisionally and amateurishly. Watkins waved a folder at me which seemed to contain such a catalogue,★ and good-naturedly, if a bit meanly, prodded my interest by hinting at great disclosures. …

I'll write again when I hear from Mr. Tyler … . I think myself that the matter is a fait accompli which Watkins either doesn't quite recognize or is not quite willing to acknowledge. … But I don't think he really has a great deal of choice, and I suspect he knows and resents it. I am determined to play up to him as much as I am congenitally able to do, since, if for no other reason, I expect to be dealing with him for a long time.

This doesn't really need an answer, and I'm sure you're busy. But if you do have thoughts or advice, in the light of this report, I would of course welcome it warmly.

My secretary at the library had informed Dick that I was in Europe and the promised second letter, written on 9 August, reached me only a few days after the first:

I now have a definite date to meet and talk with William Tyler at The Hague, during the week of Sept. 13, when I'll be at a conference in Utrecht. I would like to be as accurate as possible in my report to him

---

★This was, presumably, the listing made by Mrs. William Tyler during the summer of 1964.

about the Wharton papers at Yale, and my relation to them. My questions are these. How formal and final is my designation as the person to whom these papers will be made accessible in 1968? Who is the designating authority—you individually; or the Yale library; or the University; or who? What is the maximum period during which I shall have control over access to the papers? Can or should my designation be made more formal or legal or whatever?

I understand, of course, that you can authorize my seeing the papers, but not my quoting from them. By the way, does your authority extend in any way to the documents now at Hyères?

I realize that the situation is too complex, and perhaps even too unsettled, for you to give me an elaborate answer to these questions in a letter at this stage from Europe. But I would be immensely grateful if you could drop me a note giving me a quick general sense of things. I don't want either to underplay or overplay my hand with Mr. Tyler.

That meeting looms as all important, since Mike Watkins continues to drag his heels, to talk vaguely about "a number of other candidates," and to insist on patience, on his need to talk with other authors and publishers and so on. After a two months delay, he finally replied to my long letter of last May, suggesting my own long-range plans. He was affable as always, but spoke, as I say, of a lot of study that had to be made "before any decision can be reached as to whom the papers should be made available." I would like to be sure in my mind that *that* decision—at least as regards the papers at Yale—has already been made, and by you. I won't rub this in with Watkins; I suspect that one of the clues to his behavior is a mild resentment that in fact the main decision about the whole Wharton business has been made, and not by him. But I'd like to be sure.

I won't hold you up longer, especially since I envision you reading this standing up in the Paris American Express. But I'd like to say that I am more passionately interested every day in doing the Wharton biography, and I see ever more clearly how much advance planning must be made before I really get down to business on my next year's leave. So I'd appreciate even a hurried note about some of the questions I've mentioned.

I answered Dick's letter in longhand on 14 August, assuring him that he was the library's only candidate and stressing the importance of his coming to some understanding with Tyler as representative of the Wharton estate and owner of the Elisina Royall Tyler Wharton papers. If the estate should select someone else as biographer, Yale would be obliged to give that individual access to the Wharton papers at Yale (in order to stand any chance of eventually being given the Tyler papers). Dick had to persuade Tyler and Watkins that he was the best qualified person to undertake the job.

IV

This he was eventually successful in doing. In short order, Tyler and Watkins had given their blessing, Harper & Row had agreed to publish the book, and the Lewis biography of Edith Wharton was under weigh well before the Yale papers became available. In January 1967 Dick Lewis began work on the materials at the home of Ambassador and Mrs. Tyler in The Hague. (These were the papers Elisina Royall Tyler had accumulated in the expectation of writing her own biography of her friend.)

On the very first day of his research Dick came "on the track" of one Morton Fullerton, an American journalist, discovering to his astonishment that he and Mrs. Wharton had had a passionate love affair. From Morton's cousin, Hugh Fullerton, then director of the American Hospital in Neuilly, he learned of a poem written by Edith Wharton, describing "in a well-nigh scandalous manner" a night she had spent in June 1909 with Fullerton at the Charing Cross Hotel, London. Morton had given his cousin a copy of the poem, which Hugh led Dick Lewis to believe he had burned.

In the summer of 1968, just before the Yale papers became available to him, Dick Lewis engaged as his research assistant Miss Marion Mainwaring, a Radcliffe Ph. D. She agreed to investigate the Parisian phase of Mrs. Wharton's life, with particular emphasis on Morton Fullerton. She discovered that he had been married to and soon divorced from a French woman, Camille Chabert, and had been blackmailed by a mysterious old lady whom she guessed to be one Henriette Mirecourt. Although some of the correspondence, including twenty-two letters from Edith Wharton, seventy-one from Henry James, and a few from Rudyard Kipling, Oscar Wilde, and Owen Wister, was sold to the Houghton Library at Harvard by Hugh Fullerton, the bulk of Morton's papers had been still in his possession when he died in 1952, and Camille Chabert had carried them off. When she herself died in the 1960s, an Englishman, George Nolan, a tenant on the ground floor of her house, had taken possession of the Fullerton papers in order to save them from being thrown away.

Marion Mainwaring reported all this to Dick Lewis, and he passed the information on to us at the Beinecke Library. In the fall of 1970 we purchased the Fullerton papers as an addition to the Wharton archive. They included some forty letters to him from his cousin and one-time fiancée, who eventually became Katherine Fullerton Gerould and achieved fame as a short-story writer and essayist. There were also numerous letters from the Ranee of Sarawak. The *intimate* letters from Edith Wharton to Fullerton were not included, in either our purchase or Harvard's. They did eventually turn up— and were sold at auction to the University of Texas at Austin.

In the fall of 1971, Dick Lewis, convinced that Hugh Fullerton could not have brought himself to destroy Mrs. Wharton's poem, wrote him about it. He confessed that he did have the copy that Morton had made before he returned the original to Edith Wharton. Dick managed to persuade him to sell it to Yale. Needless to say, all fifty-two lines of the poem, titled "Terminus," were printed in the biography.

During the period when R. W. B. Lewis was at work on his book, there was never any problem with other scholars. Most of them required access to the papers for specific purposes which obviously did not conflict with the Lewis research. When the five-year exclusive period came to an end in 1973, work on the biography was close to completion.

Although when I took over as curator of the Yale Collection of American Literature in 1947, most of the Wharton papers had not been listed, the manuscripts, because they were to be available to "bona fide" students, had been roughly catalogued. Some of the shorter pieces and fragments were indexed only as groups, however, making it difficult to locate individual titles. Eventually I recatalogued most of these and, in the process, made individual cards for seventeen pages of "Fiction and criticism," which included a story fragment titled "Beatrice Palmato." I didn't examine any of them in detail, merely making a note of the size and number of pages of each manuscript.

Apparently, no one had any curiosity about Mrs. Wharton's "Beatrice Palmato" for the first thirty years of its presence at Yale; but in the 1970s, Cynthia Griffin Wolff was doing research for a book on Mrs. Wharton's fiction and had a particular interest in the novel she had planned involving an incestual relationship between a father and his daughter. Mrs. Wolff actually read the "Beatrice Palmato" fragment and discovered to her astonishment that it was a graphically detailed account of a sexual encounter between the two protagonists. She subsequently theorized that Mrs. Wharton had written it "in order to articulate fully to herself the precise nature, feeling, and history of the incestuous experience which was to lie behind and to color the actual narrative."

The astonishing permissiveness of the post-*Lady Chatterley*-decision years allowed Dick Lewis to print in an appendix to his biography the "Beatrice Palmato" manuscript. That publication, which only a few years earlier would have resulted in the suppression of the book, now contributed to its success with the public when it was issued, by Harper & Row, in 1975. Greeted by universal critical acclaim, it won for its author the Pulitzer Prize in Biography. Despite Blake Nevius's pessimistic forecast of 1949, Edith Wharton triumphantly survived the thirty-year embargo on access to her papers. R. W. B. Lewis's work, welcomed with particular enthusiasm by the feminists, may be said to have inaugurated a Wharton revival—much to the delight of Watkins, Tyler, and the author himself, who went on to publish various new editions of writings by Edith Wharton, to advise on adaptations for television and motion pictures, and, with his wife Nancy, to issue a collection of the letters.

Some other developments involving the Tyler Wharton papers were much less welcome. Wayne Andrews, during the period when he was still hoping to write a Wharton biography, had met Elisina Royall Tyler in Paris. She had not only given him access to her Wharton papers, but had allowed him to borrow some of them for further study. As luck would have it, she had left for the south of France when Andrews returned the borrowed materials. They were accepted on her behalf by her housekeeper at the Paris apartment. Mrs. Tyler subsequently fell ill and died, and her housekeeper also passed away, both within a short time. The housekeeper's heirs, claiming that the Wharton papers returned by Wayne Andrews were gifts to her from Mrs. Tyler, offered them for sale in the United States to C. Waller Barrett, in those days the principal private collector of American literature (he had already given much of his collection to the library of the University of Virginia). Because William Tyler was still United States ambassador to the Netherlands, he felt that he could not afford the publicity of a lawsuit, even to regain possession of his mother's rightful property. He declined to challenge the transaction, with the result that those important materials from the Tyler papers are now in the University of Virginia Library.

As for the Wharton papers remaining in Tyler's possession, Yale paid a price for the success of the Lewis biography. Wharton manuscript material of course increased substantially in value. Armitage Watkins's righthand woman Peggy Caulfield came to see me at the Beinecke Library in December 1975 and reported that "Bill Tyler's obligations and age are such that he wished to sell rather than make a donation" of his Edith Wharton papers. Unfortunately, at just that time all available Beinecke funds had been used in our acquisition of the archive of Richard Wright. Although there was some faint hope that we might eventually be able to find a donor, Tyler and his counsel felt that, for various reasons, it would not be appropriate to wait for possible negotiations. On 6 April 1976, Armitage Watkins and Peggy Caulfield wrote me, signing the letter jointly, to say that Bill Tyler's Edith Wharton papers had been sold to the Lilly Library at Bloomington, Indiana. The agreement with the library had been signed the week before and they wanted me to know.

My feelings about collections of an author's papers have always been ambivalent. Surely, for the scholar, it is most convenient to have the bulk of the material available in its original form in a single public institution. And yet, in these days of photo- and electronic duplication, there are numerous ways of facilitating research with documents, even when they are scattered throughout the world. Dispersed in multiple depositories, they can be used by more scholars, still well cared for, still exhibited, and all for the benefit of a vastly increased audience. I confess that my regret at losing the Tyler Wharton materials was outweighed by gratification that a Yale scholar had been the first to use an important Yale Library manuscript collection, and that he had brilliantly succeeded.

Edward Lear

Left by his friend to breakfast alone on the white
Italian shore, his Terrible Demon arose
Over his shoulder; he wept to himself in the night,
A dirty landscape-painter who hated his nose.

The legions of cruel inquisitive 'They'
Were so solid and strong, like Dogs; he was upset
By germans and boats; affection was miles away:
But, guided by tears, he successfully reached his Regret.

His welcome was prodigious: A flower took his hat
And bore him off to introduce him to the tongs;
The Demon's false nose made the table laugh; a cat
Invited him to dance and shyly squeezed his hand;
Words pushed him to the piano to sing comic songs.

And children swarmed to him like settlers; He became a land.

W. H. Auden

W. H. Auden. "Edward Lear." Ink on paper, 10¾ x 8¼ inches. Yale Center for British Art, gift of Donald C. Gallup, '34, '39 Grad.

Private Pursuits

Collecting Edward Lear
1943–1997

I

IN THE WINTER OF 1943–44, I was stationed in London with the Adjutant General's section of United States Army Services of Supply Headquarters. Active preparation for the expected Allied invasion of the continent did not intensify for us until spring, and we were allowed an afternoon off each (seven-day) week. Although the large public museums were closed for the duration, their treasures stored in the country, several small commercial galleries, many secondhand bookshops, and even the libraries of the Victoria & Albert and British museums were open. I visited some of them fairly regularly and, now and then, did a bit of research.

One afternoon, leaving the British Museum, I happened to pass the shop of F. R. Meatyard, Printseller, in Museum Street. There in the window were several small watercolors by Edward Lear (1812–88). Although I had known his limericks and some of his other poems for many years, I first learned that he had been by profession an artist from reading Angus Davidson's *Edward Lear, Landscape Painter and Nonsense Poet* in 1941. And so, three years later, I examined the sketches on display with a great deal of interest and, entering the Meatyard shop, was delighted to find a good many larger examples hanging on the walls. The small ones were priced at only a few shillings (the pound was then valued at just over four dollars), and I bought one or two of them. I enjoyed them so much that I continued to purchase a few each week.

When I came to study the sketches with a magnifying glass, I discovered that they had been done in pencil, on the spot, and then, later, inked over and colored. Pencil notations of landscape features and colors, often spelled phonetically, were also penned over. Some very small drawings were on pieces of paper cut from leaves, the versos of which had borne what seems to have been a journal, written in pencil. Almost all of the larger sketches carried numbers and dates, also entered in pencil and inked over, with even the time of day indicated.

Meatyard told me that the source of his supply was the firm of Craddock & Barnard in Tunbridge Wells, which had acquired from the Lushington family and at auction in 1929 many of the drawings bequeathed by Lear to Franklin Lushington, his executor. Another large group of similar sketches had been given to Lord Northbrook, the viceroy of India at whose invitation Lear had travelled to that country in 1873–75. These drawings had been sold also in 1929 and the early 1930s, and most of them were acquired by W. B. Osgood Field and Philip Hofer, who gave their Lear collections to Harvard for the Houghton Library in 1942. The total of such sketches left by Lear is thought to have been close to ten thousand.

It occurred to me that it would be interesting to have a series of the watercolors done over a particular period, and I asked Meatyard one day if any albums existed. When I returned the following week, he produced a bound volume containing 340 small sketches, all drawn between January and July 1867, mostly in Egypt. Because the greater part of my pay as captain was going home into savings, the price for the album made it necessary to buy it on the instalment plan. Although Meatyard was quite willing for me to take my purchase away with me, I insisted that it stay with him until I had finished paying for it.

Since almost all of the sketches I had acquired at the Meatyard shop were small, I felt that I ought to have at least one of a larger size. The Redfern Gallery in Cork Street had shown a group of Lear watercolors in the spring of 1942. That exhibition had travelled around England under the auspices of the British Arts Council and a good many of the pictures had since been returned to the gallery. I, by this time an habitué, was allowed to go over the lot of forty or fifty that remained, to select the one I liked best of those I could afford. I finally fixed upon *Tepelene,* featuring a large plane tree, with a fountain underneath at the right. It is still the best of my Lear watercolors.

In September 1944, my headquarters was transferred first to Paris, and then, after that very frigid, coal-short winter in the City of Light, to Frankfurt, Germany, where, rechristened Headquarters, Communications Zone, European Theater of Operations, we were housed, along with General Eisenhower himself, in the I. G. Farben building. My stay there was blessedly brief, for I was successful in applying for admission to Oxford for Michaelmas term, 1945, at Magdalen College under a special American army quota. At the close of those few idyllic weeks in Oxford, during which I gleaned a great deal of useful information on English literary bibliography from Professor David Nichol Smith, I travelled, on 11 December 1945, by train to London to await air transportation to the States.

The seasonal English fogs gave me a few days' grace, and I went back to Museum Street to see what might still be available in the way of Edward Lears. There I discovered that Meatyard had retired to Tunbridge Wells, and Craddock & Barnard were now established in what had been the Meatyard shop. The supply of watercolors was sadly diminished, but I did acquire another album, this one containing thirty-four fairly large, early drawings, including eight of the Lake District, of which others done in the same period, 1835–36, are in the Victoria & Albert Museum, the British Museum, and the Houghton Library.

Back in the States and once more a civilian, I accepted the offer of Jim Babb, the Yale librarian, to become curator of the Collection of American Literature, assistant professor of bibliography, and editor of the *Yale University Library Gazette*. Doing my best to meet the challenges of my three positions, I didn't have much free time during the next few years for actual collecting, although my interest in Lear continued strong. In November 1955, John Carter, then employed at Sotheby's, London, called my attention to a group of some twenty-eight Lear watercolors to be sold by the auction house later that month. I sent what I considered to be fairly generous bids, a little above the estimate in each case, on all twenty-eight, but, after the sale, I received word from Sotheby's that "the lowest figure paid for an Edward Lear drawing in today's sale exceeded your highest commission; therefore no lot was secured for you." It was obvious that the Lear market had now passed me by.

II

During the war I had paid little attention to the oil paintings, most of which seemed to me to lack the freshness and spontaneity of the watercolors. It was all too obvious that Lear had found wearisome the labor of completing a picture painted in oil, especially in the large size he felt he had to use in order to earn his living. I had acquired, in the album of early work purchased in December 1945, a sketch in oil on paper, of trees, with a hint of buildings in the distance, done at Corpo di Cava, Italy, on 28 June 1838. But that sketch did not satisfy the need I felt to have at least one finished oil painting as part of my Lear collection.

I found it eventually in London in 1949, at a bookstore in Cecil Court, off Charing Cross Road. I had asked the owner of the tiny shop whether he had anything by Lear, and he had agreed to bring in his one small picture. When I returned the following day, he had *Zagóri* (1860), showing, in the foreground, a group of natives seated at the very edge of an abyss and, in the middle distance, a small village built on a cliff, with more, even dizzier rocky heights beyond. The painting was in its original Lear frame, and I did buy it, even though I had of course to carry it with me around Europe that summer. (Lear's oils often do not ship well, his pigments having a tendency to become separated from the canvas.)

When, on a later visit to London, in 1957, I stopped to see Craddock & Barnard, I found that they had at last sold out their Lears, even though one of the partners had earlier told me that he thought they would never see the end of their stock. I managed to persuade him, even so, to rummage around in the back office, and he came up with another oil sketch, of leaves, also done at La Cava, 28 June 1838, a number of unfinished pencil drawings, along with various lists of paintings and sketches—some of them in Lear's own hand.

My next oil, *Butrinto* (1861), came from Arthur Rogers, a dealer in rare books and pictures at Newcastle-on-Tyne. Listed in one of his catalogues, it was called to my attention by my Yale colleague Dudley Bahlmann. I wrote at once to ask for the photograph mentioned as available on request. The picture proved to be a typical Lear landscape, a few shepherds among rocks and foliage in the foreground, with the lake and mountains blue and white in the distance. When the painting arrived in New Haven, the U. S. Customs inspector raised some question about the original Lear gold-leaf frame, but finally yielded to my argument that it was of negligible commercial value.

Another oil, *Corfù from Santa Decca* (1862), shows natives in a clearing in a forest, again with sea and mountains behind. I acquired it from George Dix, a Yale classmate, at Durlacher's in New York, trading him watercolors and drawings from my collection to the value of half of the price. Another, larger oil, *Corfù from Ascension* (also 1862), again with shepherds and sheep in the foreground, the forest in the middle distance, and sea and mountain range beyond, I found listed in the catalogue of Emily Driscoll, a dealer primarily in manuscripts, in New York. She had had the painting unsold for some time and seemed glad to get rid of it.

Kinchinjunga, from Darjeeling (1879), the largest of my Lears, measuring four by six feet without the eight-inch original Lear frame, became part of my collection as the result of a series of coincidences. I had happened to read in the Sunday *New York Times* in February 1951, in the account of the auctions to take place during the following week, that a sale on Saturday at the Plaza Art Galleries would include "two paintings by Edward Lear." I had already planned to be in New York the following day and stopped at the galleries, on 57th Street on the ground floor. Parked at the sidewalk outside was a large van, from which workmen were unloading furniture. I asked the manager about the Lear paintings and he said that material for Saturday's auction was just being delivered; the galleries were closed, but I could come back the next day and see everything. As I was about to explain that it wouldn't be easy for me to come back, he hesitated and added that if the Lears were "those large pictures" they were already in place and I could look at them. He led me to an office at one side of the main gallery, where the paintings were indeed hung. One was the *Kinchinjunga,* with trees, other greenery, and a band of pilgrims in the foreground, and the range of peaks now more usually spelled "Kangchenjunga" towering on the horizon. The other, of exactly the same size, was the *Plains of Bengal,* showing rivers winding away into the distance. Although I knew that hanging a picture of such size in my apartment at Jonathan Edwards College might present problems, I decided that at least I could leave a bid on *Kinchinjunga.* My decision was strengthened when the manager confided to me that he himself was expecting to bid on that picture, planning to cut the canvas down to more manageable size. I left a bid and returned home.

There was in New Haven at this time another ardent Lear collector, Ray Livingston Murphy, Yale '47 M., and I told him about the pictures. He became very much excited and insisted that we must attend the auction. It was settled that he and I would meet Bill McCarthy, a friend who then worked for the firm of Rosenbach in New York, at the galleries on the following Saturday in plenty of time for the bidding on the Lears. Coincidentally, Bill had been employed as cataloguer at the Houghton Library when the Lear collection of W. B. Osgood Field was received by Harvard. Included in it at the time were these two pictures, which Osgood Field had acquired from the estate of the 2nd Earl of Northbrook, son of the 1st Earl, who had invited Lear to travel in India, and for whom the two pictures had been painted. Bill Jackson, librarian of the Houghton Library, had regretfully decided that the paintings could never be hung in Houghton because of their size and they had not been included in the gift of the collection. They had continued to hang, one at either end of Osgood Field's gymnasium in Purchase, New York, until his death. It was these pictures and other furnishings from his estate that were being sold.

We three were at the galleries in ample time for the sale. The first of the Lears to come up was the *Plains of Bengal,* and because Ray and I had agreed that I was to have the *Kinchinjunga* as my rightful first choice, he began to bid. At one time Bill McCarthy and I had the distinct impression that he was bidding against himself, but the picture was quickly knocked down to him. Whereupon the auctioneer announced that there was another painting by Lear of identical size, also of India, and the gentleman could have it at the same price. We hurriedly agreed that he should accept, and so *Kinchinjunga* too became his, temporarily. I think he was a little tempted to claim both pictures, but eventually honored our agreement and let me have mine at the price he had paid for it. It was he who made the arrangements for the transport of both pictures to New Haven. The *Plains of Bengal* proved to be too large for his own apartment and it had to be hung in that of his cousin, George Howe, then head of the Art and Architecture School at Yale (and, later, designer of the new setting for Philadelphia's Independence Hall). The staircases and hallways in Branford College, where Howe then lived, proved to be just enough narrower and lower than those in Jonathan Edwards, where I lived, so that the *Plains of Bengal* had to be removed from its frame and the frame taken apart before it could be carried up to Howe's third-floor apartment, whereas the *Kinchinjunga* came up to my fourth-floor apartment without any difficulty.

At that particular moment in J.E. a strong interest in art among the undergraduates had resulted in the organization of the Jonathan Edwards Art Club. The arrival of *Kinchinjunga* stimulated interest in Edward Lear the artist, and I was asked to exhibit a selection from my collection in the Junior Common Room. I had no difficulty in filling the walls. The Indian landscape was the star attraction of the show: in its gold-leaf frame, spot-lighted at the end of the long room, it looked very handsome. (It was the *Plains of Bengal,* owned at that time by the late Ray Murphy's brother in New York, that was featured in December 1961 in the Grolier Club Lear exhibition arranged by Fritz Liebert. I lent forty-six items, not including my big picture, for that show. But *Kinchinjunga* was again the prime exhibit in 1968 at the Worcester Art Museum, where, at the head of a double staircase, it could once more be seen from the proper distance.)

My final two oil paintings, small, early ones, were acquired in London, from the gallery of Mrs. Charlotte Frank, aunt by marriage of the diarist Anne Frank. They are views of the Roman campagna, one painted in 1842, the other undated, but done at about the same time. They are the only oils I have that are not in the frames originally ordered for them by the artist himself. Ironically, when they were shown along with the *Kinchinjunga* and three other of my oils in the Worcester exhibition, only these two were commented upon in the catalogue as "probably framed on Lear's orders."

III

During the war, I had picked up in London copies of a good many of Lear's printed books. The various *Journals of a Landscape Painter*— *in Albania, &c.* (1851), *in Southern Calabria, &c.* (1852), and *in Corsica* (1870)—could then be had for only a few shillings each. The folio *Views—in Rome and Its Environs* (1841) and *in the Seven Ionian Islands* (1863)—and the two-volume quarto *Illustrated Excursions in Italy* (1846) cost not more than a few guineas. But a first edition of the *Book of Nonsense* (2 parts, 1846) was even then a black tulip, well beyond my means. (Happily, Yale has two copies: one in the British Art Center, the gift of Paul Mellon, '29; the other, imperfect, in the Beinecke Library, has the title of part 1 plus forty-three plates, as well as the individual title page for part 2.) Other early editions of the *Book of Nonsense,* when copies in decent condition could be found, were also priced usually at more than I could afford to pay; but, in New Haven a good many years later, I did acquire, from Bob Barry at Stonehill's, a copy of the second edition (1855).

Technically, the rarest of Lear's folio color-plate books is his *Gleanings from the Menagerie and Aviary at Knowsley Hall* (1846), of which only one hundred copies were printed. The seventeen lithographs, hand-colored by a Mr. Bayfield, were the product of Lear's four-year residence at Knowsley, during which he wrote the *Book of Nonsense* for the amusement of the Knowsley young people, the grandchildren of the Earl of Derby. The book has for that reason a special place in a Lear collector's affection. A fine copy in the original binding turned up in an English bookseller's catalogue in 1964, and a cable secured it. (I gave it, somewhat reluctantly, to Yale in 1979.)

My copy of another, much commoner, plate book, the *Tortoises, Terrapins & Turtles* (1872), in the original binding, with the plates colored, came from the catalogue of a bookseller in Boston. Forty of the sixty plates had been issued first in parts some thirty years earlier—between 1836 and 1842—under the title *A Monograph of the Testudinata, by Thomas Bell,* and they constitute another of the Lear black tulips. Happily, the Beinecke Library, in 1981, was able to acquire a bound copy on the Edwin J. Beinecke Fund. My brief note about the book appeared in the *Gazette* for October of that year.

The best known of the color-plate books is *The Family of the Psittacidae* (1832)—commonly referred to as his *Parrots*. A missed Lear opportunity came for me in 1949 when I discovered a copy in a shop window on the Quai Voltaire in Paris. The price was certainly fair enough at the time, but more than I could possibly spend without running the risk of ending up penniless somewhere in Europe. And so I resisted the temptation—to my lasting regret, for I never did acquire a copy of the book. (Fortunately, Yale has an excellent copy, received in the collection of ornithological books given by William Robertson Coe, '49 Hon.)

The *Parrots* is, even so, represented in my Lear collection. It happened that, on that same European trip in 1949, having reached London, I came across, in the shop of Walter T. Spencer in New Oxford Street, a group of original watercolors of parrots, the backgrounds of which so closely resembled those published by Lear that it seemed to me they could have been done only by the master himself. One sketch in the group at Spencer's was very definitely Lear's, with manuscript notes by him. Made on the verso of an uncolored proof of one of the lithographs for the book, it was intended, presumably, to guide the individuals employed to do the coloring. Also connecting these materials with Lear were the wrappers, the title page, and the "Names of Subscribers" that accompanied the initial instalment of the *Parrots* when it was first issued—in parts. There were as well more uncolored proofs, one with a note in Lear's hand, which gave me the idea that the whole collection might have come from the shop of Hullmandel, who had printed the plates. After a good deal of debate with myself, I bought the lot and had it sent to

New Haven. When I later showed the watercolors to Dillon Ripley, then head of Yale's Peabody Museum and later secretary of the Smithsonian Institution, he felt that the frequent awkwardnesses in the drawing made it most unlikely that Lear could have been responsible for my birds. (It had occurred to me that, since Lear had given drawing lessons to Mrs. John Gould, these might be examples of her initial efforts.) Later I took the drawings with me to Cambridge and showed them to Philip Hofer at the Houghton Library. Together we compared the sketches with studies for the *Parrots* in the Harvard collection. Phil concluded that the drawings were quite possibly by Lear himself. In any case, they continue part of my Lear collection, although I did dispose of two "duplicates" to Bob Barry (as part payment on my copy of the second edition of the *Book of Nonsense),* and gave one of the uncolored proofs to Harvard.

In February 1995, Robert Peck was at the Houghton Library as the Eleanor Garvey Fellow in Printing and Graphic Arts, working on Lear's ornithological and zoological illustrations. He came down to New Haven and examined with me my drawings, proofs, and plates relating to the *Parrots.* We agreed that the birds in the drawings had almost certainly not been done by Lear, but still reserved judgment on the much more expertly rendered backgrounds. Subsequently checking a point queried by Peck, I discovered that the paper of one of the drawings was watermarked 1839. Because the *Parrots* volume was published in 1832, the mark strengthened the argument that Edward Lear had not been directly involved in the creation of my birds.

IV

At about the same time as I acquired the *Parrots* material in London, I found, listed in the catalogue of an English secondhand bookseller at a very nominal price, an autograph manuscript of W. H. Auden's sonnet "Edward Lear," along with a proof for its first printing in an issue of the (London) *Times Literary Supplement* devoted to children's books. I ordered it, and spent some anxious moments until I heard that it was indeed available. With the manuscript and proof was an autograph letter from Auden to the editor of that issue of the *TLS,* Simon Nowell-Smith. Writing from the Hotel George Washington in New York City on 1 March 1939, Auden asked that the ninth line of his poem be changed from

His welcome was prodigious: A flower took his hat.

to

How prodigious the welcome was: flowers took his hat.

But the letter could not have reached London in time, for the sonnet was printed, in the issue dated 25 March 1939, without the correction. The change was made, along with some other alterations, when "Edward Lear" was reprinted in 1945 in *The Collected Poetry of W. H. Auden.*

The story of "St. Kiven [i.e., Kevin] and the Gentle Kathleen" is an episode in my Lear collecting that reflects no credit on either my scholarship or my knowledge of Irish literature. This was a series of eight unpublished drawings by Lear with texts in his hand, in a style resembling his "The Yonghy-Bonghy-Bò." Since I owned nothing of this type,★ I wrote Bertram Rota when I saw the manuscript listed in a Sotheby catalogue for a sale in July 1966, and authorized him to buy it for me. He was successful, and soon the manuscript arrived from England. One reason the price hadn't been higher was that a ninth drawing in the series, with two lines of the text, was missing.

For Christmas 1973, I decided that the poem would make an unusual greeting. John McCrillis, at that time designer for the Yale University Press, agreed to write out the text in his handsome calligraphy. The two missing lines presented a problem. They were from that portion of the narrative that describes the saint's flight from the determined attentions of Kathleen, who has been so unfortunate as to fall in love with him. I supplied lines to fill the gap: "Till, late at night, he's stolen now / To the wild rock of Glendalough." (Both

---

★Having spent all of my available funds on the Craddock & Barnard album of early drawings, in December 1945, I had been obliged, reluctantly, to turn down an original Lear alphabet offered by another dealer, Winifred Myers.

Peter du Sautoy and Anthony Rota later pointed out to me that my idea of the pronunciation of "Glendalough"—rhyming with "now"—was hardly correct.) The poem was eventually printed by offset—not very well, I'm afraid. At the last moment I decided that I had made an error in my transcription of Lear's handwriting, and laboriously scratched the printed text to make the correction in the copies I distributed. These were far fewer than I had intended because I spent that Christmas in hospital. I had applied for copyright in the poem on the grounds that these were verses by Lear being printed for the first time, and after some questioning from the Copyright Office, the certificate came through.

A few months later, Fritz Liebert began work on an edition he had been asked to undertake of some Lear drawings owned by the dealer Hans P. Kraus in New York, eventually published in 1975 as *Lear in the Original: 110 Drawings for … Nonsense.* There were a number of Lear's illustrations for texts by other writers, including Thomas Moore. Reading through the *Irish Melodies,* Fritz came upon the original version of the poem of my Christmas card—a copy of which I had mailed to him—and he sent me a note informing me apologetically that Moore was the author. (Lear had altered the lines, especially the first ones, just enough to convince me—and the Sotheby cataloguer—that they must be his own.) For a long time I took the easy way out and did nothing to correct my mistake.

At the beginning of November 1984, plans for a big Edward Lear exhibition at the Royal Academy in London brought Lear to the forefront of my attention. I turned out my entire collection for inspection by the organizer of the show, Vivien Noakes, whose Lear biography I had reviewed for the *Yale Review* in 1968. Mrs. Noakes was spending the major part of her time in America at the Houghton Library, which had agreed to lend from its unrivaled collection of the watercolors, but she came in due course to New Haven.

The entire university was in the midst of a strike by its clerical employees and the Beinecke Library was open only on a limited basis, staffed by administrative personnel. I managed to locate Mrs. Noakes at the Holiday Inn and she came to see my Lears in the morning. There wasn't time to complete the work of selection, but

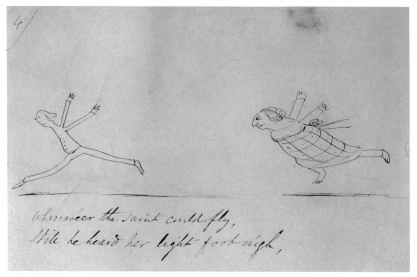

Edward Lear. St. Kiven in Flight. *Ink on paper, 4¾ x 7⅛ inches. Yale Center for British Art, gift of Donald C. Gallup, '34, '39 Grad.*

by noon she had made a tentative choice of about twenty items. Luce Marinetti Barbi had arrived that day from Italy and I had invited her and a few others to lunch at Mory's. Mrs. Noakes joined us for what proved to be a pleasant occasion. I had promised her that she would be free to leave at one o'clock with Ralph Franklin, director of the Beinecke, and they excused themselves at more or less that hour to go to the library. Between her work there and at the British Art Center, Mrs. Noakes was well occupied all afternoon, but she returned to my apartment at about six o'clock and completed her selection of my Lears. Her list had subsequently to be shortened, and only eleven items from my collection were actually shown at the Royal Academy.★

★When a very much reduced version of the exhibit came that fall to the National Academy of Design in New York, the number of Gallup items was further reduced to four; but I was delighted that details from one of my drawings, *Outside the walls of Suez, 17 Jan. 1849,* were used to decorate the invitation to the opening reception.

Edward Lear. Outside the Walls of Suez, 17 Jan. 1849. *Pencil, sepia ink, watercolor with notes on paper, 7⅞ x 5⅛ inches. Yale Center for British Art, gift of Donald C. Gallup, '34, '39 Grad.*

Somehow the show did open on 20 April 1985 and, even more miraculously, the elaborate catalogue was ready on time. My copy arrived by airmail on May Day and I cancelled my plans to attend the Senior Dinner in Jonathan Edwards College, being unable to put off the anticipated pleasure of reading it. I was proud to find that ten of the items borrowed from the Gallup collection were illustrated and that my manuscript of the W. H. Auden sonnet on Lear was featured as a very appropriate end-piece.

I wrote Mrs. Noakes the next day to express my enthusiastic appreciation of the catalogue and, later, after more careful examination, I discovered remarkably few errors. One of them was in the bibliographical listing of Lear's nonsense, which had been compiled chiefly by the dealer-collector Justin G. Schiller in New York. Although my collection of the printed books was far from complete, I found by checking my copies that the date given for the new, expanded edition of *Nonsense Songs and Stories*—1895—was off by a year. My copy was very clearly dated 1894. I ventured to write Schiller this information and received promptly an invitation to visit him. I was in New York only a week later, telephoned him, and spent an hour at his shop. He most generously gave me a copy of his facsimile of a Lear manuscript he owned, *The Tragical Life and Death of Caius Marius Esq.* (1983), and a number of his catalogues, some of them containing items by Lear.

I returned to New Haven, resolved to send Schiller a copy of my ill-fated *St. Kiven and the Gentle Kathleen,* and decided that the time had come to clean up this mess of faulty scholarship. When Fritz Liebert had informed me, in 1974, that the poem was one of Thomas Moore's *Irish Melodies,* I had compared the two texts. It was Lear's changing of Moore's "warbles" to "wobbles" in the second line "Skylark never wobbles o'er" that had closed my mind to the possibility that the verses could be by any other author than Lear. I had mislaid the notes I had made in 1974 and was obliged to look up the Moore text again. Lear's version differed in some ten instances, including his spelling of the saint's name. I was belatedly curious to discover exactly what elements of Saint Kevin's various legends Moore had used, and turned to O'Hanlon's *Lives of the Irish Saints* for more information. My chagrin at having mistaken Moore's words for Lear's was considerably heightened when I found that the poem was cited in this standard reference! Discovering that Saint Kevin's day was 3 June—only a week or so away—strengthened my determination at last to make amends for past errors.

More than four hundred copies of the Lear/Moore pamphlet had not been distributed in 1973 and 1974 (when my hospitalization interfered with Lear publication plans) and they had remained stored at the Beinecke Library after I retired in 1980. I destroyed three hundred of them, and took the remainder home for correcting.

I had two stamps prepared, one, for the title page, reading: "Words adapted from Thomas Moore," the other, for the colophon page, reading: "300 copies destroyed and 100 copies reissued 3 June 1985." I typed out some "Notes Added 3 June 1985 by an Ignorant Man," explaining my error. I signed the notes with my initials, dated them "St. Kevin's Day," and compiled a separate listing of the variants (including the original Moore lines "East or west, where'er he turn'd / Still her eyes before him burn'd." to replace my supplied lines). I had the two slips printed on adhesive paper that could be fastened to two blank pages at the end. The stamping and sticking took less time than I had feared and on 3 June all was ready. I sent off both a corrected and an uncorrected copy to Justin Schiller, and left corrected copies at the Beinecke for Fritz Liebert and Marjorie Wynne. A day or two later, I mailed a corrected copy, along with an explanatory note, to the Registrar of Copyrights at the Library of Congress and felt that, at long last, I could face my conscience in this particular matter.

In the early days of my collecting, when ordinary, unillustrated Lear letters could be purchased for a few dollars, my available funds were being spent on watercolors and books. I do have an interesting letter of 1884, written to Hallam Tennyson about the illustrations that Lear was making for Tennyson's poems. There are also a letter of 1870 to James T. Fields, the Boston publisher, mentioning a picture by Lear owned by the Fieldses, and the letter of condolence he wrote eleven years later to Mrs. Fields when he learned of her husband's death. But the best of my letters came to me along with drawings. Tipped onto the front endpaper of the Meatyard album acquired during the war was a letter of 26 May 1858 from Lear to his favorite, older sister Ann, who had brought him up. Then, in 1957, one of the Craddock & Barnard partners, in his rummagings in the back room of the shop, came up with an earlier letter to Ann, this one dated 16 January/3 February 1849. These two, each closely written on four quarto pages, are by far the longest and most important in my collection. Although typed transcripts exist, the other originals of Lear's correspondence with Ann seem to have disappeared.

V

In those years of the 1950s and even the early 1960s, in London, one still came across antiquarian shops with large stocks of miscellaneous paintings and drawings, chiefly the productions of Sunday artists. I enjoyed riffling through the drawings, especially, not without hope that I might come across a Lear sketch. On one memorable occasion I did find a small pencil drawing, measuring 17 by 25.5 cm. Depicted were some buildings at water's edge, with others up on a cliff. Here and there were characteristic notes of features of the landscape to aid the artist in recalling the scene: "Ivy," "shrubbs [sic]," "sand," "foam." The drawing was not signed, but it was titled and dated in a hand that appeared to be Lear's: "Isola di Sora / 31 March. 1842." From a published letter to the Earl of Derby of 5 June 1842, I established that Lear was in Sicily in March 1842. Isola di Sora lies about halfway between Naples and Rome on the Italian mainland. I shall leave it to some more energetic scholar to prove that Edward Lear was indeed responsible for this particular drawing.

I found at about the same time a larger sketch, 24.5 by 35 cm., in pencil with touches of white chalk, showing buildings along the shore. It was done very much in the Lear manner; but its title and date, "Castellamare / Sept. 3 1836," were inscribed in a formal italic hand that was obviously not Lear's. The drawing was stamped at the lower left margin with what appeared to be an artist's monogram, an L joined with its mirror image at top and bottom, enclosing a W.

From the resources of my own collection I could establish easily that the artist was not Lear: some of my drawings of the Lake District bore dates in September 1836, proving that he was in England, not Italy, at the period in question. I put the drawing away, and didn't get around to any further investigation until some forty years later. Then, in Bénézit's *Dictionnaire critique et documentaire des peintres, sculpteurs, dessinateurs et graveurs de tous les temps et de tous les pays,* of which a new edition had been published in 1976, I discovered that the stamp on my drawing was identical with that applied to works by William Leighton Leitch (1804–83) when they were sold at auction at Christie's, London, in 1884. From a monograph, *Wm. Leighton Leitch, Landscape Painter, a Memoir,* written by A. MacGeorge and published that same year, I learned that Leitch had travelled from Sicily to Naples "early in 1836, and ... continued there the greater part of that year, still pursuing his studies and making more sketches. ... In the beginning of November, 1836, he left for Rome... ." (p. 55) Consulting a world atlas, I discovered that Castellamare di Stabia [*sic*] is on the bay about twenty kilometers south of Naples. That seemed to me to confirm beyond reasonable doubt Leitch's authorship of my drawing. I had never heard of the artist and was astonished to learn from the monograph that he, like Lear, had given drawing lessons to Queen Victoria!

Establishing the authorship of that Leitch drawing had momentous and totally unpremeditated consequences for my Edward Lear collection. Investigating the holdings of the Yale Center for British Art, I discovered in its catalogue a number of works, including a watercolor of about the same period as my drawing. I telephoned Patrick Noon, curator of drawings at the center, and asked him to lunch, explaining that I'd like to show him a drawing by Leitch that I'd be happy to donate to the center. Noon, called out of town, was obliged to cancel that engagement, but invited *me* to lunch with him a little later on.

Although, in my will, I had directed that my entire Lear art collection was to go to Yale for the British Art Center, what might happen to the big picture had worried me. When a new gallery in

New York began running advertisements in the Sunday *New York Times* announcing that "$41,000 is what we will pay for large paintings by ... [*a list of artists, including*] E. Lear," I telephoned Malcolm Cormack, then curator of paintings at the center, to ask whether they would really want to keep such a large oil painting by this artist. He assured me that they would; but he never asked to see it; and although Duncan Robinson had been interested in Lear and had even printed a nonsense poem of his, he never during his time as director of the center, expressed to me any curiosity about my collection.

In July 1979, when Bob Kuehn sent me a newspaper clipping that reported the recent sale at Christie's, London, of the (slightly larger) Aberdare version of my *Kinchinjunga* at £77,000—an auction record for a Lear oil painting—I became a little more confident that the center might try to find room for my picture and perhaps even, once in a great while, put it on display to the public.

The opportunity afforded by an appointment with one of its officials to sound him out on the current attitude toward Edward Lear as an artist was too good not to seize. When I kept my engagement with Patrick Noon on 20 November, I took along with me to show to him not just the Leitch drawing and some other miscellaneous works on paper that I had happened to acquire over the years—drawings by Jean de Bosschère, Walter Crane, and Feliks Topolski—but a sampling of my Edward Lear collection, including a color transparency of the *Kinchinjunga*.

Noon's enthusiasm about the drawings and, subsequently, Director Patrick McCaughey's excitement about the whole collection led eventually to a visit on 17 December from both Patricks and the newly appointed curator of paintings, Malcolm Warner. They viewed practically the entire gathering of Lear materials, with the result that almost everything* was transferred on Saturday, 11

---

* All *printed* items not already at Yale had been turned over to the Beinecke Library in 1993. The remaining eighty copies of *St. Kiven and the Gentle Kathleen* were given in the same year to the British Art Center for sale in its shop. Forty-four additional printed items by or about Lear were given to the Center in 1997.

January, from 216 Bishop Street to the British Art Center. On 26 February 1997, my gift of the Edward Lears was announced by Richard C. Levin, President of Yale University. On that occasion, I read the following response:

Mr. President, Mr. Director, Honored Guests:

In June 1929, Alfred Stieglitz, at Lake George, New York, felt abandoned by his wife, Georgia O'Keeffe, who had, for the first time, left him to go off to paint in Taos, New Mexico. Her departure brought him intimations of Death—the final, inevitable parting—and worryings about the works of art in his personal collection. He wrote to her on the 27th:

> ... of your things I consider but very few "mine." The blue & white drawing ... I wish cremated with me. That's the one favor I ask ... . In a way it's criminal to ask you to have it accompany me beyond all Pain & Ecstasy—but I must take it with me—No one will ever know you as I know you. No one will see that drawing as I know it exists—for me.—So it must never leave me. And in not leaving me—perhaps when I am gone in flesh—you'll know you & I are actually together—somewhere—maybe only in the form of ashes—but the Spirit will shine from the skies—maybe in that way someday I too will be able to see Taos. ...

No fellow—or sister—artist will be surprised that the wife's drawing was *not* burned along with the husband's body when he died in 1946. Although O'Keeffe admitted more than once that it was useless to argue with Stieglitz, she had seventeen years in which to persuade him that her famous drawing must not be sacrificed to sentimentality: "Blue Lines X" is today enshrined in that part of the Stieglitz collection that she gave to the Metropolitan Museum of Art. But any collector will sympathize with Stieglitz's fond hope that even Death would not separate him from an object that he had so passionately adored.*

Although I have enjoyed living with my Edward Lear watercolor drawings and paintings over the past half century, my attachment to them has not been so close that I have ever considered requesting that any of them be burned along with my corpse. And now, thanks to the enthusiastic appreciation of Patrick McCaughey, Patrick Noon, and Malcolm Warner, I have been granted the ideal boon: having the entire collection, including manuscripts and autograph letters, become a permanent, small part of the most important and representative collection of British art in the United

---

* Sue Davidson Lowe, Stieglitz's grandniece and the author of *Stieglitz, a Memoir/Biography* (1983), the best book so far published about him and the family, considers it very probable that her uncle never repeated his request—a momentary whim occasioned by ill health and feelings of inadequacy and desertion.

States. (I can see Edward Lear in Paradise dancing with delight!) Certainly few collectors have ever been so blessed. For me, it is a source of great gratification, Mr. President & Mr. Director, that I am enabled to repay, through this and other past and future gifts to the Yale galleries and the Yale library, a little of the great debt that I owe to Yale University. Edward Lear and I thank *you*.

Elie Lascaux
1944–1988

MY OWN PARTICULAR SECTION of the United States Army was moved in September 1944 from London to Paris not long after the liberation of that city. We took over the space vacated by the Germans in the Hotel Majestic annex, off the Avenue Kléber, not far from the Arc de Triomphe. There, after our operations settled down into the usual routine, we were once more allowed the privilege of an afternoon off every seven days. I knew that Gertrude Stein and Alice Toklas were still in the country, where they had successfully, with the cooperation of their neighbors, first at Bilignin and then at Culoz, lived out the German occupation. But there was another special attraction for me in Paris beyond the prospect of revisiting the parts of the city that I had seen during my first short stay seven years before. Edward Lear was not the only artist whose work I discovered during that previous winter in London. On one of my first visits to the Redfern Gallery in Cork Street, in February 1944, I found an exhibition of pictures by a contemporary French painter, Elie Lascaux.

I had first heard of the artist through Gertrude Stein. He provided lithographs in 1925 for her *A Village,* published in a limited edition by Daniel-Henry Kahnweiler. In the mid-1930s, when Mrs. Charles ("Bobsy") Goodspeed of Chicago (later Mrs. Gilbert Chapman of New York) was president of the Arts Club of that city, she was instrumental in arranging under the club's auspices a series of exhibitions of artists represented in Gertrude Stein's collection: Pablo Picasso, Francis Picabia, Sir Francis Rose, Juan Gris, and Elie Lascaux. To create more publicity for the shows in Chicago—the scene of some of Miss Stein's most conspicuous successes during her American lecture tour—Bobsy Goodspeed persuaded her to provide brief introductions for the catalogues. This is what she wrote about Lascaux:

Elie Lascaux lived with his mother in a village and he had heard of stoves but never seen one, he always all his life hoped to have one. All his young life he had lived with an open fire place for cooking and heating and anybody who has lived with one knows how cold any very young one or any one can be with one. Now he has an apartment that is steamheated so he has never had a stove but he still dreams of one. When he came to Paris he was a very young man seventeen years old then and he was all alone and he went to the Arc de Triomphe to see everything and he naturally got there. He watched the automobiles going round round and around the arch and each time he thought it was the same one, that it was a merry go round and a most splendid one. Slowly he saw that each time it was a different one and slowly then he knew what Paris was it was a place where there were so many automobiles that each one that passed him was a different one.

All this made a Paris for him and he gets it into his pictures the white light of his pictures all the Paris that he discovered then.

It is quite an extraordinary thing that every year in painting his painting is more beautiful and developing and yet never is there left out of it the thing he saw then, when he was a young one.

His painting has a white light that is a light and anything a village, green trees any part of Paris, Bourges, all and any french thing can be in that white light which is the light that Elie Lascaux has inside him.

Bilignin, August 6, 1935

The catalogue for the exhibition bore on its front a small black-and-white reproduction of one of the paintings, *L'entrée à Bergues*. In 1937, in *Everybody's Autobiography*, Gertrude Stein repeated the story of Lascaux's first arrival in Paris. Then, in 1940, when she, in Bilignin, entrusted Kahnweiler, in Paris, with the task of choosing appropriate illustrations for her *Paris, France,* he selected Lascaux's *Sacré Coeur*—actually titled by the artist *La terrasse des Widka*—for one of the color plates. (Unfortunately, the quality of the reproduction did much less than justice to the painting.)

And so, through my work with the Stein collection at Yale in 1940–41, the name of Lascaux had become a familiar one. The exhibition of his work at the Redfern in 1944 consisted of a dozen gouache paintings and a single oil, and the quality of the light in his painting that Gertrude Stein had written about, "the light that Elie Lascaux has inside him," made an immediate impression. This was especially true of the oil, a small painting of the Church of St. Gervais in Paris, but also to an only slightly less extent of the gouaches. Returning to look at the pictures again the following week, I discovered that their interest for me continued undiminished, and I made up my mind to buy one of those I particularly liked if it was still unsold when the exhibition ended.

Although the show was not unsuccessful and a quite respectable number of items were sold, the two I liked best—the little oil of St. Gervais (the highest priced picture) and a gouache of the Church of St. Michael of Vaucelles in Caen—were not among them. At the end of February 1944, therefore, I became the owner of my first Lascaux, the two at a special reduced price. The gallery quite obviously had recognized an *amateur* (in the French sense of the word) when they saw one, and cagily arranged to hold some of the unsold pictures (I later found that they had all been consigned by Daniel-Henry Kahnweiler's brother Gustave in Cambridge), where they continued to be available to tempt me on my weekly visits. Although a good part of my salary as captain in the United States Army was going home into savings, I still had more than sufficient funds to take care of my few regular expenses. The Lascaux gouaches were quite reasonably priced, and so, between February and April, I eventually acquired three others, two more of scenes in Caen, and one a cityscape of Boulogne-sur-Seine, a suburb of Paris. One of the Caen gouaches had actually been sold during the exhibition to a couple who were looking for an oil painting for their dining room. They had had it reframed, without a mat, as if it were an oil, and had hung it for several weeks, but decided eventually that it was not satisfactory for their purposes and had returned it to the gallery. I hesitated about acquiring that fourth gouache, living as I did in a single small room in London and having already filled most of its wall space. But one day when I arrived at the Redfern I found the exhibition room a shambles. This was at the beginning of the bombardment of London by the German V-1s in April 1944 and, the night before, the Hyde Park antiaircraft guns had opened up against them. But the V-1s came in at such a low angle that the guns, far from being effective, caused considerably more destruction than the rockets. A shell from Hyde Park had hit the building housing the Redfern Gallery, and broken plaster covered everything. The few remaining Lascaux were safe, though dusty, in the basement, but this narrow escape put an end to my indecision and persuaded me to buy that final gouache—not very logically, for the painting was obviously a good deal safer in the Redfern basement than in my third-floor room.

A friend of mine in the G-2 section of army headquarters to whom I had shown the Lascaux gouaches later told me that he had wondered whether I had some advance knowledge of the Allied plans to invade the European continent because three of the four had been painted in or near Caen, one of the principal points of the Allied attack. Increased activity in connection with the planning of the invasion soon put an end to my afternoons off, and it became apparent that my time in London was limited. Reluctantly I removed the Lascaux from their frames, gave the frames back to the gallery, rolled the gouaches, and sent my "collection"—except for the small oil, which I kept with me—to Connecticut for safe-keeping.

At the Redfern I had been told that Lascaux's pictures were handled in Paris by the Galérie Louise Leiris, founded as the Galérie Simon, after World War I, by Kahnweiler. He had been the artist's dealer from early in 1920, soon after Lascaux began to paint. With the German occupation of Paris, Kahnweiler, as a Jew, had been obliged to flee from the Nazis. He sold the gallery to his wife's sister, Mme Michel Leiris, a French citizen by birth and his associate in the gallery for twenty-one years.* It had become the Galérie Louise Leiris, and continued to take all of Lascaux's production. In 1944, it was indeed the one place in all the world for viewing his work.

My first free afternoon came on a Monday and I made a beeline for the gallery, then at 29 bis, rue d'Astorg, only to find that this was the weekly closing day. The front door had a glass panel and, peering through it, I could see two or three oil paintings obviously by Lascaux hung tantalizingly on the wall opposite. I was careful to

---

*It was only after Kahnweiler's death, in 1979, that it became known generally that Louise Leiris was actually the Kahnweilers' daughter.

choose Tuesday for my afternoon off the following week and found the gallery open. Although Kahnweiler himself had still not returned to Paris, Louise ("Zette") Leiris—to whom Erica Brausen at the Redfern had given me a letter of introduction—made me welcome. On that first day I was quite content to limit my examination to the seven or eight Lascaux that happened to be on view. (The gallery had frequent one-person exhibitions of its principal artists—Picasso, Léger, Masson, Beaudin, Kermadec, Suzanne Roger, Laurens, Manolo, and Lascaux—but a few representative works by the other artists were always to be found.) On that first visit I added to my collection another small oil, *La riche cuisine* (1943), a still life featuring a well-stocked kitchen table before a fireplace. The French franc was then valued at only two cents and the price for this small picture—of the same size as my *St. Gervais*—was only thirty dollars.

During those fall and winter months of 1944–45, my collection grew rapidly. Although I soon exhausted the supply of small pictures, there was an almost limitless cache of larger ones that Kahnweiler (who returned to Paris in October 1944), Mme Leiris, and Germaine Lascaux (the artist's daughter, then at school in Paris and working part-time at the gallery) were quite willing to bring up for my consideration from the basement storeroom. Soon I was allowed to consult the complete photographic record the gallery maintained of Lascaux's oils. Although many of them had over the years been sold or at least consigned to other dealers, many others, miraculously, could be produced from that seemingly inexhaustible basement supply. In November I was surprised to discover that *La terrasse des Widka,* the original of the illustration in Gertrude Stein's *Paris, France,* was still available, and in April 1945 I came upon *L'entrée à Bergues,* which had not sold in Chicago; it gave me special satisfaction to add those paintings to my collection. In March I had found an oil, *Les halles à Dives,* painted in the early 1930s, years that I had come to regard as particularly happy ones for Lascaux's art. Kahnweiler himself agreed that this was one of his brother-in-law's most successful and characteristic paintings. Later that spring, when the publishing house of Gallimard exhibited a small group of pictures by Lascaux in their seventeenth-century hôtel in Paris, the

Elie Lascaux and Daniel-Henry Kahnweiler, 19 October 1949. Photograph by Carl Van Vechten.

gallery asked to borrow from me this painting for inclusion. Gertrude Stein and Joe Barry went with me to visit the exhibition, and I was proud to have them see my picture hanging on the panelled walls.

In April, Lascaux himself came up to Paris for a short visit from St. Léonard, where he and his wife were then living (he was a native of that part of France, having been born in Limoges). I was happy to meet him at last and find that he had many of the qualities reflected in his paintings: a zestful enthusiasm for living, a delight in ordinary places and events, and a keen sense of humor. On my afternoon off that week, he gave Germaine and me a conducted tour of his old haunts in Montmartre. He had first begun to paint as a prisoner of war, befriended by a German officer, who had provided pigments and brushes. After the Armistice, Lascaux had come to Paris to live and work as an artist. He had been helped by Suzanne Valadon and Maurice Utrillo, and had met that champion of so many artists, Max Jacob. It was Jacob who had introduced him and his work to Kahnweiler.

Lascaux, Germaine, and I walked up and down the streets of Montmartre that afternoon, visiting places that had been important to him in his early days. We saw a wall decoration he had painted at one of the cafés, visited the Sacré Coeur, and had apéritifs in an open-air restaurant. It was a memorable afternoon, sunny and warm. As I walked away from them after we had said goodbye, I came upon a street vendor offering the first lilies-of-the-valley, the French *muguets*. I bought a bouquet and rushed back to overtake my friends and present the flowers to Germaine in celebration of our afternoon together.

The Lascaux continued to live in St. Léonard during the time I was stationed in Paris, but I received occasional news of them through Germaine. Her father painted a picture commemorating his brief return to Paris in which I was delighted to find figures identifiable as "le commandant Gallúp" (his camera hanging from his neck), Gertrude Stein, and Alice B. Toklas among the persons shown promenading near one of the Paris fountains. He later sent me by way of Germaine an ink drawing of the Prévoté des Seychères at Aureil, inscribed in memory of our first meeting.

That summer the Lascaux moved from St. Léonard to an apartment in Boulogne-sur-Seine on the outskirts of Paris. I visited them there in September, on my way from Germany to England and Oxford, and Lascaux gave me a number of his original pencil and ink sketches for paintings that I now owned. I saw him again, briefly, on 1 December, at the printer's, where he was at work on the lithographed illustrations for an edition of André Gide's *Isabelle* being published by Gallimard, and he gave me a proof of one of the chapter headings for the book. Later that same month all the paintings I had acquired in Paris accompanied me to the United States. (They were not very large and, without frames, could be tied easily into a compact bundle that weighed surprisingly little.) *L'entrée à Bergues* and *La terrasse des Widka* provided spots of color for the Stein memorial exhibition at the Yale Library in 1947. Becoming a resident fellow in Jonathan Edwards College in 1948, I acquired a roomy apartment and with it display space for both my Lascaux and my Lears. The Galérie Louise Leiris sent me photographs of Lascaux's new work from time to time as they received it, and I acquired additional pictures as I could afford them, bearing in mind the not inconsiderable cost of having them shipped from Paris.

Lascaux was a devout Catholic and had at one time done a series of drawings of the seven deadly sins. Now, during the winter of 1947–48, he made each one the subject of a small oil painting. The complete series was shown at the gallery, and an article about them by Georges Limbour appeared in one of the Paris journals. Lascaux very much hoped that the pictures could be kept together. Kahnweiler sent me photographs, which I liked; the Gallup collection seemed an appropriate repository for the seven, and my order arrived in Paris before any other collector had decided to acquire them.

II

I used then to let my vacation time—one month each year—accumulate at the library in order to spend every fourth summer in Europe. My first trip back to Paris came in 1949. I visited the gallery several times at the end of June and then took the train to Marseilles to visit the Lascaux at Carquéiranne, where they were spending that summer. Our reunion was a joyful one, with a most convivial dinner to celebrate the American Fourth of July. The Lascaux always made friends quickly wherever they spent more than a few days at a stretch, and I met a good many of them in Carquéiranne. We swam in the Mediterranean and took walks in the countryside (one, to the nearby village of La Garde, later memorialized by Lascaux in a drawing that he sent me as a souvenir), and I was regretful when the time came for me to be on my way.

In January 1951, I arranged in the Jonathan Edwards College Junior Common Room an exhibition of practically my entire Lascaux collection. There were thirty-four oil paintings, sixteen drawings, watercolors, and gouaches, three lithographs, and eight illustrated books. I prepared and had printed a broadsheet catalogue, which folded into an eight-page pamphlet and featured on the outside the drawing of the artist and me en route to La Garde two years before. I had got permission from the Chicago Arts Club to reprint Gertrude Stein's introductory preface of 1935, and added a short biographical note of my own about Lascaux. It was, up to that time, the most extensive retrospective of the artist's work.

The Lascaux spent the summer of 1952 in Vallauris, where Elie had become fascinated with pottery-making. His friend Picasso, also working there, had given him one or two lessons, and Lascaux was eager to see what he could do on his own. From New Haven, I commissioned a bowl and six small plates, featuring, respectively, fish, birds, fruit, garden implements, musical instruments, and a landscape of Vallauris. *Le service Gallúp,* as Lascaux called it, came out quite well, but he was never sufficiently comfortable with the ceramic technique to take advantage, as Picasso invariably did, of occasional mistakes, making those part of his design. Although he did accept a commission from Christofle in Paris for two plates and used for them simplified drawings of the fish and bird motifs of my "service," his desire to experiment with pottery-making was satisfied and, so far as I know, he never went on to anything else in that line.

On my European trip the following summer the presence of my nephew Richard Gallup, aged twenty, made it feasible for us to buy in Paris a "Quatre Chevaux," the smallest size Renault. The Lascaux were again at Vallauris and we stayed a few days with them there. The four of us made an excursion to visit the friends in Carquéiranne and had lunch that day with the Guigues (he had been mayor of the town). Back at Vallauris, the Lascaux took us to see the pottery that Picasso was creating at the Madoura factory and, in the salesroom, we met Jacqueline Roque, who soon afterward became the second Mme Picasso.

Four years later, in 1957, the Lascaux were in Venice, and I spent several days exploring with them the fabulous city. I remember boat trips to Merano, Giudecca, and the Lido; a convivial cocktail hour at Harry's Bar; and an interminable evening concert in the plaza before

St. Mark's. But Lascaux did not stay long enough to produce memorable pictures there, and he came to consider ill-advised the few attempts he made to record the city on canvas.

At the time of my summer trip in 1961, I found my friends living in Antibes. They were occupying an apartment, owned by the gallery, on an upper floor of a new, modern building, "La Résidence des Fleurs" (where Graham Greene was a fellow tenant), overlooking the harbor. Here again we spent afternoons on the beach, went for walks exploring the old town, and sat on the balcony watching the water-skiers. That year I had come by train from Geneva and had had my first—and last—experience with something called a *couchette*. The train was scheduled to leave at midnight and I was the first occupant to arrive in the compartment, at about 11:30. At each side was a tier of three berths. Mine was the lowest on the left-hand side, and I took off my jacket, tie, and shoes, and lay down. To my surprise the next person to arrive was a middle-aged lady, who seemed to take the presence of a man as routine. We were eventually joined by four other travellers, all women, who also appeared to accept the situation as normal. And so I spent that night, the only man in a compartment with five women.

A Guggenheim grant made it possible for me to visit my friends again in October. Now happily established in Paris in an apartment on the Boulevard St. Germain, Elie was freshly recording many of his old haunts in the city. There we celebrated Bero's birthday. My gift to her for that occasion was a small painting by her husband. To this gesture of mine Elie felt he must respond. He had, in the late 1920s, done a series of pictures of scenes at Versailles in Marie Antoinette's hamlet, the rustic village that she had had built in the grounds of Le Petit Trianon, where she and members of her court diverted themselves with peasant pastimes, dressed in country costumes. Lascaux knew of my eagerness to find one of these pictures and spent a good part of the night following Bero's party making for me an ink drawing of *La Maison du Bailli au Hameau de la Reine*, inscribing it the next day "Pour Donald Gallup en souvenir de sa visite chez son vieil ami Elie Lascaux Paris Octobre 1961."

The train trip from Geneva to Nice in 1961 had given me my fill

Donald Gallup, Berthe and Elie Lascaux, Piazza San Marco, Venice, June 1957. Collection of Donald Gallup.

of *couchettes* and, in 1965, for my visit to the Lascaux, I *flew* from Switzerland to France. My problem on that visit was that I had been served a meal on the early evening flight, only to discover when I reached Nice that Germaine Lascaux and her husband, Picasso's nephew Javier Vilató, were waiting to drive me back to Antibes in time for a late dinner with her parents and some friends. It was difficult for me that evening to do justice to Bero Lascaux's excellent cooking.

We made an excursion that summer to the Léger museum near-by, only recently opened to the public. The Vilatós were living in Vallauris, and we spent an afternoon and evening with them there, seeing Javier's studio, and enjoying a splendid dinner cooked by Germaine, accompanied with constantly replenished pitchers of cold sangria.

The visit with them in Antibes in 1965 proved to be the last time I ever saw Elie. He and Bero had come with me in my taxi to the airport at Nice, but I asked them not to wait to see the plane take off, having no liking for noisy farewells in the midst of madding crowds. Lascaux was then seventy-seven and although he still worked every day at his painting, his health, both physical and mental, was quite obviously deteriorating. He continued nevertheless to get a great deal of enjoyment out of life during the next two years, delighting especially in the grandson that Germaine and Javier gave him. He celebrated his eightieth birthday on 5 April 1968 and died a little more than six months later, on 28 October. He lies buried in the Cimetière Montparnasse.

III

In February 1988 the Galérie Louise Leiris was planning an exhibition to commemorate Lascaux's centenary. I was more than a little flattered to receive a letter from the manager of the gallery:

Dear Mr. Gallup,

It seems to us that you have been one of the most fervent collectors of the work of Elie Lascaux, a painter whose centenary our gallery will celebrate with an exhibition to open, at the very latest, at the beginning of May.

Raymond Queneau and Michel Leiris wrote prefaces for two earlier catalogues, and, this time, we should be happy and flattered if you, the leading foreign amateur of this painting, would agree to write a brief introduction (for a fee, of course) for the catalogue of this third exhibition of which the theme will be very probably "Paris and the Ile de France." We believe that all admirers of Lascaux would be much interested in what it is that has appealed to and retained the interest of an American academic of your standing in the artist and his work.

If for some reason you do not care to write this short preface, would you be willing to select from your Lascaux letters those that seem to you most revealing of his sensitiveness and the means he has used to achieve his aims?

With best wishes from the Leirises and me.

Maurice Jardot

This was an invitation that I could not very well refuse. Because I had been given a choice and because I wanted in any case to review my correspondence with Lascaux in deciding what I should write, I prepared both a prefatory note and a selection of passages from the letters. This was the introduction:

Gertrude Stein, in her preface to the catalogue of Lascaux's Chicago exhibition in 1936, wrote of the white light in the pictures and called it "the light that Elie Lascaux has inside him." Because it is such an integral part of his painting, this light is at once the key to the charm which his work holds for his admirers and a hindrance to his gaining the appreciation of those who do not instinctively understand him. For unless one knows that this light is not sentimental, naïve, nor merely decorative, that it is part and parcel of the artist's painterly self, one cannot look at his work with complete sympathy. The light of Lascaux's pictures is essentially the aura lent to familiar objects by their presentation not as actually seen, but as experienced, after having passed through the transforming processes of the painter's mind. It is Wordsworth's

> The light that never was on sea or land,
> The consecration, and the Poet's dream.

Objects are quite realistically presented, but they are endowed with a deeper significance which was inherent in them all along but was only revealed to us by the painter's keener perceptive powers.

Although he wrote regular articles on painting in London between 1917 and 1920, Ezra Pound is not generally thought of as an art critic. It was he who, as early as 1910, wrote (in *The Spirit of Romance)* of two kinds of beautiful painting exemplified by works of Burne-Jones on the one hand and Whistler on the other:

> one looks at the first kind of painting and is immediately delighted by its beauty; the second kind of painting, when first seen, puzzles one, but on leaving it, and going from the gallery one finds new beauty in natural things—a Thames fog, to use the hackneyed example. Thus, there are works of art which are keys or passwords admitting one to a deeper knowledge, to a finer perception of beauty ...

The supreme quality of the work of Elie Lascaux is that it combines these two kinds of painting. His small picture (32 x 24 cm.) of the Church of St. Gervais, painted in 1935, gives to this rather drab and austere façade an immediate, extremely pleasing beauty that is not at all apparent to the casual passerby in Paris. In the painting Lascaux, a pious Catholic, looked above and beyond the actual image to discover the true essence of the building. Architecture and landscape in his pictures share the characteristics of a still-life and, oddly enough, his still-lifes have some of the appurtenances of architecture and landscape.

Almost all of Lascaux's work has this quality. In the main, he was content to portray only scenes long familiar and well understood: the streets and buildings of Paris, especially Montmartre and the Ile de la Cité, Versailles, Limoges (where he was born) and the surrounding towns and countryside. In these pictures there is a sureness, sensibility, and sincerity, born of deep knowledge and true affection, set down in his own inimitable, unique way.

Picasso, that master of a truly amazing number of ways of expressing himself, is reported to have commented about his old friend that "Elie peint toujours des Lascaux"; and the artist himself once remarked to me about one of his gouaches, "Ça, c'est moi!" On this 100th anniversary of his birth, surveying these pictures he painted of the city he loved most of all, we rejoice in the staunch integrity that caused Elie Lascaux, in spite of what he sometimes felt to be a lack of understanding and appreciation, but always with Kahnweiler's unwavering support, to continue painting in the way that he knew to be right for him.

And these were the passages I chose from Lascaux's letters (presented in my own, rather halting translation):

Thank you again for the additional photograph [*of Montmartre*], but I don't plan to paint another picture inasmuch as the first commemorates my return to La Butte after five years. Painting ought to mark the life of the painter, just as a writer writes the hours of his existence. (Saint Léonard de Noblat, 23 June 1945)

This evening, listening to a radio program reviewing the exhibition of the Surindépendants, we were delighted to hear my name coupled with praise for my work. And so perhaps La gloire will finally knock at my door! (Boulogne s/Seine, 15 November 1945)

I keep on painting and it only becomes more difficult for me: I put a great deal of thought and effort into my pictures and have only scant return. I am quite certain that I'm making progress, but even so one mustn't repeat oneself.

As you see, my dear friend, I am a little discouraged. Let's hope that it's just a temporary setback that will soon pass, for at bottom I have faith in my work. Long live conscience and simplicity, as Corot used to say, but my goodness how difficult it is to be simple! (Boulogne s/Seine, 28 July 1946)

I must tell you, dear friend, that your letters are esteemed: they do me a great deal of good and I feel less alone before my work, not being accustomed to such sincere encouragement. Your letters give me courage and the assurance that I am accomplishing something. I've struggled for thirty years and my work is still not understood in my country. I do have Kahnweiler, and now Raymond Queneau who defends me admirably. (Boulogne s/Seine, 16 March 1947)

For several weeks and especially after having painted two bad pictures, I was completely disgusted with my work when, recently, the exposition of

Elie Lascaux. Le balcon des Lacourière (1947). *Ink on paper, 6 x 7 inches. Collection of Donald Gallup.*

the Impressionist masters opened at the Jeu de Pommes of the Tuileries. ...
I left the exhibition completely enthralled, having only one thought—to
take up my brushes again. Of all the artists shown, Manet seems to me the
greatest, then come Renoir and Cézanne. (Boulogne s/Seine, 6 June 1947)

Do you show my work to your friends? What do they think of it?
Perhaps they, like certain Parisian critics, find it only the window-display of
a *pastry-cook*. I know very well that Renoir was treated as a *butcher* and today
no one would dare say the word. I must therefore wait and while waiting I
work with the joy of having friends like you and Kahnweiler, who finds my
last pictures very well done. (Boulogne s/Seine, 30 July 1947)

I received your comforting letter just as I had begun a new painting. I
had gone to Montmartre to study dry point and etching at Lacourière's
under the direction of my friend [André] Beaudin. After having worked

hard with meager result (which, incidentally, Lacourière and Beaudin considered good), Lacourière invited us to lunch. From his balcony I had a view over Paris with Le Moulin de la Galette in the foreground. I made a very detailed drawing and the next day, 15 August, I started the canvas that I have just finished. There are good things in it, but it is not a complete success. ... (Boulogne s/Seine, 10 November 1947)

As you know I don't paint in winter-time, in November and December, the days are too short. I begin again about 15 January, and so I've been working. My first canvas is the view from 53 bis Quai des Grands Augustins [*the apartment of Kahnweiler and the Leirises*], a view that I've wanted to paint ever since my return from St. Léonard. I don't yet know what Kahnweiler thinks of it, but I'm sure it has some good things in it. ...

I have just had during last December a show in Stockholm. All the pictures and even some drawings were sold. (Boulogne s/Seine, 30 January 1948)

As for my work, I have just completed the "Seven Deadly Sins." Now, looking at the pictures, I am like the crow watching the fox go: "jura, mais un peu plus tard, qu'on ne l'y prendrait plus" ("swore, but a little later, that he'd not be caught again"). The other paintings are landscapes of Paris and a view of a Limousin château under snow. Among these landscapes are the view from the window at 53 bis Quai des Grands Augustins and the old church of Ivry s/Seine that I discovered on the day of Antonin Artaud's burial.

As you see I've worked hard; now we'll see whether quantity equals quality. (Boulogne s/Seine, 5 April 1948)

We are living in a small house with a fine view of the sea. ... As for my work I find myself confronting this landscape like a beginner and in spite of my flood of joy at being in this beautiful country I tremble at the thought of repeating myself. (Carquéiranne, 24 April 1948)

Today I can tell you that I have worked well and may even have made some lucky hits. And so you have a *happy Lascaux,* with the additional joy of knowing that my "Seven Deadly Sins" are with my American friend, which means that they will never be broken up. And so I am full of courage to continue the series of paintings of Carquéiranne which, according to Kahnweiler, has been so well begun. (Carquéiranne, 1 June 1948)

Your valued and affectionate encouragements join those of Kahnweiler who, when he stopped here, found that my efforts had yielded fruit. "You have succeeded," he told me, "in introducing cubism into landscape." Those are very important words for me because, as you may judge from my small drawing of the old clock tower at Draguignan, the triangular movements for me only reinforce the colors without attempting to take away from the character of the object that I wish to paint.

It is therefore without wishing it that I manage to effect the entry of cubism into the landscape without deformation of the subject. I'd be truly happy to show that the great lesson of cubism is valid. For me, as you know … it is above all since my meeting with Juan Gris that I have used the play of shadows but still not daring to make use of them except very timidly. Now I'm going at it more frankly, with the result that in my work at Carquéiranne there will be more failures, but I'm sure there will be two or three successes. … (Carquéiranne, 5 July 1948)

I worked a lot in November and December on landscapes of the old quarters around Notre Dame. Some of these areas were to be torn down. The demolitions began before the war but were not completed, so that great sections of wall rise in the air, giving glimpses through their gaps now of the towers of Notre Dame, or the clock-tower of the church of St. Gervais, or the bell-turrets of the ancient Hôtel of the Bishops of Sens. Just behind the Lycée Charlemagne, surrounded by these ruin-like walls, there is a playing-field. Many strangers think these walls resulted from bombing. These are the corners that I am painting just now. I've found tranquillity again and believe me you have had a hand in this. (Boulogne s/Seine, 31 December 1948)

At last we have moved from Boulogne! It's sad to say, but I left the place without regret, save for the memory of fine times with Juan Gris and also at the Kahnweilers' where I met a great many people. Now I am in the Faubourg St. Germain and feel as if I'd lived here all my life. It is true that I often came here either to visit old friends or to go to the Quai des Grands Augustins.

I have already been working, hard, on drawings and two small canvases (still-lifes). It's truly a renewal in my life, and I venture to hope that it will be the same with my painting. When I have finished work in the evening, I go for an apéritif at the "Deux Magots," the café at the foot of the Church of St. Germain, that you must have known. In a word, the Lascaux are happy.

As for the exhibition in London, I have no news as yet. I only know that Gertrude Stein's preface is to introduce the catalogue, and I am delighted at that. (Paris, 19 November 1950)

Last week Picasso asked to see me: he is always splendid. He wanted to collaborate with me on some pictures. For example, he would paint a window and I would execute the landscape seen through that window. I don't know that he will follow out this idea, but as you see he does not forget me. (Paris, 17 December 1950)

Alas! I can't tell you anything about the exhibition in London. Kahnweiler and Mayor have gilded the pill by telling me that it came at a bad time, with strikes, the grippe, and Londoners talking only of war. I don't believe them for, in a brief notice in *Time,* the journalist continues to consider me a naive painter—a treatment I've always protested against.

Don't think that I am cast down by this bad luck that pursues me for, with friends like you I still have courage and, according to Kahnweiler, my last things are very good. And then the quarter where I am now, this old corner of Paris, makes my need to paint break out and I feel like a dog whose muzzle has been removed. (Paris, 19 March 1951)

I have worked hard and well since we moved here to 72 Boulevard St. Germain. I think Kahnweiler has written you, for he has only praise for the last pictures. At first I was very much inspired by the roofs and high chimneys that surround me. I've been working on this motif, for the chimneys make me think of organ pipes. Then, our windows open on the old Rue Daumas where there are still houses of the 17th century (in ruinous condition, of course). The poor souls who live there, since they have no refrigerators, put everything on their window-sills. And so I've been working on this subject too. Right now I'm painting some still-lifes, inspired by the poor tramps who live along the Seine. They have always with them a bag, containing bread, a liter of wine, some newspapers or books, old shoes, etc. I am not unhappy with these things. (Paris, 4 May 1951)

I have worked hard here and have even done several ceramics—five or six. Kahnweiler wants to include them in my next show. As for me, I don't think them very important, for to accomplish anything in ceramics you'd have to work at them for two or three months.
As I've been working under the patronage of Picasso, the first plate I did was one showing the Place de *L'homme au mouton* [*a sculpture by Picasso*] using only black, and then a second with green and ochre. Picasso considered them well done, even the first; but he asked me to give him the second. This was most encouraging for me and for that reason I've kept on. As Heini [Kahnweiler] is going to photograph the other plates, you will be able to choose among them.
I sha'n't be calm until after the new exhibition, and then perhaps unhappy. Goodness knows painters are difficult to understand! (Vallauris, 25 September 1951)

Well, the exhibition is over—a good show, but a great success especially for the drawings. ...
I can't tell you how glad I am that the show is over. I could no longer live, no longer work, and now I have taken up my brushes again, as Léger has taken my place at the Gallery. ... That opening was today. (Paris, 28 November 1951)

The great painters discover ... Lascaux searches, and always hopes to find. To experience the joy of a successful canvas would make me happy. Alas, I'm always thinking that the next picture will be that, and then it still isn't. A few friends like my American friend give me courage to continue to paint for, basically, I am sure that my painting is good. (Paris, 11 January 1955)

Some good news to tell you.

I knew from Kahnweiler that a dealer in New York was very much interested in my painting. In November he came to Paris, and returned to New York carrying several of my pictures. In the early days of January Heini received a letter from this dealer, Schoneman, reporting that he had sold them all. All my canvases? Yes, all of them, and he wants to have a show in his gallery. He is to come back this month and I am impatiently looking forward to his return. I'll send you a catalogue.

The second bit of good news: there'll be an important exhibition of my things at the museum in Limoges. There will be about twenty canvases of mine along with others of the gallery's artists to give variety during the months of July to September. (Tourists take note.)

The third item: a collector in Nantes who already has several of my pictures wants to arrange a show in that city. He was a friend of Max Jacob.

What do you think of all this? I'll keep you posted. (Paris, 26 January 1958)

I am making great strides thanks to the joy in my heart, it seems to me that I must succeed in my work. (Paris, 14 September 1958)

Yes, my dear American friend, yes, dear first big collector of my pictures, your friend Lascaux has had a tremendous success in his show. Of the sixty-five canvases hung, forty-six have been sold. ... On the hanging day two of your countrymen, two Americans, selected twenty paintings. I was already happy about that, but on opening day there was a veritable stampede to buy my canvases. I still don't understand this, for people bought things who had known my work for a long time, and could have purchased pictures for several years. During this madness I thought of my American friend. Berette and I are crazy with joy. Miss Toklas was delighted and all the family. I know this will certainly give you pleasure. (Paris, 20 March 1959)

Your congratulatory telegram arrived on the very day of my seventy-first birthday. Thank you, thank you, dear friend. Yes, the celebration continues: from the day of the opening it has been an enchantment. Successful in sales, successful in reviews—we are in a state of perpetual joy. (Paris, 5 April 1959)

I sent both the introductory note and the quotations from the letters off to Paris on 5 March, leaving it to the gallery to choose between the two, explaining that I certainly did not want to be paid, that I was only too glad to do this small thing for Lascaux; if they wished to make some payment to Germaine, I'd be delighted. A cable on 16 March announced that they would use the preface. In May, I was very much touched to receive from the gallery in tribute to my 75th birthday a handsome framed gouache specially chosen by Zette Leiris as typical of the artist at his best. Germaine and her son, Xavier, thanked me by cable soon after the exhibition opened, praising the introduction as "so right, so true, so warm." Included in the show was the painting Lascaux had completed at St. Léonard soon after his visit in April 1945, entitled *Le retour à Paris,* with Gertrude Stein, Alice B. Toklas, and me in the foreground. A few weeks later I was delighted to receive from Germaine and Xavier a large color photograph of that picture.

Collecting Lawrence Durrell
1955–1986

IN 1955 LAWRENCE CLARK POWELL, head of the Clark Library at the University of California, Los Angeles, and longtime eloquent publicizer of books and book collecting, had talked with contagious enthusiasm of the writing of Lawrence Durrell, author of *The Black Book* (Paris, The Obelisk Press, 1938). That novel had been praised, as I well knew, by T. S. Eliot as "the first piece of work by a new English writer to give ... any hope for the future of prose fiction." Larry has always been a most effective persuader, and I promptly placed a standing order with Bertram Rota in London for Durrell's first editions. As they arrived from England I read them dutifully, with interest and a good deal of pleasure, but without any real conviction that Larry was right in his estimate of Durrell's importance. Even at that time, the first edition of *The Black Book,* sharing as it did some of the notoriety of Henry Miller's Tropic books from being then publishable only in Paris, was expensive. As I reached the point of feeling that I could afford to pay x dollars, the book seemed to be available only at x-plus a considerable amount. I eventually acquired my copy through the agency of Henry W. Wenning, whose career as a New Haven bookseller and publisher, although brief, was memorable. Asking substantial prices for what he believed to be worthy books, he was quite prepared to accept and give good value for items offered in exchange.

It happened that John Slocum, after the exhibition at Yale of his Joyce collection, which I had helped to arrange, had given me one of the several copies he had acquired from James Joyce's brother, Stanislaus, of the rare broadside *The Holy Office* (1904 or 1905). Because the Slocum—now Yale—collection was well supplied with copies, there was no obligation for me to give this to Yale, and I knew that John would not object to my disposing of it. My acquisition of *The Black Book* when Wenning turned up a copy in 1960 thus became possible: in return for the Joyce broadside, Henry allowed me a substantial credit toward the Durrell item.

With *The Black Book* in place on my shelves, I became more active in trying to fill the gaps in my collection. My enthusiasm had been stimulated by the publication of first *Justine* (1957) and then the other three novels constituting *The Alexandria Quartet*. Now, at last, when I asked New York booksellers if they had anything by Durrell, they at least recognized the name, although it would still be several years before they could bring themselves to believe that my pronunciation of it—with the accent on the first and not the last syllable—was anything more than affectation.

Another stimulus to Durrell collecting came in 1960 with the appearance in the *Book Collector,* London, of a checklist of his books compiled by Larry Powell and Alan G. Thomas. From that listing I discovered that I had, unwittingly, purchased *two* copies of one of the author's rarest works only four years after publication and at the published price. In London in 1937, on my first trip abroad, I had stayed just around the corner from the Faber & Faber offices in Russell Square at the large, moderately priced Russell Hotel (which still exists—though no longer so moderately priced). In the same block was a bookstore, specializing in contemporary belles lettres, at which I had of course inquired for items by or about T. S. Eliot. The clerk produced *Bromo Bombastes: A Fragment from a Laconic Drama,* by Gaffer Peeslake (London, The Caduceus Press, 1933), in part a parody of Eliot's *Sweeney Agonistes: Fragments of an Aristophanic Drama.* Although the edition had been limited to a hundred copies, the book was priced at only five shillings. I purchased a copy for myself and another to give to Henry Eliot for the collection of his brother's work he was then building up for Harvard. When I got back to New Haven that fall, I sent off the extra copy to Cambridge and placed the other among my Eliotana. It was of course still there when I learned from the *Book Collector* checklist that Gaffer Peeslake was a pseudonym of Lawrence Durrell. Apparently, during the war, German bombs had destroyed the bookshop along with most of the copies of *Bromo Bombastes,* thus making it a genuine rarity. Ironically, it was almost the only title by Durrell lacking in Larry Powell's collection.

The author's first novel had been *Pied Piper of Lovers*, published in London in 1935 by Cassell. It was so poorly received that when the second, *Panic Spring,* was accepted two years later by Fabers, they persuaded Durrell to let them publish it pseudonymously—as by Charles Norden. But *Panic Spring* also failed to sell, and both books are, in the words of the secondhand booksellers, "seldom met with." It took me a good many years to secure fine copies of them in their original dust jackets.

Some other rare items I acquired from Frances Steloff at the Gotham Book Mart in New York. One day in July 1960 she showed me a folder, produced from the nether regions of her shop, containing several Durrell pamphlets marked "N[ot]. f[or]. s[ale]." They were *The Parthenon* ([Rhodes, 1945])—a poem dedicated to T. S. Eliot, of which only twenty-five copies had been printed; *Zero and Asylum in the Snow* (Rhodes, 1946); and five issues of the magazine *The Booster* (the later numbers retitled *Delta*), which Durrell and Henry Miller had produced in Paris in the 1930s. Remembering the rare Eliot broadside similarly marked and how Frances had told me later that I should have placed it firmly under my arm and walked out of the shop, I was determined not to make the same mistake twice: after examining the Durrell pamphlets carefully and commenting on their condition and rarity, I calmly gathered them up with some books that I had already purchased, told Frances to send me a bill, and did indeed walk quite deliberately out. Her cries of "Stop, thief!" as she made a show of coming after me, sounded so convincingly genuine that I almost turned back; instead I merely repeated to her the advice she had given me about the Eliot broadside, and continued on my way. Several days later, in New Haven, I received a bill from the shop for the Durrell items, accompanied by a letter:

Dear Don Gallup,

I never dreamed that you could be so cruel and unmanageable; when I find the other Durrell pamphlets [*she had told me that she thought she had some others around somewhere*] you may view them only through the glass door. …

I turned down [an offer] for the Durrells, & was asked to name the price, but I said if anyone were to have them you would be the one. I hope they make you happy.

Bromo Bombastes

A fragment from a laconic drama

by

Gaffer Peeslake

which same being a brief extract from
his Compendium of Lisson Devices

Here printed for the delectation and subtile
enjoyment of the author's friends

London
The Caduceus Press
16 Grenville Street, W.C. 1
MCMXXXIII

[*Lawrence Durrell*] Bromo Bombastes (1933). *Beinecke Library, gift of Donald Gallup.*

Two other ephemera came to me from Barbara Howes, editor of *Chimera,* and herself a fine poet. These were inscribed copies of *Zero and Asylum in the Snow* and *Six Poems from the Greek* (also Rhodes, 1946). Durrell had sent them to her for possible use in her magazine. Once when I happened to mention to her my interest in this particular author, she had told me about the pamphlets, and I had asked her to let me know if she ever wanted to sell them. A few years later, after she had divorced Bill Smith, she wrote me that she was turning some of her books into needed funds and would be glad to let me have the Durrells.

It was Bertram Rota who supplied my greatest rarity, *Transition: Poems* (1934)—miraculously the dedication copy with the author's inscription to his brother, "For Leslie, who liked one and will I hope like another, from Larry." When I mentioned this copy to Alan Thomas, an old friend of Durrell's and himself a bookseller, he explained that it had probably got into the rare-book market by accident: Leslie Durrell had almost certainly not sold it, but, far more likely, had merely left it on a bus.

Although I never yielded to the temptation to collect the innumerable foreign translations of the books and acquired only a few first American editions, Durrell's output has been substantial and his generosity almost unbounded in supplying prefaces and introductions for publications by his friends. By 1986 my collection had grown so large that the only solution I could find to the space problem was to turn the books over to Yale, all thirteen feet of them, expecting that the Beinecke Library would give them careful attention not very far short of the devotion I had lavished upon them over thirty years.

That I was not wrong in my expectation was demonstrated first by Ralph Franklin: he promptly attempted to acquire for the Beinecke a copy of Durrell's very first and rarest publication, *Quaint Fragment* (London, The Cecil Press, 1931), lacking in my collection. I knew from Margie Cohn that she had sold a copy to Bradley Martin for his collection of important books by English authors. Ralph wrote to Martin (whom we both knew from his being a fellow member of the Grolier Club), but he was not inclined either to give or sell the Durrell item to Yale. After his death, when his collection was sold at auction by Sotheby's, the Beinecke Library placed substantial bids for both *Quaint Fragment* and *Ten Poems* (1936), another early Durrell publication that I did not have. But both books sold for prohibitively high prices. Fortunately, in 1988, not long after Durrell's death, a copy of *Ten Poems* was listed at a much more reasonable price in the catalogue of a rare book dealer in England. Vincent Giroud, who had succeeded Marjorie Wynne at the Beinecke as curator for contemporary British authors, received an airmailed copy of the catalogue, noticed the Durrell item, telephoned an order, and was successful in securing it. There aren't many libraries that have the time, the concern, or the funds to keep gift collections alive and growing in this way.

The Flowers of Friendship
1947–1979

I

THE EXHIBITION I arranged at the Yale Library in 1947 of the Stein correspondence gave me the idea that a wider selection of the letters would make an interesting book, a reflected portrait of Gertrude. Items in this mass of material would shed light on her early life in California, Cambridge, and Baltimore, detail graphically her struggle to get her work printed, document her friendships and her quarrels, and trace the process by which she finally achieved the fame ("*la gloire*") that she had always coveted.

I discussed the letter project on a number of occasions with Carl Van Vechten, wrote Alice Toklas about it, and received from both enthusiastic encouragement and unqualified support. Over a period of several years, in the evenings and on weekends, I completed my reading through most of the correspondence, and chose many additional letters that I had not had space to show or had not known about in 1947.

That was the easy part. Making the necessary copies, in those pre-Xerox days, was wearying and time-consuming; and the checking of the transcripts for typing errors was destructive of my eyesight. Carl Van Vechten had reported my project, not long after I had started it, to Alfred Knopf, his own publisher, who had written in September 1947, asking me to let him see the manuscript with a view to his firm's considering it for publication. Four years later I managed to complete and briefly annotate my selection of the letters and sent it off to New York. Alfred Knopf himself read the manuscript and, on 14 November, he and I conferred about the book. He was willing to publish it, but wanted no more than 100,000 words. He suggested that I supply connecting links for the letters and reduce the number of footnotes to the absolute minimum possible. He objected to the rather excessive praise of Gertrude Stein in some of the letters—even those of Carl Van Vechten, hoping that it could be cut down, and complained also about Marsden Hartley's "going on and on."

Of course I went through the torture suffered by all authors and editors when they are asked to cut anything, but eventually produced setting copy of the agreed-upon size. Now I faced another difficult task: establishing correct, current addresses for the correspondents or their heirs, and securing permission to print the letters.

Writing these individuals gave me the opportunity to ask them on Yale's behalf for any of Gertrude Stein's letters they had kept. Some of the college friends reported their correspondence thrown away long since, they having had no idea that Gertrude would ever become famous; some of them provided interesting information; and a number actually gave letters to Yale.

There were remarkably few outright refusals of permission. Laura Riding and Robert Graves had passed from a phase of great admiration for Gertrude Stein and her writing into one of almost complete rejection of it and a denial of its importance. In 1952, they simply did not wish to appear in my book. In helping to promote the Francis Rose exhibition held under the auspices of the United States Air Force in Paris in 1945, Gertrude Stein had written to my old commanding general, John C. H. Lee, inviting him to attend the opening. I had included his answer merely in order to represent the show in the book. When General Lee, now retired from the army and a vice-president of the Brotherhood of St. Andrew, asked me not to publish his letter, telling me that it could add nothing to the value of my publication, I had no choice but to agree.

Some individuals, like T. S. Eliot, gave permission grudgingly. He was not very happy at the prospect of seeing his letters in print, considering them to be rather trivial. I suspect that as strong a reason may have been the rather surprisingly complimentary remarks he had made in one of them about Gertrude Stein's writing (he had described them to me as "possibly more courteous than sincere"). The sole occasion on which the two had met—in 1924—was memorialized by Stein in her "portrait" of Eliot, "The Fifteenth of November" (the title recording the date of their meeting), published in 1926 by Eliot himself in his *Criterion*. Neither had been much taken with the other. He commented to me that he had found her rather inclined to make sweeping statements for immediate effect, and recalled particularly her assertion that "Anthony Trollope was the only English novelist of his period who could write good English."

Getting permission from some correspondents involved rather complicated negotiations, by far the most difficult of which were those with Ernest Hemingway. In spite of the vicissitudes of their friendship, Gertrude Stein confessed to having always retained a fondness for Hemingway. One of the principal reasons for her affection was his obviously sincere admiration for *The Making of Americans,* proven by the tremendous effort he had made in Paris in 1924 to get a substantial part of that long novel printed in Ford Madox Ford's *Transatlantic Review.* Hemingway himself had copied part of the manuscript and kept applying pressure on Ford first to continue printing the instalments and then to pay Miss Stein for them at the agreed-upon rate. Eventually, financial problems became insoluble and the *Review* ceased publication; but thanks to Hemingway, sections of *The Making of Americans* appeared in each issue from April right up to and including the last, in December 1924.

It was obvious that my book ought to include representative Hemingway letters. But he was already known to be difficult about giving authorization, either not responding at all to requests or refusing permission. In 1950, Charles Scribner, Jr., his publisher, had acted as intermediary in arranging for the inclusion of quotations from a Hemingway letter to Stein in the article on *"The Making of The Making of Americans"* that I had written for the *New Colophon;* but my need now to use whole letters rather than a sentence or two altered the situation. Since I couldn't very well ask Charles Scribner for help with a book being published by Alfred Knopf, I wrote Hemingway myself, enclosing copies of the letters for which I hoped to receive permission.

He was then living in Cuba and since even airmail was apt to be slow, I didn't expect to have a reply for several weeks. When the weeks became months, I forced myself to accept the fact that he was not going to answer. Not one to give up easily, I wrote again, enclosing an international-airmail-reply coupon. Hemingway must have been in a receptive mood when the second letter arrived, for he responded at once, returning the coupon, but telling me he had decided not to allow any of his letters to Gertrude Stein to be printed while Alice Toklas was alive. Then, as he phrased it, "to make the letter a collector's item," he went on to explain why he felt as he did about Alice, giving the details of a visit to 27 rue de Fleurus during which he had happened to overhear a domestic quarrel between her and Gertrude—an account later repeated in his *A Movable Feast* (1964).

Although this was naturally of great interest to me, it seemed to end any hope of my being allowed to print the letters. But there was nothing to be lost in making a final appeal, and I wrote Hemingway again, pointing out how essential it was to the plan of my book to have his role in the periodical publication of *The Making of Americans* represented. And counting upon the effect that a dramatic, attention-catching gesture might have, I returned his letter, disclaiming any interest in the collector's item he had offered in place of the permission I so badly needed. Again Hemingway must have been in a good humor, for he replied promptly, saying that he didn't want to "louse up" my book and giving me permission to print the letters.

My triumph was gratifying but not entirely unmixed with regret that by the trick that had got me what I wanted, I had lost a letter that anyone interested in either Hemingway or Stein would be very happy to own. For years the loss rankled. When Carlos Baker came to Yale to do research for his biography of Hemingway, I asked him if he had noticed "my" letter in the Hemingway papers then deposited at Princeton. He reported that he had indeed seen it, and so I knew that it hadn't just been thrown into the closest available wastebasket.

Some time later, when I had occasion to write Mary Hemingway for permission to reprint the Hemingway quotations in my article on *The Making of Americans*, I told her the story of the lost letter and asked if I could have it back, explaining that I certainly had no intention of selling it and would give it eventually to the Yale Library.

She replied promptly that she'd gladly let me have the letter but it was not immediately locatable in the files; if and when it turned up she would see that I got it.

There the matter rested for a year or so until I was once more in correspondence about Hemingway letters, this time with Jo August, who was organizing the Hemingway papers for the Kennedy Library, to which Mary Hemingway had given them. Enclosing a copy of her letter to me, I asked Jo August to be on the lookout. A few months later she wrote me excitedly that she had found the letter. Not wishing to entrust it to the mails, she came down from Boston and, at lunch at Mory's, turned the familiar piece of paper over to me. I felt a momentary, slight twinge of embarrassment at having eaten my piece of cake in 1952 and getting it back twenty-three years later. (Carlos Baker included its text in the selection of Hemingway letters that he edited in 1981.)

It was after an almost identical time span that I received the reply to my letter to Mina Loy. She had written out her answer but hadn't got around to mailing it. Joella Bayer found it among her mother's papers after her death and sent it to me in May 1975.

Other correspondents, especially the painters, seemed to feel the need to give me detailed explanations. Eugene Berman was hesitant about allowing the publication of the one letter of his that I wanted to use. He explained that this note of thanks to Gertrude Stein for hospitality during a visit at Bilignin actually masked his conviction that her interest in his painting had "come to a sudden and startling end and probably couldn't be revived." He had made no reference to his fears, preferring not "to jump too quickly at too disheartening conclusions." The letter, he felt, would be misleading and, without extensive footnotes and comments, would give an incomplete idea of his relationship with Miss Stein and its break-up. He invited me to come to see him in New York so that he could tell me more of the circumstances. A subsequent pleasant conversation led to his finally allowing the letter to stand as he had written it.

Stuart Davis wrote me that his letters made him sound more stupid than he would admit to being, and supplied some background information. He explained that Elliot Paul, then editor of *Transition,* had built him up as one of the top American artists with an article about him and reproductions of some of his paintings in the magazine.★ Miss Stein had expressed a real interest in his work, more than simply polite, and appearing to be sincere. Paul had taken him to see her twice. She had suggested that as soon as he had made a few things in Paris, she would visit his studio and select something for her collection. Viewed in this light, his two letters inviting her to come to see his work and referring to the bad state of his finances would be seen to be entirely natural.

Pavel Tchelitchew insisted on seeing not only the original French of the selections I proposed to use, in translation, from his letters, but also all of the omitted parts. He and his friend Charles-Henri Ford spent a good deal of time working over them. Pavlik explained to me why extensive corrections were necessary:

When I say: je suis un nègre de russe, I don't mean I am a Russian Negro, but: I am a Russian, who is treated by the French as the Amer[icans]. treat the Negroes! ... I am as different in my approach to the words as I am in my approach to the forms, lines, and colors. It is not because I don't know the language properly, but because I use metaphors and invent unusual situations. I am not a usual person, as you know. Therefore I would ask you to keep my corrections, otherwise the letters are not mine—they lose color, light, and form.

He asked me to restore some sentences that I had planned to omit, explaining that

It is very little to add—but it gives the letters more *my* character and explains many things, which not knowing me nor Gertrude and our relations, seem to you unimportant. Later, when you will be an old man and I will be no more there, lots of things will be clearer, will be re-judged and put on a plane where they belong, so then you will see *why* I put [back] those few extra lines and *what* they mean. I, in writing letters not only say things that happen. In "*how*" I say it (your French is not up to my own—I *think* in French—that explains *all*) is the reason "*why*" I say it. Being American, you respect *action,* but being brought up and born in Europe, I respect "thought" first. ... After all, dear Donald, my letters have to have a bit of savory and not sound like [just] anybody's letters.

★"Stuart Davis, American Painter." *Transition*, Paris, 14 (Fall 1928) 146–48, plus 4 plates on 2 leaves, and a cover illustration, reproducing 5 paintings by Davis.

THE *Flowers* OF *Friendship*

LETTERS written to
GERTRUDE STEIN

Edited by DONALD GALLUP

Before the Flowers of Friendship Faded Friendship Faded
TITLE OF A BOOK BY
GERTRUDE STEIN
PUBLISHED MAY 1, 1931

ALFRED A. KNOPF   NEW YORK
1 9 5 3

II

With permission problems settled, I turned the typescript in to
Knopf's, and their production people took over. They were determined to make an attractive book—in the well-established Knopf
tradition—and assigned it to the distinguished designer W. A.
Dwiggins. The type he chose was handsome, his arrangement of the
letters was attractive and eminently readable, but the title page he
first proposed looked to me cluttered and struck me as quite unworthy of either his or the firm's imprimatur. I let Herbert Weinstock,
my editor for the book, know of my disappointment. He was reluctant to question the design, explaining to me (what I very well
knew) that "we like to give [W. A. Dwiggins] free rein when we ask
him to undertake the design of our volumes." He did however agree
to let Dwiggins know of my reservations about the title page, but

THE
FLOWERS of FRIENDSHIP
Letters written to
GERTRUDE STEIN

Edited by DONALD GALLUP

Before the Flowers of Friendship Faded Friendship Faded
(TITLE OF A BOOK BY GERTRUDE STEIN)

1 9 5 3
ALFRED A. KNOPF   NEW YORK

warned that "the final decision must be left with him." Fortunately, Dwiggins himself hadn't been quite happy with his design: he had tried "to do 'a rose is a rose is a rose' stunt in type," but didn't like the result. The subsequent revision, while still by no means my favorite Dwiggins title page, represented at least a considerable improvement.

Both Carl Van Vechten and Alice Toklas were pleased with the finished book. Carl gave it an extremely generous review in the *New York Post* for 16 August:

The editor has done a skillful (brilliant would not be an exaggeration) job, creating an exciting juxtaposition, linking the material with helpful comments. So far as I can discover there are no errors of fact; even typographical errors seem to be lacking. The index itself could scarcely be improved. As an editor Mr. Gallup leaps with one bound into the front rank.

[He] … has given us a picture of a wonderful woman who perhaps had more effect on her generation and those that followed than is generally realized. He has built this portrait up little by little through the words of other people, artfully assembled and artfully arranged until, at the end, the reader rises, firmly convinced that he has been reading the biography of a genius.

Gertrude Stein's friends, who are legion, her readers, and the generations to come who can study her work in the Yale University Library, can thank Mr. Gallup for his loving and understanding effort. Most of all, Gertrude Stein, wherever she may be, should thank him for giving the public some accurate idea of what an important and distinguished figure she was in the history of American literature. "The Flowers of Friendship" is her accolade!

The book contained a printed dedication "For Alice B. Toklas /who was there when they came/and who knows what they meant." I had visited her in Paris in June, but had gone on to Spain before her advance copy of the book arrived. She wrote on 3 July, addressing her letter to me in care of the American Express Company in Seville. It followed me to Rome, back to Paris, and finally to New Haven, where I received it on 21 October:

Dear Donald—

The Flowers came yesterday afternoon. When I turned out my light (hour unknown) I'd read most of it. It is immensely impressive. You have achieved a complete accurate unbiased picture of Gertrude by an unfailingly happy choice of the material. There is of course more than this but I want to thank you with all my heart for your tribute to Gertrude, your faithful loyal friendship, all the constant flower of which the book is touching evidence. My warmest, most grateful thanks to you always.

Thank you for sending the book to me and by air, which really I should have stopped at the first suggestion you made of doing it. The dedication is [a] precious possession to me, but that too should have been nipped in the bud. Your wishing to do it was more than I deserved. You see how your goodness to me is embarrassing. There is however one thing that fusses me seriously—acknowledgment to me!—Oh no, and in the same breath as to Carl. My pillowslip was scorched. You—oh dear there are no complaints you understand but deep embarrassment.

What a sleuth you are—there are things I never knew—for example that it was Mildred [Aldrich] who introduced Cook. How you uncover the facts—oh marvellous—good friend.

With all gratitude, love, appreciation and admiration

Alice

Another enthusiastic reader was Fania Marinoff Van Vechten. She wrote to Alice a characteristic letter about the book:

At night I couldn't read Flowers of Friendship. The letters & the people who wrote them (many I had met), what they said and felt about Gertrude, stimulated me too much, I couldn't sleep. I've just finished the book (in the daytime). I've never read a richer collection of the history of struggles, ambitions, hopes and achievements of so many marvelous people. So many, whom "The Mother of us all" aided, encouraged—whose final recognition she made possible—and the story of the slow, sure ever growing glory of her own triumph.

I learned a great deal more about Gertrude thru these letters. I kept feeling these should be read by everyone who has never read Gertrude Stein (and of course [they] will be read by everyone who has). For me it was an emotional experience of many kinds of emotions. ... And Alice darling, I felt your presence, spirit and influence on every page everyone wrote after you shared each other's destiny. ...

The book was widely noticed and, on the whole, well received by the critics. Kathleen Cannell had a particularly warm review in the *Christian Science Monitor,* and William Saroyan published a comment—mostly about himself (one of his own letters was included in the book)—in a new periodical, *The Reporter.* Knopf's told me in late September that there had been perhaps forty or fifty reviews in papers all over the country. But, although the firm was for a time noncommittal about how the book was actually selling, in the end there was no denying that it had failed to interest the book-buying public. Malcolm Cowley, in his review in the *New York Herald Tribune,* suggested the trouble was that the title really didn't apply:

Are these letters really "The Flowers of Friendship"? Doesn't friendship imply a relationship among equals—or at least among persons who are equal as friends, even if they occupy different positions in the world? If we apply that test to the book, only the early letters from Miss Stein's classmates, and a few later ones from Paris connections like Mildred Aldrich, could be described as flowers of friendship. The relation of other correspondents to Miss Stein is that of clients to a patron or pupils to a teacher or noblemen to their absolute sovereign or even of adoring nephews to a maiden aunt who might leave them some money.

. . . they shamelessly flatter the author and her work. ...

Along with this glorification of Miss Stein and this disparagement of every other writer who might dim her luster, many of the correspondents—including the best of them—indulge in a peculiar form of self abasement.

Friends don't write to friends in exactly that style. Friends try to be candid with one another, whereas one detects in many of these letters—even those from good and honest writers—a special form of insincerity that seems to be based on a high regard for Miss Stein and a sensitive feeling about what she would like to hear them say. Her true story has to be read by indirection.

The true story, it seems to me, is of an extraordinarily vital and persistent woman with a passion for achieving not greatness but glory. ...

Whatever the reason for the public's failure to buy the book, sales were disappointing and returns downright frightening. I ventured to express to Alice Toklas the hope that the book would escape the fate of being remaindered: "I should hate to see it for sale in the corner drugstore at $1.89." But I had to endure an even worse ignominy: in October 1954, after the book had been out a full year, Alfred Knopf acknowledged that he had been too optimistic about the reception the volume would meet and had printed far too many (4500) copies. He announced in his quarterly newsletter, *Borzoi Books,* that his firm, while its present stock lasted, would supply this "charming" book postpaid at 50¢ each (the published price was $5.00). When I ordered fifty copies, the sales department, forgetting that their president had promised to send the book postpaid, attempted (unsuccessfully) to bill me for the shipping charges.

More blows to my pride came when I discovered that, in spite of Carl's and Alice's praise for my facts, I had got several of them wrong. Alice had been quite justifiably surprised to read my statement that Mildred Aldrich had introduced William Cook to Gertrude: Cook himself explained that it was Leo Stein who had done the introducing. One of the most difficult problems had been dating the undated letters, and I had erred at least twice. I had taken a letter from Etta Cone about *Three Lives* to refer to her helping with the cost of the first publication of the book in 1909, whereas it actually concerned Etta's possible purchase of the manuscript. This was fifteen years later, in 1924, when the newspapers had widely reported Dr. A. S. W. Rosenbach's acquisition (for $1975) of the manuscript of James Joyce's *Ulysses* in the auction sale of John Quinn's library. I had dated a letter of Katharine Cornell in which she mentioned having seen Thornton Wilder in Salzburg, "full of thrilling things" Gertrude Stein had said, as having been written in 1933—almost two years before Thornton and Gertrude had met! The correct year was 1937.

I found out later that Alice had not liked my referring to Gertrude's final illness as cancer, she holding that the correct diagnosis was calcification of the uterus. She also felt that the sculptor David Edstrom should have been represented. (I had been aware of his importance in the early Paris days, but had not found any of his letters interesting enough to print.)

The Flowers of Friendship was actually reprinted in 1979, but I was given no opportunity to make corrections. Farrar, Straus and Giroux published it in their reprint series, Octagon Books, merely reproducing the Knopf volume photographically. I am sorry to have to report that their edition met with about the same lack of appreciation that had greeted the book a generation earlier.

Virgil Thomson, 4 June 1947. Photograph by Carl Van Vechten. Beinecke Library, gift of the photographer.

Virgil Thomson

1945–1989

REVIEWS BY VIRGIL THOMSON, printed in the *New York Herald Tribune,* of various musical events in New York and elsewhere were part of my education while I was in New Haven between 1940 and 1941, and after my return from the army in 1946 until Mr. Thomson resigned as music critic in 1954. This man obviously knew whereof he spoke, and if his dicta were expressed occasionally in terms verging on the autocratic, they had almost always—to my untutored ear at least—the authentic ring of truth. This impression was reinforced by his replies in the *Tribune*'s correspondence columns to indignant protestations and carping attacks. (For me, the Thomson contributions to the New York paper recalled now and then the write-ups of musical events in New Haven published in the *Yale Daily News* during 1933–34 by my fellow Trumbullian John Hersey, although his ex cathedra judgments, formed also on a base provided by an excellent musical training, often couched in a terminology just as impressively high-flown, lacked the authenticity of experience.)

Besides the *Tribune* columns, my work with the writings of Gertrude Stein in 1940–41 had informed me about Thomson and especially his celebrated collaboration with her on the opera *Four Saints in Three Acts.* He and I met twice at her apartment in Paris in 1945, and the historic second occasion, already reported in *Pigeons on the Granite,* had the eventual consequence of enshrining us both as characters in the other Stein-Thomson masterpiece, *The Mother of Us All.*

It was that opera, after its première performance at Columbia University in May 1947, that prepared the way for our third meeting. Again as recorded in the previous instalment of my memoirs, Mrs. Kenneth Simpson gave a party later that year for the composer and the cast, and kindly invited me to attend. I went with Fania Marinoff and Carl Van Vechten (he had already photographed several cast members). My hostess soon afterwards placed on deposit at Yale a bust of Gertrude Stein by the French sculptor Antoinette Champetier de Ribes. Bernard Faÿ, friend of both artist and subject, acting as agent for the artist, had left the work with Mrs. Simpson for possible sale. It became eventually a permanent addition to the Gertrude Stein collection.

My next dealings with the composer were in connection with the book of letters to Gertrude Stein, *The Flowers of Friendship,* that I was then preparing for publication. Although in October 1951 I had not yet found a publisher for the book, I wrote Virgil, enclosing the typed transcripts I had prepared of five of his autograph letters: four about the two operas, and one that reported on a concert performance in New York in February 1929 of his setting of her *Capital Capitals. Four Saints* was then about to be revived under the auspices of the American National Theatre and Academy, with a reconstitution of the Florine Stettheimer sets by Pavel Tchelitchew, and I offered to look up anything that might be needed in the Stein or Stettheimer materials at Yale. Virgil replied promptly, saying that he would be pleased to appear in my volume of letters:

Whenever you find a publisher for them write then for my formal permission. I should like to check the ones you sent me against my manuscript. There are two words that do not seem to make sense. I suspect a misreading of my script. Also, I think the name of [X] ... should be omitted, since the matter discussed was a business deal that did not come through.

He thanked me for my offer of help with the sets, but proposed to come up to New Haven later himself, bringing Tchelitchew with him.

That visit did not take place, but Virgil did give a lecture in New Haven later that year. He had hoped to come to the Sterling Library to look over the *Four Saints* materials, but his crowded schedule did not allow it. Instead, he invited me to his talk on 8 December, and I was happy to hear, at last, a sampling of his fabled "performance" of the opera, singing all the parts with a success that was altogether remarkable. I later sent him photocopies of some of Florine Stettheimer's notes about the sets.

During the following ten months, I completed my editing of the book of letters to Gertrude Stein and, with Carl Van Vechten's help, found a publisher in Alfred A. Knopf. I reported to Virgil in September 1952:

There has been some progress on the book of letters addressed to Gertrude, and it now appears that Alfred Knopf will publish it if I can cut it down to a hundred thousand words. I still want to include those letters of yours, however, and have checked their texts with your original manuscript. ... Of course I plan to check all the letters in proof against the originals just to be sure.

He had forgotten that I had sent him copies of his letters and asked me to send another set.

At just this time, Carl, with Alice Toklas's and my enthusiastic approval, had asked Virgil to write the introduction for *Bee Time Vine,* the third volume of the Yale Edition of the Unpublished Writings of Gertrude Stein. He wrote me on the 25th of September:

I have written a preface and some notes for the Stein volume. I shall send them to you as soon as I can get them typed. There is some obscurity about the line "Rose as [*sic*] a rose etc." Alice says its appearance in "Lifting Belly" [*one of the Stein pieces, dated 1915–17, in the third volume*] is its "first and only" appearance in Gertrude's writing. Is this true? If so, it makes a mess of "Lifting Belly" as to the apparent dates of composition, since the stationery bearing the device already existed in 1914–15.

I answered on the 29th:

I sent you copies of the letters on 31 Oct 1951. ... To save time, I'm enclosing my third carbons of the letters, but I shall have to ask you please to return them since they are the only ones I have left besides the manuscript itself.

I'm delighted about the preface. Alice's formidable memory has failed in this instance, I'm afraid. The first appearance of "Rose is a rose etc." was in "Sacred Emily," written according to Gertrude in 1913. We have the manuscript—the piece was printed in *Geography and Plays*—and the phrase is there.

On 7 October he wrote me again:

Here are both copies of my letters. All the emendations are proper excepting the insertion of the word *as* on April 15, 1946. I still do not know what *boule* and *garden* mean.★

Thanks for information about the rose passage.

I brought from Europe for you at Alice's request the complete Paris press on *Four Saints*. At the moment I cannot find it among my things, but it will surely get to the surface before long. When it does, I should like to send it to you for mimeographing.

The preface will be coming along in due time. Meanwhile I should appreciate a copy of the new volume just issued.

I answered on 9 October:

I didn't mean that you were to return *both* sets of copies. I'll make all the emendations … . The word which I translated "boule" stumps me; I have traced it with the enclosed result. Could it be "book" or what? The difficulty is that the final curl is definitely added.

I'll be glad to see the press on *Four Saints,* and am even more eager to see your introduction. I have asked the Press to send you a copy of *Mrs. Reynolds.*

He replied on the 14th, suggesting that the word "boule" must be "boob" ("garden" remained a mystery to us both)★★, and sent the promised reviews of the European production of *Four Saints*. These were followed on the 11th by a typescript of *Four Saints,* showing Virgil's cuts for the opera, that had been, he reported, in the possession of James Thrall Soby ever since the Hartford première in 1934. We acknowledged it on the 19th as Virgil's gift for the Stein collection.

On the 25th of November, he forwarded to me the completed introduction for the third volume of the Stein edition, complaining that he still did not have the promised copy of *Mrs. Reynolds.* This had been sent to him at the *Herald Tribune,* but he had never received it. The press was obliged to furnish him a replacement.

★These were the words that, in my transcripts, hadn't seemed to him to make "sense." In a letter of 26 February 1929, he had reported that the audience's way of taking the *Capitals* proved to him "the possibility of having a regular boule[?] success with the opera [*Four Saints*]". In his letter of 19 July 1928, he had written: "I hope you get your garden." (There was no context to help explain the reference.)

★★It remained a mystery to me only until 1971 when we acquired Gertrude Stein's letters to Virgil. In her letter to him, postmarked Belley, 13 [?] July 1928, she had written: ". . . we almost had the use of a garden with immured sisters only we haven't, but perhaps we will."

For some time, Alice Toklas had been exerting polite pressure on Virgil to give us his letters from Gertrude. In 1960, he did place them at Yale on deposit, and I agreed to make and send him transcripts, as well as a microfilm of the originals.

In May of that year, Virgil Thomson was to be inducted—along with Eero Saarinen and Robert Penn Warren—into the American Academy of Arts and Letters. For several years the Yale Collection of American Literature had had on deposit with the Gertrude Stein collection the original ink manuscript for the opera *Four Saints in Three Acts,* the property of Mrs. Briggs W. Buchanan, wife of an old Harvard College friend of Virgil's, to whom he had given it. With her consent, we lent the manuscript to the academy for an exhibition of works by newly elected members. I went to New York for the induction ceremonies on 25 May and heard Virgil give the Evangelina Wilbur Blashfield address, "Music Now." At the reception after his talk, I had the opportunity to congratulate not only him and Red Warren, but also H. D., who had received the Award of Merit Medal for Poetry on the same occasion.

In December 1939, Lord Berners had regretfully decided that he could not write the music for Gertrude Stein's "Dr. Faustus Lights the Lights," as he had hoped to do, and suggested that the piece be offered to Virgil Thomson, who, for various reasons, declined then to undertake the assignment. Subsequently, Carl Van Vechten, acting after Gertrude Stein's death as her literary executor, authorized a young New York composer, Meyer Kupferman, to write the opera. He completed the task, but was not able to find either producer or publisher for his work. In September 1962, Virgil changed his mind about "Dr. Faustus," and decided that he could, after all, find a way to set the Stein text. But Carl had not thought to put a time limit on the authorization he had given to Kupferman, who consequently continued to control the work. Virgil consulted with Arnold Weissberger, a legal specialist in such matters, and for a time, from 1962–64, contemplated challenging the Van Vechten authority to execute such agreements as that with Kupferman on the grounds that Gertrude Stein in her will had empowered Carl merely to edit her unpublished writings and had not actually made him her literary executor. Had Virgil taken the threatened action, he'd have cast into limbo all posthumously executed contracts for Stein publications. Upon reflection, he decided not to go ahead with his challenge—and I breathed a sigh of relief!

In 1965 Virgil had just given the pencil manuscript for *Four Saints* to the Library of Congress, getting a generous valuation from the library for use as a deduction on his income-tax return (as was then still allowed). With nary a warning to me, he advised Mrs. Buchanan to withdraw her manuscript from Yale and give it to the Library of Congress. I found out about this in time, and protested to Virgil—who answered that he merely wanted Mrs. Buchanan to get the best possible valuation for her gift. I was able to find out from my friend Frederick R. Goff, in charge of rare books and manuscripts at the Library of Congress, the exact amount of the valuation the library had given Virgil for his pencil manuscript. Armed with this information, Henry W. Wenning, then a dealer in books and manuscripts in New Haven, was quite willing to set a similar appraisal on the ink manuscript for gift to Yale. As a result, Yale—not LC—became the permanent owner of the manuscript.

On 12 December of that year Virgil wrote inviting me to a buffet dinner at his apartment for two nuns, one of whom "produces Gertrude Stein plays in Los Angeles. They are far-out and very devoted to Gertrude." An account of a dinner party at the Chelsea Hotel would certainly have enhanced considerably the readability of this narrative but, unfortunately, I was just then working against a deadline and had to decline the invitation.

On 3 March 1971—four years after the death of Alice B. Toklas—Virgil announced to me that he had decided, because of the recent ruling by the IRS that "self-created" items, including letters received, were no longer a legitimate income-tax deduction, to *sell* his Gertrude Stein letters. The decision did not come as a surprise, for Henry Wenning had already informed me that Virgil had asked him to appraise the letters for this purpose. Virgil set the price at $12,500, explained that his letters from Alice Toklas were *not* to be included, and asked that I give him Yale's decision in just twelve days—by 15 March. Fortunately, the Beinecke Rare Book

Committee agreed that this was a purchase that we must make and I was able to surprise Virgil on 9 March with a favorable reply.* I knew that he was negotiating with New York University for their acquisition of his entire archive (they had promised him a special room), and was prepared for his plea, on 20 June, that the sale of the Stein letters not be publicized: "It might be a shade inconvenient." But when he asked me, in August of that year, to have all the Stein letters photographed so that he could place copies of them at New York University, I made clear to him my reluctance to comply with his request. The complicated negotiations with the university progressed though certainly not at a rapid pace: it was not until three years later, at the end of March 1974, that I received what was obviously a form letter from him:

Dear Donald,

I have made a gift to New York University of my musical and literary manuscripts, my correspondence files, and similar records of my professional life. In the University's new library on Washington Square a section has been designated for the preservation and exhibition of all these, to be known as the Virgil Thomson Room.

I am hoping that my own materials (now being organized for transfer to their permanent home in this handsome new building designed by Philip Johnson) may be augmented by gifts from friends and colleagues.

According to the present tax laws, as I understand them, the commercial value of letters, drawings, and the like is not deductible when they have been received directly from their authors. Nevertheless, they do have historical value; and New York University hopes to gather an impressive assemblage of memorabilia, manuscripts, and related materials from the worlds of music, art, theater, journalism, and films, to be known as the Virgil Thomson Collection.

May I urge that you seriously consider adding to this Collection any letters, manuscripts, photographs, art works, or other materials that you may possess relating to my work or to my life and background.

Whatever you are willing to part with will be deeply appreciated by the University and duly acknowledged in the listings, catalogs, and other pub–

---

*One item he didn't include in the correspondence sold to Yale was the Stein calling card that began, in 1930, a nearly four-year break in their friendship. Below the engraved "Miss Stein" Gertrude had written: "declines further acquaintance with Mr. Thomson." Preparations for the 1934 production of *Four Saints* effected a reconciliation. The card was found by Virgil's biographer in the small wooden box in which it had been carefully preserved.

lications that will be issued regarding the Collection. In the case of items that the owner does not wish to lose touch with, Xerox copies can be made available in return for the originals.

The Collection will be ready to exhibit early in 1974. Until then, I suggest that gift items be sent either to my home address or to Ms. Elizabeth K. Miller at the Elmer Holmes Bobst Library of New York University, 70 Washington Square South, New York, N.Y. 10012.

Ms. Miller will also be happy to answer inquiries.

Very sincerely ever,

[signed] Virgil
Virgil / Thomson

The prospect of being listed in some future New York University exhibition catalogue did not present to me a temptation that I was unable to resist, and I sent no Thomson memorabilia to either Virgil or Ms. Miller. What success his appeal may have enjoyed with other friends I cannot say, but three years later I received another long letter, dated 8 August 1977:

Dear Donald,

Now that I am eighty and with memorabilia of all ages crowding my house, I am looking toward a sensible distribution of these things and wondering if you might help me with a bit of advice.

The loot consists of:

1. my musical manuscripts—10,000 pages of original holograph (mostly pencil) all card-catalogued by a trained music librarian and filed in non-acid folders in 25 filing-boxes (12″ x 14″ x 4″).

2. 105 filing-boxes of correspondence:
   a. special items and family documents from before 1926,
   b. letters received 1926–1940 (excepting the G. Steins, which you have),
   c. correspondence 1940–1977 complete, almost all with copies of my letters attached. This includes 200 from Alice Toklas, of which I do not have mine to her but which you may already have,
   d. all contracts since 1924 for music publication, book and magazine publication, theatrical and film production, conducting and other personal appearances,
   e. certificates of musical and literary copyrights, with renewals,
   f. bank accounts and royalty statements from 1921–1977.

3. a large number of books both French and English with endorsements by their authors.

4. 6 filing-boxes of photographs (V.T., his family, friends, and profes-

sional associates, also of V.T. opera productions),

5. a complete collection of V.T.'s musical and literary works, published and unpublished.

6. complete materials—manuscripts and proofs—of all V.T. books.

7. 27 boxes of clippings and reviews, 1920–1977.

There exist also paintings, drawings, sculptures, and objets d'art, but these I intend to dispose of separately.

It is the V.T. relics that need a home. Obviously, consulting them would be easier if they were all in one place. Actually they invite consultation in all the fields that my professional life has touched—namely, music, theatre, ballet, journalism, and letters, as well as the visual arts, where I have had many close friends.

If you feel inclined to advise with me, I can come to see you in New Haven. But if you would prefer to cast an eye on the collection itself and its catalogs, everything is in my New York flat except the musical manuscripts, which are being kept in storage for me, against fire damage, at the New York Public Library branch in Lincoln Center.

Do let me hear from you if you have a free moment.

I replied on the 31st, upon my return from vacation in Switzerland:

I am astounded: I thought you were to have a special room at N.Y.U. for the papers that you hadn't already given to the Library of Congress. Certainly you did give some things to the Library of Congress, didn't you?

Before I can advise, at least so far as Yale is concerned, I'd need to know whether the papers would be sold or given, and if sold at approximately what price? It's certainly an important archive and I'd dearly like to see it at Yale.

We have only a few of your letters to Alice after Gertrude's death—seven or eight. What happened to the others, I have never known. There was talk of some of Alice's correspondence having been sold to the American Library in Paris or to Texas.

He wrote me on the 12th of September:

New York University was so dilatory about equipping my room with drawers, cabinets, and locks (they wasted four years ...) that I backed out of the agreement. Also, a rare book dealer in California ... , whom you probably know, tried for some time to find a customer for buying the collection, but without success.

He was asking $150,000 for 10,000 pages of composer's holograph. If you think Yale would like to acquire it at some more realistic figure, I should be happy to consider that. I should also be willing to accept payment in five, or possibly even ten, annual installments. I am planning, moreover, to leave in my will some money for establishing fellowships at a major university, and Yale might very well be considered for this benefaction. If the purchase price could be directly assigned to this purpose, it might not have to go through me as taxable income. Do let us look into all these possibilities.

I should also be inclined to give them free my 100 or so boxes of correspondence, my purpose in this being to keep my manuscripts and other significant papers, so far as possible, all in one place. Yale already owns, I may add, an ink score of "Four Saints" entirely in my hand.

The Library of Congress owns my pencil sketch and original orchestral score of this opera.

I am sorry we do not know where the letters received by Alice Toklas, if she kept them, have gone. In any case, hers to me, which are even more numerous, I think, than my letters from Gertrude, it would certainly be appropriate to deposit at Yale.

Do let me know your thoughts on these matters and what possibilities you may find for purchase.

To which I replied on the 16th:

Many thanks for your letter. It's too bad the NYU plans didn't work out, and that … [X] couldn't sell the manuscripts for $150,000; but perhaps all the past disappointments will be more than compensated for if the Virgil Thomson Archive and the Thomson Scholarships end up at Yale.

I was in Indiana when your letter arrived yesterday or the day before (I got back in the early hours of this morning), but I have lost no time today in laying the matter before Harold Samuel, the Librarian of the Music School. He tells me that the Dean is very actively involved in a program for new scholarships and he is most hopeful that something can be arranged along the line you suggest. He has copies of your letters and will write you as soon as he has had a chance to discuss the proposition with the Dean.

As you know, the Music School Library already has the manuscripts of Ives, Ruggles, Ornstein, and several other important composers. Thomson would be a splendid addition.

Besides the long Four Saints ink manuscript, we have several other short ones received as part of the Stein papers: "Alice Toklas," "Film: 'Deux soeurs qui sont pas soeurs'," "Lady Godiva's Waltzes," "Miss Gertrude Stein," "Piano Sonata No. 3," "Portrait of F.B.," and "Preciosilla." Of course copies of all of them can be easily supplied to make the Thomson Archive as complete as possible.

I certainly hope that all of this can be brought about, and without too much delay.

It was a great relief for me during the last years of my curatorship of the Yale Collection of American Literature not to have to deal on business matters with my friend Virgil Thomson. And I rejoiced in the success which rewarded Harold Samuel's labors. He was able somehow to meet all of Virgil's exacting demands and yet keep his good will. The complicated negotiations came to a happy culmination in 1978 with the sale and gift of the Thomson archive to Yale. In 1979, the Virgil Thomson scholarships in the School of Music were established, and a big Thomson exhibition opened at the Beinecke Library. Virgil himself came up, and I joined him, Sam, and Kathy Moretto for a tour of the show. On 23 April, he gave a talk in the Law School auditorium, "Music Does Not Flow," and the next evening there was an elaborate celebratory dinner in the Presidents' Room in Woolsey Hall. John Houseman, Virgil's long-time associate, gave the principal address, ably seconded by Betty Allen and Bill Zinsser.

Seven years later, on 2 December 1986, Virgil came back to Yale to receive the prestigious Howland Medal for "distinguished achievement in the ... fine arts," and to give another talk, "Words & Music," later published by the Yale University Press. It was my honor and privilege to introduce him on that occasion, and this is what I said:

As composer and critic, Virgil Thomson needs no introduction to this or any other university audience—especially as we join in observing his 90th birthday, an occasion that has already become one of the most celebrated events of the 20th century.

But some of you may not realize that Yale is now THE center for Thomson studies. In 1946, just before she died, Gertrude Stein sent off to New Haven the final lot of her papers, including the letters from Virgil Thomson that tell the story of the two Stein-Thomson operas, *Four Saints in Three Acts* and *The Mother of Us All*—operas that have made musical history. *Four Saints* had its world première here in Connecticut in 1934 and *The Mother of Us All* in New York in 1947; if they haven't received the accolade of production at the Metropolitan Opera House in New York, the reason is, I am sure, that the Metropolitan plans a surprise for Virgil on either his 95th or 100th birthday.

Along with the Thomson letters received in the Stein papers, there were also manuscripts of Thomson musical portraits and settings for Stein poems and of his Third Piano Sonata, written for Gertrude to improvise on the white keys of her piano (she disliked using the black keys). Mr. Thomson himself gave us a typescript of the Stein libretto for *Four Saints* and turned over to us his Stein letters. With his blessing, Mrs. Briggs

SOTHEBY'S
FOUNDED 1744

Property from the Estate of
Virgil Thomson

NEW YORK
THURSDAY, OCTOBER 11, 1990

Buchanan gave us the ink manuscript of *Four Saints*. Florine Stettheimer designed the famous cellophane décor for the first production and, again with Virgil's blessing, Miss Ettie Stettheimer gave us her sister Florine's dossier on the opera, which includes a good many photographs.

In 1978, the Music School acquired the bulk of the Thomson manuscripts, and he gave all the rest of his correspondence. In 1979, Yale established the Virgil Thomson Scholarship in the Music School and presented a memorable concert of his works. He has lectured here on a number of occasions in the past.

Virgil Thomson returns to New Haven to receive the Henry Elias Howland Memorial Prize this evening and to speak to us this afternoon on a subject that has been close to his heart and mind for almost all of his ninety years, "Words and Music." Mr. Thomson.

Yale's Virgil Thomson celebration continued the following afternoon with a "conversation" between the composer and Tim Page, music critic of the *New York Times,* and concluded that evening with a concert of his music presented by students, alumni, and fellows of the School of Music, featuring performances of his portraits, his *String Quartet No. 2* (1932), and *Capital Capitals* (1927).

Virgil died on the last day of September 1989, just two months before his 93rd birthday. He departed this life, as his biographer has pointed out,

just the way he had hoped he would: at home [*in his apartment at the Chelsea Hotel in New York*], in his sleep and in time to make all editions of the Sunday *New York Times*.

Laura Riding Jackson (1977?). Photograph by Lowber Tiers. Collection of Donald Gallup.

Laura Riding Jackson

1952–1991

I

THREE OF HER letters to Gertrude Stein had provided the occasion
for my first brief exchange with Laura Riding Jackson. As Laura
Riding, she and Robert Graves had been for several years warm
admirers of Miss Stein and her work and had even set by hand and
printed at their Seizin Press in London one of her abstract compositions, *An Acquaintance with Description,* issued in 1929. Miss Riding,
by the time of her attempted suicide in that same year, had come to
regard Gertrude Stein as one of her perhaps five closest friends, sending to her from hospital a series of long, warmly intimate letters.
Returning to the United States in 1939, she had, in 1941, married
Schuyler B. Jackson, the critic and former poetry editor of *Time*
magazine. I had chosen three of her letters, all relating to *An
Acquaintance with Description,* for inclusion in *The Flowers of Friendship*
(1953), the book of letters to Gertrude Stein that I was preparing,
but Mrs. Jackson refused to give me permission to print them, making her reasons clear in two typed instalments. The first was dated 30
July 1952:

I do not agree with your judgment that [the letters] ... are worth publishing; ... .
  Whatever contribution I made to the making public of Gertrude Stein's
writings is represented by my share in the printing and publishing of *An
Acquaintance With Description;* I prefer to let that contribution stand as
made, without the personal, private accents that the three letters in question, if printed, would lend to it. ... I find the letters in quality not such as
to justify an expense of book-material, book-space, and the attention of
people upon them. Furthermore, the personal correspondence of which
they are initial letters terminated in irritations on my side and undoubtedly
similarly on Gertrude Stein's side—so that these letters, if printed, would
make a false picture of the whole of our relations ... .
  In my dislike of having thus to impose a restraint, I console myself with
the thought that from your point of view my refusal can result in little loss:
I hope that you will have that view of it.

Of course I accepted her decision. But in the words I used, Mrs. Jackson found cause for "a persisting uneasiness" that resulted in another letter. On 17 August she thanked me for the cheerfulness of my response, but she felt that I had made some wrong assumptions about her view of her association with Gertrude Stein:

the manner in which I wrote allowed you to think that my view of it was such that I could take pleasure in having letters of mine to her published. That is not the case. I withheld an expression of my aversion to the publication of any letters of mine to her from a desire to confine my answer to what I considered to be the principle involved: whether those particular letters could justly be regarded as of particular usefulness, histor-ically, regardless of my aversion. In trying thus to be just to your own interest in them I kept my feelings too much out of the picture, confusing to some degree reticence and cordiality with justness.

I look upon my association with Gertrude Stein with sorrow and shame, for my complaisance in it towards her—both in respect to her work and her personality. I know now that instead of helping her—by perceiving the unwholesomeness of her word-compositions—I con-tributed to her self-satisfaction in them—adding to others' indulgence of her foibles one more bad service in the name of friendship.

I can find no other way of correcting my failure to safeguard the words of my previous letter from giving out untrue implications ... besides that of communicating to you my view of my association with her. I apologize for thrusting it upon you. I attach no special importance to it, or to your knowing what it is, except in the sense that anything untrue lodged any-where in human life does harm. I write not to reopen the subject of the three letters that have passed between us, but with the feeling that [the correspondence] ... was not properly closed and the wish that it may now be so.

And that was most certainly that!

II

Almost a quarter century later the Stein-Riding letters were again the subject of an exchange between Laura Riding Jackson and me. (She was now a widow, Schuyler Jackson having died in 1968.) On 28 December 1974, she wrote to the Yale Library asking

whether you have any manuscripts of mine, or manuscript material per-taining to me—or my work. If you do, I should care to know, besides the nature of any such in your possession, what the conditions would be for my obtaining copies of them.

I reported to her early in January 1975 that we had none of her manuscripts, but that we did own her letters to Gertrude Stein, their use
restricted; and I reminded her of our earlier exchange. Her typed
response, dated 10 January, was prefaced by a handwritten note:

This letter is a very untidy typescript: I apologize for this. It has been written at a somewhat unwell time, with work-fatigue present, besides, at day's
end.

Her typing did indeed leave a good deal to be desired: peppered
with restrikes and manuscript corrections, the letters, already
couched in a characteristic fastidiousness of word-choice that I
found occasionally obfuscating, became here and there, extremely
difficult to puzzle out. That first, long letter (which I quote with
extensive omissions) was typical:

Indeed, it pleases me rather than otherwise, in a personal respect, that
there are no manuscripts of mine in your special American collection.
Much of my manuscript ... and other material ... also, came by circumstances to be separated from me, with later repossession ... not pursued
because of circumstances moving me to let the matter of it stay dormant.
But it did not; and eventually I became aware that much ... had been sold
and distributed, a good deal finding its way to libraries. ... not until recent
years did I turn to investigate little by little what had been going on behind
my awareness, as it were, and also in the field of literary records generally
in my regard. From the early Forties onward for very many years my interest, my activity, was centered in studies in ... problems of language in dis-
sociation from literary involvements. Your request as to those letters of
mine written to Gertrude Stein came in that period. (It surprised me, your
telling of this: I had no recollection of it at all.) My feeling about such
things in the present time does not differ generally from what it then was.
But it is qualified by a few considerations, a very important one of which
is my having resolved in the last few years to do all I could without serious
interference with my work-devotions towards correcting factual and other
mistreatment of my work and ... myself that has got incorporated in the
literary records and academic and literary-world attitudes.

This lengthy commenting is not idle. Your reference to these letters
of mine to Gertrude Stein falls close to a matter of letters of hers to me
only recently come into my possession, thirty-nine pages, belonging to 25
items. ...

The ... letters ... [are] pledged to Cornell University Library, where
there is a collection of varied material ... pertaining to my work, and
myself ... ; and some personal effects of my husband's ... . The originals of
the letters will be soon sent from London to ... Cornell ... . I have xerox

copies here ... ; I have so far only glanced hastily at the pages. I do not know ... whether I shall find reason for making public any portion of them, or all; my inclination is towards letting them be, at least, of an unrestricted status at the Library in Ithaca. I have serious and sad feeling about Gertrude Stein, and the relations of friendship that for a time existed between us. I have something written on her, that I have not been able yet to put into final state, in which I try to identify the perverse purpose in her life-zest and labors ... .★

She concluded by requesting copies of her letters.

I sent them, but felt that Yale was justified in asking something more in return than just photocopies of the Stein letters; and Mrs. Jackson subsequently agreed to provide us with detailed notes about the entire correspondence. She explained, in a letter of 4 February 1975:

I think that when I have made my comments on my letters to G[ertrude]. S[tein]. and ... her letters to me . . . , there may be useful points of inter-reference apparent to me, that I could form into a set of notations for you, and Cornell. ...

I return a little to my sense of the righteous procedure of your holding those letters in restriction. ... Why, even dear Mr. [George] Healey, who started the collection of my writing at Cornell, and received my decision to give everything possible to Cornell Library with joyful cheer, had acquired a sizable collection of letters of mine, and the question of restriction was never raised with me. When I learned of the Library's possession of these, the actuality of the sale of them by one whom I had served devotedly as friend,★★ Mr. Healey set against my feelings about the betrayal of confidence (they touching on much of the personal) stout consolation on the ground of their showing a remarkable generosity to a younger writer. But that *good* man had no thought of restriction, at any time.

And she added, as a final note in signing the letter:

I am pleased to be treated well in these things (not the universal academic rule, by my experience) ... .

The problem of restriction was a recurring one. In a letter of 16

★"The Word-Play of Gertrude Stein" was eventually published in *Critical Essays on Gertrude Stein* [Edited by] Michael J. Hoffman (Boston, G. K. Hall & Co. [1986]), pp. 240–60. In "Addenda B" to the essay, page 258, Mrs. Jackson quotes a sentence from one of the notes she had sent me on the Stein-Riding correspondence.

★★Alan J. Clark, Mrs. Jackson's authorized bibliographer, informs me that the friend was James Reeves.

February, Mrs. Jackson gave me a progress report:

My inspection of [Gertrude Stein's letters] ... so far suggests nothing calling for restriction; but I shall have to think carefully as to this in a general way, for I have put restriction limits on all my correspondence lodged at Cornell ... with a few exceptions that I am only now making where there has been ill-behavior of a public character towards me, and the correspondence provides some balance of fact against this. I am in general horrified by stresses of special personal importance on this or that manuscript material, according to public-interest value of it, rather than according to values of intellectual bearing, and, especially so where values of personal honor and friendship's claims or gratitude's or all of these are brushed aside by the potency of market yields. ...

She expressed again her "grateful satisfaction" in my "scrupling to hold ... [her] letters to G. S. restricted," and promised to include in her comments "anything of useful relevance to the letters of mine that I find in the letters of hers." As evidence of "not neglecting these responsibilities undertaken," she sent to me on 29 May 1975 her typed comments on the correspondence from its start in 1927 through her own letter of 8 January 1929. She put no restrictions on these early letters, but asked that, at least for the present, nothing after that last letter be shown to readers. Her notes were almost exclusively concerned with the proper dating of the letters. She apologized for any repetition, explaining that

I have had to work this intricate task into an over-complicated work and life schedule, and have been unable to keep to it in long unbroken spells of attention.

She replied to my acknowledgment of receipt of the notes on 7 June, and assured me that "I shall complete the operation to my best of management of the time-needing problem."

Over the following months, Mrs. Jackson sent me her reflections upon the Stein letters. A brief note added to one of them by Robert Graves brought forth an extended analysis of his and her relationship and of their brief friendship with Gertrude Stein. In sending me these and other comments on 23 October 1975, Mrs. Jackson explained:

I have continued to introduce interpolations of critical reflection and personal narrative and analysis. ... it has seemed to me that presenting them here ensures some keeping straight of things for consulters of the material, whether they come into contact with what I may otherwise write and publish, of an autobiographical reference, or critical judgement.

When she had sent me nothing over a considerable period, Mrs. Jackson, on 23 April 1976, reassured me:

I have not at all lost hope of achieving the completion of my ... notes, with correlations between the two sets of letters; and, please, do you not lose hope. I have been, and will continue to be, overworked ... . I am dogged by what seems to be virus hound-packs harassing a facial-nerve area of itself a permanent paining phenomenon, and I walk with difficulty and discomfort, which hampers me a good deal in my solitary maintenance of this domestic establishment, but, somehow, 'it' goes.

In a postscript to that letter, Mrs. Jackson asked me about drafts, in the Yale collection, of three of the Stein letters to Laura Riding. I replied frankly on the 28th:

As for the Stein drafts, I am a little hesitant to send copies of those because (1) they are so difficult to decipher, and (2) there's a slight feeling of treachery to Gertrude in revealing first thoughts which were obviously superseded by second and even third; but still you may find all this of interest if not of importance to your process of annotation.

She responded sympathetically:

I do understand your hesitating to send me the rough-trial sheets. And your trust of me in doing so cheers me. The four very rough ones ... are her first scrawlings for a letter responding to my letter expressing annoyance at a Paris (was it not *Herald Tribune* in those days?) English language report of myself and Robert Graves' being in Paris as 'Mr. and Mrs. Robert Graves'. I had reason to connect this with Virgil Thomson, in my feelings.— Gertrude played with what riled her quite elaborately; I did not give things that riled me any other character in my dealing with them than what they were, in the bare. This was rather early in our relationship. After that there was no ruffling of relations-waters between us. The final, as you may know, was my protest over what she did with Basket's unwellness as communication material: it was writing *writing,* not writing a *letter,* to her friend. After that: no more passed between us.

She signed herself: "Believe me to be glad in how it goes, in our communicating."

III

In October 1975, Howard Woolmer, a bookseller-bibliographer from whom I had acquired materials for both the library and myself, wrote to offer a collection of Laura Riding typescripts, amounting to 239 pages of original and 130 pages of carbon, all of it unpublished. The price was reasonable, but because Woolmer explained that the author "has expressed an interest in publishing some of this material at a later date" and, more importantly, because the Beinecke was in the process just then of negotiating the purchase of Richard Wright's papers from his widow, we declined the Woolmer offer. Shortly afterwards, a letter from Mrs. Jackson, written on the 23rd, made it clear that Woolmer had been acting as her agent in offering to us the typescripts. In my reply to him I had made reference to a "major acquisition" for which available Beinecke funds had been earmarked. Mrs. Jackson accepted our decision concerning the typescripts, but with a reservation:

I have only a private aftermath of some balking at that term 'major'—which poses to me a question as to whether … material related to myself is by general routine of 'minor' status. … I am experiencedly aware of there being certain academically and literarily established categories of attitude to my work and myself … . I have felt that, since we, you and I, are in correspondence to a degree personal because of the character of this letters-material, I owed it to the fresh air of the correspondence to say that I do not function, in correspondence or in any other activity, under a 'minor' classification with myself. Which is not to say that I wear to myself a badge labelled 'major'—or any badge. The presentations that I am making to your Library in the form of these voluntarily recorded glosses are made in simple sense of duty to the truth of the readings that may be made of the material in question … and without any deferring to conceptions of the relative importance of the two correspondents. I yield no dominance, in importance of contributions to the human capability of truth of consciousness of the human reality, to Gertrude Stein, in any coupling notion of the two these letters may stimulate.

Please, entertain what I have written as just an interlude of private word of mine to you, in these special proximities centered in these letters-collections.

Of course I reassured her that I had used "major" merely in reference to the size (and price) of the Richard Wright archive, and she accepted my explanation without further question.

The notes that Mrs. Jackson had sent me on the Stein–Riding correspondence had made it clear that she was eager belatedly to rectify the general critical attitude toward herself and Robert Graves, especially in its downgrading the importance of her contribution in works that they had published jointly. In a telephone call of February 1976, followed up by a letter, Mrs. Jackson asked me for "some word of explanation" of an "anomalous circumstance" that had just then been called to her attention. From a scholar who had used the Stein papers at Yale she had received word of a card in our manuscript catalogue that referred the reader to the entries under Graves for additional material by Laura Riding. She explained the grounds for her concern:

I have learned, gradually, much about manoeuvres with manuscript material by Robert Graves, directly, and by intermediary figures, including dealers, acting in relation to complexities of distribution of large-scale quantities of 'Graves' material. ... It is [all] ... of an order of things which has rooted itself here and there quite firmly, that is indelibly offensive to me.

Fortunately, I was able to reassure her:

When the [Riding and Graves] letters first came in just after Gertrude died, the person in charge of sorting [*I didn't confess that I had been that person*] placed both ... [groups] in the same folder because some of those just after your accident were written [for you] by Graves. We have never allowed readers to examine the letters, and although the Graves and Riding [letters] were separated long ago, the corrected catalogue cards seem never to have been "written up." They are now in process and I shall ... send you copies of the new cards as soon as they come through.

But this did not completely satisfy her, and she wrote me again on 13 March:

My interest has been excited in regard to what you describe as the Graves letters. Up to 1939, and well into 1939, the only correspondence that had, by my knowledge, occurred between Robert Graves and Gertrude Stein consisted of the letters he wrote to her to apprise her of my state after the falling of April 1929. ... If he wrote any to her in the pre-forties period other than a few giving word of my state, this was done secretively by him. ... —She died in 1946. This leaves about seven years of possible writing by Robert Graves to her, after I terminated the working association that had been between him and myself and all personal contact, also. ... I have never thought about the possibility of his correspondence with G.S., after 1939 ... . Is it possible for me to see these letters of Robert Graves to Gertrude Stein? ... I am resting upon wonder if the extensive invidious—in my regard—procedures of Robert Graves do not inject a principle of moral justification of my being allowed to have acquaintance with those letters of his of which you tell?

Mrs. Jackson explained that various problems of hard work and ill health continued to delay her in completing the task of annotating the letters, and I assured her once again that she must not feel any pressure to finish the annotation except as she could do it without discomfort. I reported to her that

There are only two letters to Gertrude Stein from Robert Graves written after 1930 and they concern his *King Jesus* and so must have been written in 1946, just before Gertrude died. In the second letter there is a reference to you:

"No, I don't regret a moment of the life I spent with Laura. I was learning all the time and she was a wonderful poet at her best and as good to me as I deserved, I suppose."

Mrs. Jackson responded on 29 March 1976:

I am grateful to you for what you have written to me ... on the matter of correspondence between R.G. and G.S. ... I, contrarily to the insidious lying sense of his remark ... as to what I 'was' as a poet ... , 'was' through to the end of the relationship and from the very beginning good to him beyond anything he could have merited ... . This changed him from what he fundamentally was to one endeavoring to take on the *credit* of being laudably otherwise. Those who knew him well, the basic person, were astonished at the appearance of change to cleanness, kindness—which had its counterpart in the *show* of his writing. ... every so often he has bleated about my being 'the best poet of her age' ... . Occasionally it has been 'best woman poet of her age'. In private letters of the 'forties recently on sale at Sotheby's he advises his correspondent to read me as against reading Auden—me as very good, but 'a poet's poet'!!!!!!! This leaving Graves of course center-stage. ... In those ... letters there is also said of me, quite lyingly ... that I was 'born in a slum'. This is malicious invention, going well with being 'a poet's poet'!—just not main-line, like the regular guy Graves, with a little 'von' in the ancestral directory.*——— ...

Let this letter not be as a Pandora's box. When you put the reading-lid down, all will have flown instantly back—of the swarmy—into my keeping.

---

*Alan J. Clark informs me that the reference here is to letters from Robert Graves to Arnold Snodgrass, lots 403 and 404 in Sotheby's sale of 15–16 July 1974.

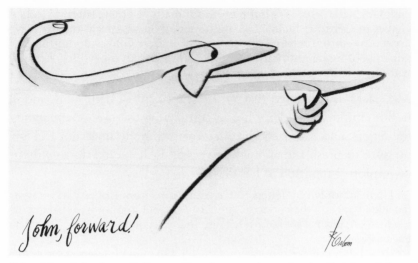

John, forward!

Robert Osborn. John, forward! Crayon with wash on paper (mounted on board), 8⅜ x 11 inches. Beinecke Library, gift of Mrs. John Farrar.

IV

During this period Mrs. Jackson was busy with the revision of her and her husband's book on language,★ but she took time, in 1976, to react to my Christmas message of "Courage!":

'Courage' is a good banner, and I shall carry my version of it (the word, the meaning) the better for knowing it specifically (although I think I have known it implicitly) as a banner-word of yours. ...

I replied:

I'm delighted that you find "Courage!" acceptable as a banner-word. For me it is a variant, for use when the way is harder, on Gertrude Stein's "Continuez!" Another version, possibly falling between the two, has just arrived in the form of an Osborn drawing made for John Farrar (see enclosed Xerox ...). And a slightly snobbish variant on that is its Italian form: "Avanti!"

★*Rational Meaning: A New Foundation for the Definition of Words,* published by the University Press of Virginia, Charlottesville, in 1997.

All this, just as the new year begins, should indeed set us upon our respective ways with a vengeance!

She responded in the same vein on 8 January 1977:

How good you are to me—this is a thorough kindness of sharing of special learning in the pharmacopoeia of word-medicine, special-section learning. I have enjoyed looking at the Osborn drawing. I cannot but treat it as a present. Forgive my Spanish way of hurrying to make return present-compliment. ... It does not fall into the banner-word field of interest, but it is of end-of-year reference. I made it the closing piece of the contributions to the magazine *Chelsea,* issue #35 ... [*This was* "A Letter For Everyone / End of Year, 1975," *a two-page typescript, inscribed:* "For Donald Gallup / at beginning of year, 1977 / with happy regard"]

Her letter continued:

I must tell you that your developing the banner-word theme turned my thought after a little to a word of precious connotation, for me. It is not a banner-word, but, rather, a talisman-word, that opens its entire potency where the mind allows it the virtue of promising what it means, allows it its possible all of propitious meaning. It is the keyword of my book *The Telling*'s propitious message. (I sound it in the dedication.) It is: *further.* Can we say that this word is the reward-word, *courage* having been called by us as a word we have earned the right to call to us?

I thank you for taking the theme further. I am glad about this!

Of course I thanked her, and agreed that the "talisman-word," *further,* is indeed precious:

I think at once of Browning ("A man's reach should exceed his grasp / Or what's a heaven for?") and Goethe ("Wer immer strebend sich bemüht / Den können wir erlösen"). ...

To this Mrs. Jackson was, on 20 February 1977, "moved to add a postscript to our deliberations on progression of a certain sort":

I wonder if there is not a catch in that Browning version of the matter, the concision suppressing an implicit/necessary verbal sense 'A man's (ideal) reaching (i.e., what he reaches *for*) should exceed his (actual) *reach* where he[,] it[,] encompasses the *graspable?* This being the implicit sense (what else could [it] be, the sense not being just a muddle?), does not this make 'heaven' a figure of the unreachable, to conceive of as the ideal/reachable? Do we have here a poetical/tailored paradox?

By the way, that 'further' is in my terms of progression '*the* further'. I.e., what there *is* to reach, the value being not just *on* progression, or in an ideality. ... this is just to tell you that I am putting your letter away now with fresh pleasure in the fact of those deliberations in which we engaged. May you be doing well in *your* progression plans, arrangements, attainments!

At Christmas time that year we exchanged greetings, and Mrs. Jackson reported that

The unfinished work of collation on the letters (mine to G. S., hers to me) is very seriously scheduled with me for attention in the new year. *This* year has been an overburdensome one for me. Happy prospects! I keep you in good remembrance.

And early in January 1978 she sent me "something for a general greeting—to tuck away in your little remembrance file." This was a photograph of her by Lowber Tiers, which she had inscribed: "For Donald Gallup / in friendship".

It was late November before I heard from her again. She remarked on the lapse in our correspondence, explaining that she had "had a rather strength-straining time of it in the past year … ," and asking me to be "among the four that have proposed themselves to me as suitable persons for the [National] Endowment [for the Arts] people to consult as to my qualifications for a fellowship". This was for support for a book reporting on her experience as a "worker in the field of literature," which she hoped to complete within a year.* I wrote her that I'd be honored to second her proposal and hoped that it would be successful. She thanked me promptly and assured me that her "commitment to complete the ordering, collating, of the two groups of letters" had not been forgotten.

V

A little more than a year and a half later, in mid-July 1980, I was surprised on returning from lunch one day to find Barbara and Jim Mathias, who had both been in Yale graduate school with me back in the thirties, waiting at the Beinecke to hand over an inscribed copy of Mrs. Jackson's *A Poem … How a Poem Comes to Be (For James F. Mathias),* which had just been printed as a broadside by the Lord John Press in Northridge, California. In acknowledging to her the

---

*Alan J. Clark reports that these memoirs remain "chiefly unpublished."

gift of the poem for the collection, I explained that I'd be retiring as curator on 1 September but expected to be working at the library on various projects. She wrote me on 10 August:

It pleases me that you will be stationed at the Beinecke Library, doing work of your own. Oh, I wish I had got my notes on the two sets of letters ... completed within the time of your Curatorship; but I have had huge difficulties in the conduct of all the elements of my work and related responsibilities ... . When I do get this task completed, ... I shall notify you ... , for the sending to you of the material, for your seeing first—if this suits you, and fits the circumstances.

Jim Mathias had told me that, having retired as vice president of the Guggenheim Foundation, he planned to devote himself to writing a biography of Mrs. Jackson. She spoke of this in the same letter:

Yes, this plan of Jim's writing a biography of me, what we think of as a story of my life embracing the story of my work, developed wonderfully, to the surprise of us both. ... There will be no conflict between his story and the memoirs I am working on, for these are concentrated on my literary-world experiences, and my views, based on them, of the relationship of my work to that world, and of the state of that world.

I answered that I was certain that Jim's "energy, intelligence, and good humor will insure his being able to complete the undertaking successfully and promptly."

But the arrangement with Mathias did not, in the end, work out. More than four years later, on 17 May 1985, Mrs. Jackson had a sad story to tell me. She had become gradually aware of

a very strong tendency [in him] to assume a managerial command-post in my affairs, a drive to 'take over', and a jealous attitude towards persons with whom I had normally good relations. ... but there seemed a persisting will to do the honorable and the correct: I bore all that long while with the inappropriate and unacceptable in his behavior with what seemed to me an indulgence—and fundamental *trust* that he, and the whole of the circumstances, justified. ... He accumulated a growingly large file of materials. All that he might need to know I took care to record for him ... ; I arranged for his having right of access to and copy of material in various libraries; I allowed him to make copies of letters to me ... , and of my replies ... . I let him have copies of all new writing of mine ... . As I have indicated, there was manifested on his part, a certain zeal, and care to meet the requirements of the commitments involved, and the pledge of personal appreciation professed; but ... I understood that this was a man holding much inner disturbance under control that sometimes gave way. ...

In August 1983, Mathias had "suddenly exploded," without apology or explanation, and now he was refusing to return to Mrs. Jackson any of the materials she had confided to him. She wrote me that there had been a general understanding between them that,

in ultimate case of emergency, such as his death, all the material was to go to The Berg Collection. ... but when the complexities resulting from his withdrawal were understood there ... that possibility of resolution vanished.—My authorized bibliographer Alan J. Clark ... offered to act as good-will moderator between J.F.M. and myself for the breaking up of the material into just portions of rightful property. This was refused by J.F.M. Also refused by him has been an offer of the Cornell University Library ... to house the material ... with, at my suggestion, credit to J.F.M. as for compiler. ... J.F.M. has also indicated to me—this some time ago—that letters from me on this great matter are unacceptable, for him!

She added that resort to legal means seemed beyond her reach financially. She had no one in mind to succeed Mathias as biographer who could "present himself—or herself—to James Mathias as the rightful custodian of material put into his care as a committed biographer." And she wrote that she would be "happily grateful" to me for "any least word of suggestion or counsel."

I replied on 22 May 1985:

I wish I could suggest some easy solution for the unfortunate situation, but I can't. I agree with you that resorting to the expensive, worrisome, and time-consuming machinations of the law simply cannot be contemplated: the effect upon you—your health, and your state of mind—would be catastrophic; and "the law's delay" has certainly diminished not one iota since the seventeenth century!

Although having such important and vital materials for your biography in JFM's possession now that he is no longer your authorized biographer is obviously intolerable and a source of great discomfort, it seems to me that it might be best to wait to do anything drastic for at least the time being. As it becomes gradually known that Mathias is no longer the authorized biographer, you will, I am sure, hear from various persons who would aspire to that role. *Deo volente*, one of them will be well qualified, and he or she may well be able to achieve through tactful patience and understanding a solution to the problem. I devoutly hope that this will be the outcome.

Mrs. Jackson was pleased with my reply. She wrote me on the 28th:

Your letter ... kindled for me a joy I had not been expecting to feel in this particular phase of my life-experience. I was moved, by it, to want to write a response to a pronouncement people are given to making as they are confronted with curiosities of human behavior not pleasing but felt to be better passed over than complained of. The pronouncement goes something like this: "Well, Everybody's different. If people weren't, all, different, they wouldn't be human." I have never made peace of heart or mind with this axiom of resignation to 'differentness', but the feeling your letter stirred in me took the word-form of pronouncement of distinct countersense to the common one on difference. When, it goes, someone behaves with a beautiful readiness in what one identifies with the best sense of what is 'human' ... or finely characteristic of a quality of being not other than human, ... what is manifested ... is *not* a supposedly natural 'difference' in human beings, from one to another to another: it is the wonderful, miraculous sameness that constitutes the essential distinction of nature that bears the name 'human,' along with a mélange of associated accidents of individual biological peculiarity subsumed in the name in linguistic helplessness—as the case is with names that acquire a meaning-potency as *words*.—

I felt I must report to you the general joy your letter gave me not describable in other terms than those I use above. That experience of the sameness that is the human is rare. But the rare experience of it sharpens the consciousness of fragmentary manifestations of the same, elsewhere, and one's own stubborn holding to the reality of the miracle of what 'human' *means*.

She told me that she had asked the Carcanet Press to send me a copy of the new edition they were just then issuing of her *A Trojan Ending*, first published in 1937, and sent me an inscription to put with it:

'A Trojan Ending' / for Donald Gallup / with grateful feeling / and most serious regard / Laura Jackson / May, 1985 / Wabasso Florida

Later that same year, Mrs. Jackson did consult the Authors' Guild on her difficulties with Jim Mathias, but she reported to me on 13 September that

For all their considering the case, and sympathy with me in the distressing circumstances, they cannot go further than reckoning on what securities of copyright control I might count on and, for the rest, advising the consulting of someone legally well-informed in such a problem-area.—I have so much of unpleasant to deal with ... that I dare not let any one unpleasant matter claim more than some of my consideration on what-to-do. ... I myself am predominantly troubled by the general state of the human sense of right and wrong—of which the special wrongs that converge upon oneself personally are but exemplifications.

VI

Reciprocating, in May, for her gift of *A Trojan Ending,* I had sent Mrs. Jackson a copy of my edition of *The Journals of Thornton Wilder,* just being published by the Yale University Press. Ill health and the pressure of work kept her for a time from reading very much of it, but she gave her first impressions in a letter of 13 September:

I have been thinking that Thornton Wilder was-is an extraordinary kind of American, having … a strong leaning to the *indeterminate* in his positioning himself to problems of judgement, and choice. One can understand the attraction, for him, of personalities such as Gertrude Stein. But he was a far more thoughtful person than she was (she, all verbal pragmatics). I like the report of his difficulty in finding something definite to say on Kierkegaard (himself a thoughtful man caught in a sense of need of much indetermina-cy of position.)—So, thanks for all the promise of revelations stored in the book, beside the solid fact of it itself!

Mrs. Jackson returned to the subject of the Wilder *Journals* on 10 October:

I have found myself drawn on and on, by straight-ahead reading, and read-ing from index promptings, into comprehending efforts: his diagrams of thought-problems, estimation of his own make-up and of a hypothesized American nature, with seeking for determinate answers the while leaning to a generalized indeterminacy as to the practical mold of truth: what a drama of conscientious perplexity it is! — The continual figuring of Gertrude Stein in his programmes of *some* adequacy of determinate think-ing interested me, of course, because of my experience of contact with her. She aimed at behaving and performing from scenes, contexts, rid of what might involve challenge to her intelligence. This made for a bigotry of self-sufficiency disguised as strength of mind and character that has taken in generation on generation.—Wilder was strictly honorable in his constant striving for the adequate 'everyman' generalization—honorable about his own predicament of resorting to indeterminacy as the immediate, practi-cal, solution. (With rare exceptions.)

A week later, on the 18th, she wrote me still another letter about the *Journals:*

Wilder's position bears seriously on the problem of just *what* the American version of human identity is, or should be. I have for some time thought of an American impulse (have written on this) to *define* the human being, seeing this as figuring on the healthy side of spiritual vigor, also on the side of the merely pragmatic, or brash. Wilder at least saw that definition was at issue, but he could not face the strain of the responsibilities of definition.

There was intellectual honesty in this, besides uncertainty of *himself,* I think.

I thanked her for her letters:

I was delighted to have more of your reaction to the Wilder *Journals*.... They are indeed a "drama of conscientious perplexity," though possibly rather more dramatic, conscientious, *and* perplexed than was actually the case: Thornton's mind was, I am sure, playing upon a good many possible points-of-view, some of them not very seriously entertained, others only tentatively adopted.

The figure of Gertrude Stein *does* loom large in these pages, and your comments on her role are especially interesting for me. Indeed she did not brook challenges to her intelligence. Thornton was quite willing to act the part of humble disciple because he valued her friendship and conversation so highly. When I first met her in 1945, I must admit to having been extremely skeptical; but those eyes, that voice—indeed the sheer magnetism of her personality won me over (of course it was all too apparent that I offered no challenge to her intelligence!).

And this brought from her further comment on 1 November 1985:

Your experience of G. Stein came about 15 years after mine closed!— I have long thought that the late modern conception of 'literature' made a mix of personality and literature of an impossible hybrid identity—with the nature of literature and that of the human person becoming both more and more wilfully and arbitrarily conceived of.—This may have been one of the puzzlement areas of Thornton Wilder's private and tentative journeys in thought-experiment.—Anyhow, your *Journals* present a very serious much of an attentive observer of critical human times. The book is of much interest—of much historic interest.

In another letter on 16 November Mrs. Jackson commented upon Harry Levin's review of the Wilder *Journals,* along with a recent biography of Wilder, in the current issue of the *New York Review of Books:*

It pleased me much to find good space of reviewer attention given [to it] ... . I was uncomfortable with want of distinction by the reviewer of your work and the biography, between the two, and with his failure to identify the great service of inner-man portraiture that you extracted from your treatment of the *Journals.*—For me, though I say this without having seen the biography, it is your work that paints the picture, unfolds the essential story.

I replied on the 21st:

As for the Levin review-article on the Wilder *Journals*, I was only happy that he chose to discuss it at such length. I am uncomfortably aware that another editor would have produced from the same material a quite different book, possibly a better one. ...

And she wrote me on the 29th:

it pleased me to know that you felt contentment with the review ... . I find the ... book, as edited by you, an elegant and important piece of editorial and bibliographical workmanship, and, besides, a very helpful depiction of the inner 'position' of Wilder as person, and writer.

In the letter of 18 October, Mrs. Jackson had complained to me of the lack of critical attention being paid to the new edition of *A Trojan Ending:* her publishers had sent out 25 review copies, which had so far produced only one review—and that an "outrageous" attack—in the *Philadelphia Inquirer,*

sneering at the work as 'revisionist mythology' of Graves inspiration, and declaring it inferior to the Claudius writing of Graves★ (and rather Hollywood in its picturings of the people). What use is pointing to the prefatory thanks of Graves to me as responsible for what virtues of style the Claudius writing had ... —the prefatory tribute eliminated in later publications?★★ ... In large part ... I think, the treatment of the reproduced *A Trojan Ending* is also explicable as near-total loss of innocence in the reading habits of human minds of our time. All predisposition is externally stimulated. There is no inner curiosity.

I thanked her for her letter on 4 November:

I am sure you are right in your diagnosis of the illness that affects the average American reader—lack of inner curiosity. Of course he accepts being told what to read because of the plethora of reading matter being offered: he throws up his hands in despair at the bewildering array of books, and seizes upon whatever guide is most easily available. ...

It is shameful that *A Trojan Ending* should be treated so cavalierly. You must take cold comfort in your knowledge that the book makes a genuine contribution and will of course endure.

★Graves's novels *I Claudius* and *Claudius the God* (both 1934), narrated by the emperor himself (10 B.C.–A.D. 54), were the bases for a widely viewed BBC TV series.

★★Alan J. Clark informs me that Mrs. Jackson "appears to have been mistaken on this point. Graves had indeed eliminated Riding's name from his revision of [his autobiographical] *Good-Bye to All That*, 1957, but not from the 1930s novels." In all reissues known to him, "both of the Claudius novels and of *Count Belisarius,* 1938—RG's original thanks to & acknowledgements of Riding remain unaltered."

VII

In one of my letters to Mrs. Jackson I happened to mention two papers I was preparing on Ezra Pound. She commented, on 18 October 1985:

I myself have many reservations about Pound, but I am sure that your kind of scholarship is essentially pro-scholarship, not pro-Pound.—

A month later she wrote me that our exchange had reminded her of a book in her library:★

I have a copy of Pound's PROVENÇA ... published by Small, Maynard and Company, Boston, 1910. My husband Schuyler experimented for a while in his earlier days in bookbinding, and this copy is his first production—all intact save for the spine, tightly sewn still, but the brown covering extending from the edges of the blue-gray cover boards is missing. ... I have wondered as to the bibliographical value (I don't mean 'monetary') of this issue of the PROVENÇA, in relation to my decision as to the allocation of it. If you can, without undue exertion, give me a ... clue as to the status of this little book, I'd be very glad in the help.

I replied on 21 November:

Pound's *Provença* ... is an interesting book and an important one as being his first to appear in the United States. There were two printings ... . If the reading in the section title on pages 53 and 55 is "Laudante" and "Laudante."—rather than "Laudantes"—then the book is probably the later printing. But either printing is rare.

She thanked me on the 29th:

I am grateful for what you have written to me on Pound's *Provença*. The copy I have, on those pages, has 'Laudante,' not 'Laudantes' and is, therefore, as you say, probably the later printing. ... I like much knowing what you have told me about it.

Do you have a copy of the book, of this printing? If you do not, and it would please you to have one, it would please me to present the one I have described to you. ... I would write a brief note to go with it, to cover the fact of the binding and the little information-piece ... [Schuyler] wrote into it. ...

I responded on 9 December:

I was ... very much touched that you should offer the precious example of your husband's binding [to me]. As it happens, I do not have in my Pound

★She had first mentioned the book to me four years earlier, on 28 December 1981.

collection a copy of the second printing of *Provença* and should value this one especially because of its provenance. But I can't accept your gift without offering something in return. I wonder if you'd like a copy of your *Though Gently* (1930)? My books are scheduled in my will to go to Yale, but I am trying to find appropriate homes in libraries for those items that Yale already owns. Yale has a copy of *Though Gently*★ and it would be much more fitting—and welcome—for *you* to give it to some library of your choice, if you so wish, rather than for me to try to select one. ...

Please do write about the binding [of *Provença*] for it would be most meaningful to me—and to Yale.

The death of Robert Graves had been reported in the *New York Times* the day before, and I ended my letter "With all best wishes and thoughts of you occasioned by yesterday's headlines."

She replied on the 12th:

I am writing close upon the coming to me of your letter of December 9th—with gladness in the fitting of ... the little book into your collection. ... I shall join to the book ... a simple account of the binding of it by my husband. This was done long before we came to know each other. I can only describe what he told me, how he was given binding apparatus by a friend skilled in such doing, tried his hand, with his *Provença*—and achieved little more than the beautifully treated copy of 'Poetry of The Bible'—which has on the back cover, in gold lettering, his mother's initials. He made the book for her. After her death, it came back to him. He wrote a presentation word in it for me on the day before I was scheduled to arrive in New York, from France (after thirteen years of life abroad). We had been corresponding for a little while. So far as I know, no other examples of binding-work of his exist. He was interested in fine printing. Studied with Bruce Rogers for a planned Open Road Press project, for the printing of American regional poetry; had engaged Frost, Lindsay, Bynner, others, of differing regions to assist him editorially. Nothing was ever brought into publication, his youthful finances failing. But he had been very serious about the project.

Your thought as to ... providing me with ... your *Though Gently* for presentation to a library of my choosing is a lovely idea. I am sure there is a copy at Cornell, I think it is my own copy... . Let me take a little time for thinking on this. ...

★I had had in my library for several years a group of the Seizin Press books, acquired not from any particular interest in Graves and Riding, but because I had happened to find them listed for sale at bargain prices. There were two titles by Laura Riding, *Though Gently* and *Laura and Francisca* (1931). I had checked them in the Beinecke catalogue and, when I wrote Mrs. Jackson, remembered that *Though Gently* was at Yale. My letter had already been mailed when, on rechecking, I discovered that it was *Though Gently* that Yale needed. Unfortunately, I couldn't very well ask to have the book back!

It moved me with thankful feeling that you made ... reference to ... the death of Robert Graves. ... Alan Clark, to whom I confided the task of building a bibliography of my work, ... telephoned ... from London ... and touched on the just-reported death. I said "It will clear the air." I have written, in various contexts, on the literary-world attitude to this man of lies. They, there, have not been in comfort with him but unable, because of their own evasions of the laws of truth, to dare to treat him as a perpetrator of frauds. The only announcement of his death that I have so far seen was in the paper of the county in which I reside. ... 'I Claudius' was of course featured in the title of the news-report. When he wrote that book, he and I were in comradely working partnership. I labored ... over the stylistically crude text—the dialogue especially was sloppily unreal. In consequence of my labor, he felt obliged to make note of it in the preface to the first publication, crediting me with what merits of style it possessed. In all republished forms of the Claudius affair (coming after my terminating the association of almost thirteen years), he eliminated this acknowledgement.★—Fundamentally it is an insincere work, dressed up in buffooneries for theatrical effect and appeal.—

(To note that my pledge as to the collating of the letters of mine to Gertrude Stein and hers to me ... [is] only part-fulfilled: this is among the much with which I keep myself charged in desire and will to fulfill. In all this I am continually delayed, by bodily discomforts and severe limitations in needed help, secretarially and managerially. But none of it is other than a continuing call for me.)

I answered on the 17th:

I shall look forward to receiving the *Provença* with your account of its binding ... . I shall ... mail ... you my copy of *Though Gently,* which will be *your* book to present to a library of your choosing.

There was a long notice of the death of Robert Graves in the *New York Times.* I thought of clipping it and sending it to you, then decided against it, thinking you would probably receive it from some other source.

I am glad that you plan to continue the collating of your letters to Gertrude Stein, for the documentation will be valuable for future scholars. But of course you must do this only as you can.

Mrs. Jackson wrote me on the 29th:

Your ... copy ... of *Though Gently* came ... . — I have not yet decided on the repository for it, but have two-to-three in mind. It touched my feelings to see the book again,—. . .

Your kind thoughtfulness in making reference to the death of Robert Graves I am very grateful for. I *have* seen the *N.Y. Times* obituary. I could

---

★See second footnote on page 160.

not reply to you on this without candor. But I feel you would not want me to write on the subject of Robert Graves to you in any other way. The *N.Y. Times* notice was relatively free of the usual misrepresentation of me in the Robert-Graves context, but it was full of misreport of him—as all writing on him, especially in recent years, has been, and could not otherwise be—the lie in the man's makeup having been endlessly used by him as ambition-sustenance, and provided incitation to malice and worse against myself, in quarters of personal spite and literary-world moral indifference. I have seen a few other U.S. obituary notices, and I have written in comment where I felt I must, although such corrections as human honor impels me to attempt are rarely published. ... —I doubt you will see my comment on the *N.Y. Times* obituary in print. And I want not to burden you with the sense of what I wrote in comment on it. I am much consoled, amidst the trials of recent years in my experience, by your generosities of understanding and sympathy. ... It gladdens me that we have this good feeling towards each other.

The note on *Provença,* which arrived with the book a few days later, was dated 31 December 1985:

I provide this note on this copy of Ezra Pound's *Provença* on presenting it to Dr. Donald C. Gallup, in token of the fullness of regard in which I hold him, and of my happy sense of the kindnesses he has shown me, unfailingly, over the years.

And she went on to give the circumstances of its being bound by her husband.

I thanked her on 4 January:

I am sorry that you had to go to all the trouble of getting a box for the ... *Provença,* of writing the explanatory note, and of mailing the package, but am happy to report that it arrived safely today. The note covers everything beautifully and I shall keep it enclosed with the little volume in my Pound collection ... . I have already begun to turn the collection over to Yale and have provided in my will that anything not already at Yale when I die shall be delivered to the Library by my executor.★ I am glad to know that *Though Gently* reached you and happy to think that it will eventually be in a Library of your choosing.

I am glad ... that you have received the Graves obituaries ... . I agree with you that one can't very well ignore lies and vilifications that are published about one in the public press. It is unfortunate that some papers like the *New York Times* on occasion, having published the charges, seem to

---

★I gave my entire Pound collection, including the Jackson *Provença,* to Yale between 1985 and 1992.

feel no responsibility for similarly publicizing corrections, but at least there is the satisfaction of feeling that one has done everything in one's power to put things right.

Her answer was dated 10 January:

Your (so prompt) report of the coming to you of the little book pleased and comforted me. I am glad about the book's being now yours, and the eventual assignment of it you have described. And your sympathetic comments in your letter on literary press betrayals of literary and human decencies are of fortifying effect. For the most part my friends take the view that I waste my powers on corrective offerings in these cases—that I should be concentrating on my 'work' exclusively. I do not make such separations. I care about all this debasement of literary-world honor and proper concerns inseparably from my caring about literature as a central domain of human functioning. ... But, forgive my lingering on this unpleasant matter. I want, have wanted, in writing in reply to your kind letter to stress my gratitude for all your kindness towards me. I will have sense of it in store with me as I proceed in this year's course, in which immediate trials seem likely to persist. ...

A note from her a few weeks later reported that she had sent *Though Gently* to the Berg Collection of the New York Public Library. I applauded her choice and assured her on 11 February that I was delighted:

I knew John Gordan [*the first curator*] well and have known Lola Szladits [*his successor*], since the days when she first began to work as his right hand. She has carried on superbly the tradition that John began. I am glad to think that the book will be part of that distinguished collection.

Mrs. Jackson's last letter to me was written on the 22nd:

I am grateful for your word on my decision as to the presentation of the copy of *Though Gently* you gave me ... . I indicated that I was acting ... from very serious regard for the Berg Collection and a special personal esteem of Dr. Szladits. ... What you record in your letter on her performance at the Berg comforts and cheers me. As one who cares much for and about her, I am aware of the strains she has put upon herself to maintain a best of everything at the Berg, despite all private difficulty.★
... I wish you much ease and cheer in this year's further, and ever.

★Lola Szladits died of cancer on 30 March 1990.

Mrs Jackson's "further" did not, in 1986, or in the few other remaining years before she died of cardiac arrest on 2 September 1991,
include the long promised completion of the notes on the Riding-
Stein correspondence. Her physical ills became eventually so inca-
pacitating that she could no longer write. A new authorized biographer emerged during those years in the person of Elizabeth
Friedmann, and, after Fall 1991, a Board of Literary Management,
provided for in Mrs. Jackson's will, in due course found solutions for
some of the problems that had vexed her final days.

AFTERWORD, MARCH 1997

It was only when this account was being prepared for printing that I
learned from that most helpful of editors, Christa Sammons, of the
happy culmination of Mrs. Jackson's friendly relationship with Yale.
Insulated from the real world in the ivory tower of my retirement, I
had not been aware that, early in the year of her death, the judges for
the Bollingen Prize in Poetry of the Yale University Library had
awarded one of the two prizes for 1991 to Laura Riding Jackson,
thus honoring her lifetime achievement. In their announcement, the
committee described Mrs. Jackson as "a poet of seminal importance,
… the only survivor of the great first generation of American mod-
ernist poets," and stated that "She has created a poetry of pure intel-
lect that is at the same time unexpectedly sensuous. Her originality
continues to astonish."

Some European Pursuits

At Renishaw Hall with the Sitwells
1949

IN THE SUMMER OF 1949, after having attended both the first and second nights of T. S. Eliot's *The Cocktail Party* at the Edinburgh Festival, I took the train to Sheffield, in Yorkshire, where Edith Sitwell had promised to hand me, for the library, her letters from the Russian-American artist Pavel Tchelitchew. This had come about through Lincoln Kirstein, a long-time friend of the Yale Collection of American Literature and a strong advocate for its attempt to gather and preserve documentation of twentieth-century belles lettres. He had given Yale the *Hound & Horn* and Gaston Lachaise archives, as well as some of his own manuscripts, and it was he who persuaded Charles-Henri Ford to turn over to us papers relating to the magazines he had edited, *Blues* and *View*. Tchelitchew had worked closely with Ford on *View*, and Lincoln got him to give us the letters he had received from Miss Sitwell. I went to New York to see the artist at the apartment he shared with Ford, and he handed me a large, carefully wrapped package marked "Not to oppen [*sic*] before year 2000." The date for the sealing had been mutually agreed upon by him and Miss Sitwell. Although subsequently Lincoln persuaded Tchelitchew and attempted to convince Miss Sitwell that they should allow him to edit a selection of the letters for publication, she was at that time determined that the correspondence not be available until the specified date.

I had met both Edith and Sir Osbert Sitwell in New York at the Kirsteins' apartment on their first triumphant reading-and-lecture tour of the United States, and on a repeat performance the following year, both had come to New Haven for public appearances. Edith read from the manuscript of her book on Shakespeare, although it had already been published in England. Those in charge had responded to the unprecedented interest in the event by scheduling her reading for Woolsey Hall, the largest auditorium on the campus. Although they had taken care to place a microphone on the table at which Miss Sitwell was expected to sit, almost her first move after the applause subsided was to pull her chair away so that the audience, especially the large number of ladies present, could get an unencumbered view of her costume. This was a long flowing robe of emerald brocade, set off by a multitude of bracelets and assorted rings on her arms and fingers, a large, flat silver ornament hanging around her neck, and on her head a multicolored turban. The effect was spectacular, but her move away from the microphone meant that very little of the subsequent reading was audible beyond the first few rows. Further, she held her folio manuscript in her left hand and its upper portion, every now and then, flopped down against the microphone, making a loud report. The first time this happened, Miss Sitwell paused in her reading, looked up, and asked "Was that a bomb?"; the subsequent noises she simply ignored.

Lincoln had suggested that I ask Miss Sitwell to place at Yale, to complement her own letters to Tchelitchew, those she had received from him. I wrote her in the spring of 1949, soon after she and her brother had returned to England, and received a gracious reply: she would be glad to give the letters to Yale, subject of course to the same restriction of not being available to scholars until the year 2000. In subsequent correspondence it was arranged that I would collect the letters from her that summer.

Tchelitchew happened to be in Paris that June, and I called at the apartment on rue Jacques Mawas that he occupied with his sister Choura. He gave me for the Yale library his letters from Gertrude Stein, the document of nobility of the Tchelitchew family, and for the Yale Art Gallery a palette that he had used for pictures painted in the 1930s. This kidney-shaped object, heavily encrusted with dried oil pigments, proved to be a little too large to fit into my suitcase, and I was obliged to carry it under my arm, checking it at various railway stations and hotels throughout the remainder of my European trip.

I later discovered that Edith Sitwell had written to me in care of Alice Toklas in Paris, but had apparently made some mistake in writing my name. Alice had shared Gertrude Stein's feeling that Edith, after her first efforts at publicity in England for Gertrude and her writing in 1926, had proceeded to use her chiefly to promote the Sitwell literary career. In any case, Alice apparently endorsed the envelope "I know of no such person" and put it in the post for return. When I got to London, I happened, by mere chance, to visit the shop of Maggs Brothers, antiquarian booksellers with whom I had had only a very slight relationship. There I was told by Mr. Ernest Maggs that the firm had a telegram for me from Edith Sitwell. I had been expecting to see her and pick up the Tchelitchew letters at her club in London, the Sesame, but the telegram explained that she and Sir Osbert would be at Renishaw Hall and asked me to come there and spend the night.

Having for years read and been told of the long-established English custom of dressing for dinner, I could think only that I was not sartorially prepared to accept the Sitwells' invitation. And so I answered, thanking them for their offer of hospitality, but explaining that, travelling without the proper clothes, I'd have to refuse. In subsequent correspondence Miss Sitwell assured me that she and Osbert never dressed for dinner and that whatever clothes I had with me would be quite acceptable.

Still it was with some foreboding that I in due course stepped off the train in Sheffield. To my surprise I was met not only by a car and driver but by Edith Sitwell herself. It was exciting to see the fabled estate for the first time. Sir Osbert took me for a tour of the grounds, laid out by their father, Sir George, and showed me a good many of the pictures, especially those by John Piper, which I remember as hanging chiefly crowded around the main staircase. As Edith led me into the drawing room I noticed the celebrated Sargent painting of the family, hanging over the doorway, and said that I had always liked it. "Oh, have you?" she replied quickly; "I've always loathed it. But then, you see, I always hated my father and mother."

Both Edith and Osbert were the personification of English hospitality. I was shown to the bedroom that would be mine (it was that formerly occupied by their mother), and was told that dinner would be at 8:00. I cleaned up and changed into my most formal costume (a dark business suit) and joined my host and hostess in the drawing room. In spite of her comforting assurances to me in her letter, Edith was dressed in a long flowing costume, with the usual adornments of jewelry, and Osbert was wearing a dinner jacket. We dined by candlelight, I the only guest, seated at Osbert's right, Edith at his left, across from me, with the highly polished table stretching away into the shadows. I remember grouse as being one of the courses of a sumptuous meal. We talked then and in the drawing room later of T. S. ("Tom") Eliot, Alec Guinness, John Lehmann, and other friends and associates. We retired early and I passed a very comfortable night in Lady Sitwell's bed, untroubled by dreams.

I had been told that breakfast would be served me in my room at 8:00 the next morning. When the butler came to take away the tray, he brought a large—and heavy—metal safe which, he explained, contained the letters. I was appalled at the prospect of having to carry this object all the way back to New Haven, but when I meekly asked if there wasn't some lighter container that could be used, he answered: "Oh, no, Sir, Miss Edith sent in to Sheffield twice before she selected this one." I did later point out to her that the United States Customs in New York would certainly ask to have the safe opened, and she consented to let me have the key. The safe was loaded into the car along with my suitcase (I had checked the Tchelitchew palette in London) and Edith insisted on driving with me to the railway station. There we said goodbye and I, with a sigh of relief, settled down in the train for the ride back to London.

The Sitwell safe was, as it turned out, even more of a problem than I had feared. I had sailed on the *Queen Elizabeth I* and of course declared the Tchelitchew letters as material that I was bringing into the United States as agent for the Yale Library. At the dock in New York there was the usual milling crowd with trunks and suitcases under the letter "G" and it took me some time to find a free inspector to examine my luggage. The palette was no problem, although I did have to unwrap it, but the inspector insisted that the safe be opened and asked in what language the letters were written. Deciding that I'd not be violating restrictions if I glanced at one to identify the language, I found it to be French. The agent agreed that there would be no duty to pay, but there remained the question of the category under which the letters would be admitted. He spent a good deal of time poring through his book of instructions, only to give up and tell me that he would have to consult his supervisor. This took even more time, for that officer was for the moment otherwise engaged. Eventually he became free, had the problem explained to him, and in turn resorted to the printed regulations. His final decision was that the letters could be entered as engravings. I agreed that this was the correct solution (not in the least convinced, but willing to agree to anything that would get me on my way). I insisted that the inspector relock and reseal the safe and add his certification that the original seal had been broken in his presence. And at last, some four hours after the ship had docked, I was free to make my way by taxi to Grand Central Station and then by train to New Haven. There my first order of business the next day was to hand the safe over to Marjorie Wynne, librarian of the Rare Book Room in the Sterling Memorial Library, where it joined the package of Sitwell letters given by Tchelitchew in the manuscript vault.

I made a special trip that same day to the Art Gallery to entrust the Tchelitchew palette to Lamont Moore, the director. Now there is an ironclad rule that every item intended for the gallery's permanent collection must be presented to a committee on acquisitions for its approval. Some months later, Lamont came one day to my office, rather shamefacedly bringing with him the Tchelitchew palette. He explained that the committee had voted unanimously that the Collection of American Literature in the library seemed to them a more appropriate place for the palette than the Art Gallery. I pointed out to Lamont that I had merely been following Tchelitchew's instructions in handing the object to him for the gallery's collection. If the committee did not wish to accept it, it would be his responsibility to inform the artist and, presumably, return the item. Lamont, characteristically, never summoned up sufficient courage to write

Tchelitchew and, so far as we both know, the kidney-shaped, pig-ment-encrusted palette, if it still exists, is tucked away somewhere in the gallery's basement.

Edith Sitwell died in 1964 and the bulk of her archive was acquired for the Humanities Research Center at the University of Texas in Austin. Bertram and Una Rota were charged with the responsibility for the selection and transfer to Texas of the Sitwell papers. Bertram wrote me on 13 January 1966 that, in going through many trunks of miscellaneous correspondence at Renishaw Hall, he and Una had found some Tchelitchew letters which he was certain Dame Edith intended for addition to those already at Yale. He was sending them, "almost as a posthumous gift from her," and asked that we put them with the rest, under the same conditions, treating them as if they were part of the original group.

I answered on 2 February:

I'm delighted to have the letters from Tchelitchew to Dame Edith for the Library and extremely grateful to you and Una for making this possi-ble. It was in 1949 ... that I went to Renishaw to collect the Tchelitchew letters for Yale, and these that you have found are doubtless the ones she received between 1949 and Tchelitchew's death. I agree with you that Dame Edith would have felt that these later letters belong with the earlier ones and it is very kind of you to let us have them. They will join the oth-ers under the same restrictions (not available until 2000) and I know that scholars of the 21st century will utter prayers of thanksgiving that these 44 are not physically separated from the bulk of the correspondence. Pavlik's sister, incidentally, has agreed to let us have the later letters from Edith that Pavlik received after he had turned over the earlier ones to Yale, and the entire exchange will therefore be available when 2000 rolls around all in the same place.

The subsequent history of the Sitwell-Tchelitchew correspon-dence illustrates some of the complications that often arise when a library accepts restrictions of access to its manuscript materials. Eventually, in March 1978, Marjorie Wynne was obliged to reply to all queries with a prepared statement "To Whom It May Concern":

Subject: The Edith Sitwell-Pavel Tchelitchew Correspondence

In 1949 the Yale University Library received a sealed packet with the following label:

> 'Letters from Edith Sitwell to Pavel Tchelitchew. Given to the Yale University Library by Mr. Tchelitchew, 26 February 1949, on the absolute condition that they not be unsealed by anyone, except himself, until the year 2000 A.D.' A note written by Tchelitchew directly on the wrapping paper says: 'Not to oppen [*sic*] before year 2000. P. Tchelitchew.'

In the same year we received another sealed packet [i.e., the Sitwell safe] with the following label:

> 'Letters from Pavel Tchelitcheff to Edith Sitwell presented to the Library of Yale University. Not to be opened until the year 2000. [*Signed*] Edith Sitwell. D.Litt., Litt.D.'

The restrictions attached to both of these gifts were accepted and agreed to by the Yale University Library. The Library, therefore, cannot under any circumstances break faith with the donors by opening the packets before 2000.

In 1965 Dame Edith instructed the Library to open the packet that *she* gave and to allow Mr. Parker Tyler to examine the contents for his biography of Tchelitchew. Only Dame Edith had the right to give such instructions, and the Library followed them to the letter.

Now that Dame Edith and Tchelitchew are dead, no one else—either relative or literary executor—has any authority over the sealed packets or any reason to expect the Yale Library to open them before 2000.

Olga Rudge in her office at the Palazzo Chigi, Siena. Collection of Mary de Rachewiltz.

Pursuing Pound in Italy and England

WITH OLGA RUDGE IN SANT' AMBROGIO
1957

I ARRIVED IN Rapallo on 17 June 1957, planning to spend six days, and at once began to worry that I might not be able to get in touch with Olga Rudge, the principal reason for my visit. I had written her at Siena, where she was still serving as secretary of the Accademia Chigiana, and she had answered from there, saying that she would be in Rapallo at the time of my visit; but she did not give the address. I had assumed that she would be listed in the local telephone book, but a thorough search was unrewarding. The desk clerk at my hotel knew of no such person.

I first went to Ezra Pound's old address, 12 via Marsala. There the old lady who answered the bell knew of neither Pound nor Miss Rudge (I found out later that the street numbers had been changed), although her son or grandson recognized the name of Pound as that of "*il grande poetà*"; he suggested that I try the local information center. I found it after some difficulty, and the official in charge, who spoke some English, admitted to having "listened to" the name of Olga Rudge. He suggested that an American lady, Dr. Frieda Bacigalupo, at the Anglo-American Pharmacy, knew everyone in Rapallo and would probably be able to help me. The shop proved to be just across the street from my hotel, and a lady who was obviously Dr. Bacigalupo was very much in evidence behind the counter. Elegantly dressed and rather elaborately made up, she was helping an English-speaking couple locate a friend. This involved a number of telephone calls and was eventually successful, but Dr. Bacigalupo seemed about to leave the shop. I apologized for bothering her while she was so busy, and asked if she knew Olga Rudge. "But Olga Rudge is one of my oldest and dearest friends. I am Dr. Frieda Bacigalupo." "Yes, I know; they told me at the Information Center that you knew everyone in Rapallo." "But how did you know that I was Dr. Bacigalupo?" I turned this off as best I could with a mumbled explanation.

She told me that Miss Rudge was going to Genoa that evening for a concert, but would be back afterward. She lived in Sant' Ambrogio, a good walk up the mountain, and there was no telephone; one had to call the owner of the house and leave a message. Eventually Dr. Bacigalupo telephoned for me, asking Miss Rudge to call her in the morning. Dr. Bacigalupo would call me at nine o'clock.

Thinking that I had done all I could do for the day, I wandered off to café-sit and dine by myself. When I got back to my hotel at about nine, I found a note from Miss Rudge, which she had left just before catching the 7:40 bus for Genoa. She asked me to go with her to the concert if I got her note in time (of course I didn't) and to come up the hill for lunch the following day. I was to take the 11:40 bus for Zoagli and get out at Brugo, from where there would be a fifteen-minute walk to her place. I gulped a little at the simple instructions to cover what I suspected would be a complicated procedure, but went to bed cheered by the thought that we had at least established contact.

I was some three-quarters of an hour early for the bus the next morning and had the usual indecision about where to wait. But by the time it came in, I and about forty others, most of them laden with packages, were ready to board. As I entered I tried to get reassurance by repeating "Brugo?" and received a number of "*si*"'s and affirmative nods in reply. When I repeated the name, the ticket-seller broke into violent and rapid Italian, none of which I understood. I did find one man who, as nearly as I could make out, was also going to Brugo, and I stuck as close to him as the sardine-packed crowd permitted.

As the bus approached our destination he and I made our way to the front and, at the stop, managed to get out. Brugo seemed to be just another bend in the curving road. When I asked my companion for Sant' Ambrogio, he nodded, pointing in the general direction of the very top of the mountain. I started up a steep flight of stone steps and eventually, with the help of a couple of young girl guides—who at first tried to turn me down the hill again to a Signora Ruggio—I got to the "casa" of which Olga Rudge occupied the top floor. It was a plain little house built in the native style of painted stucco, with steps leading up to her apartment. The door, or rather the upper half of it, was open. As I walked up the steps, sweat pouring from my face and my jacket damp, I heard a pleasant, musical voice even before I caught sight of its owner. I remembered her from our brief meeting in Siena eight years before as vivacious, with sparkling eyes. Her gray hair was cut in a bob, her head tilted as if in anticipation, but also with an air of repose. She had not been able to catch the bus she had planned to take back from Genoa after the concert and had missed the last one from Rapallo to Brugo. The hour's climb at three in the morning had been "very romantic, but, after all!" We walked up the hill to a little inn, where we were served a very acceptable lunch by the boy who, it turned out, usually accompanied the mule up the hill with the provisions. The service was slow, and our conversation skipped from subject to subject. D. D. Paige, who had edited the published volume of Ezra Pound's *Letters,* was mentioned, and Miss Rudge expressed her annoyance that her own letters to Pound should have been left out at the via Marsala apartment for him to see: Dorothy Pound ought to have put them into a sealed box. Many things from that apartment had already been taken to Tirolo, where Mary de Rachewiltz, Ezra Pound's and her daughter, lived, but a great number were still here in the little house, to which they had been trekked by Pound himself and others when the family had had to leave Rapallo during the war. Miss Rudge happened to mention a friend of Pound's, Father Desmond Chute, and suggested that I ought to meet him. She telephoned from the inn and he invited us both to lunch with him three days later.

We walked back to the house slowly in the hot sun. There Miss Rudge showed me first the Gaudier-Brzeska sculptures (the *Embracers* had stuck to the red paint of the bookcase on which it was placed). Here in the sitting room the furniture generally was of a very primitive kind, with a table and two chairs actually built by Pound himself. There were books everywhere, and we rummaged through the cases, finding several items that I set aside for detailed examination. I think Miss Rudge was disappointed when I showed little interest in anything not within the scope of the bibliography (which was to list only printed materials). I hardly turned my head to look at manuscripts of the *Cantos*. The Fenollosa notebooks *did* interest me, and the original plaster life mask of Pound, with a bronze cast made from it, by Nancy Cox McCormack, each in its special wooden box. (The bronze was later given to Yale by Mary de Rachewiltz.) Here were presentation copies, one or two from Joyce, several from Eliot, but mostly Pound's file copies of his own publications.

All fifteen hundred copies of the first edition of his *Guide to Kulchur* (1938) had been bound and were ready to be published when Faber & Faber (his English publishers) decided that certain passages in the text were libellous and must be deleted. Publication was delayed from June until July while at least fifteen leaves were reprinted, the originals excised from the bound copies, and the new leaves pasted on to the resulting stubs. Only six copies escaped this cancellation process. I was delighted to find two of the unexpurgated copies, along with, happily, one of the copies as published. This enabled me to make a hurried comparison of the two and thus establish the differences between the first and second states of the book.

There were at least fifty copies of *"If This Be Treason ..."* (1948), the selection Miss Rudge had had printed from Pound's talks on Rome Radio during the war, and some forty copies of the original Italian edition of *The Economic Nature of the United States*. And there were many periodicals, some of them extremely obscure, with Pound's contributions.

I examined these and other books on this and a subsequent visit the next day, when we again had lunch at the inn, this time with Miss Rudge as my guest. When I left that afternoon, she went with me into Rapallo and introduced me to Signor Macchiavelli, proprietor of a bookshop there, who, I had been told, owned a complete file of *Il Mare,* a paper to which Pound had contributed a literary column. No, he didn't have, but there were files at the Biblioteca della Società Economica in the nearby town of Chiavari and at the University of Genoa; it would be easy to see them there. I bade goodnight to Miss Rudge and she agreed to stop at my hotel for me on Friday just before our one o'clock luncheon appointment.

FATHER DESMOND MACREADY CHUTE
21 June 1957

Father Chute had lived for ten years not far above the center of Rapallo, in a vaguely Victorian house set on the hillside amidst a veritable jungle of garden: palms and banana trees, gardenias and camellias, bougainvillea, geraniums, and cacti, all in that careless profusion which gives the impression that Nature, left to herself, has been allowed to run rampant. Father Chute later described the garden as his "wilderness" and the trees and shrubs as varieties that could be left to grow by themselves, but in almost the same breath he referred to his gardener. Certainly the task of watering daily all this vegetation must have occupied a good deal of someone's attention.

The interior of Father Chute's castle was much like its outside: something of a hodgepodge of furniture and pictures. He, himself, in his black priest's cassock, appeared at first much too big and heavy for such a setting. He wore a visor to shade his eyes, and glasses with special protective shields, and had a gray beard and close-trimmed moustache. He asked us to sit down, and offered us gin with an air of gracious hospitality. His voice was not unmusical but rather high-pitched and apologetic, so that one had to listen carefully to catch the final phrases as they trailed away behind his beard.

We hadn't much time for our gin, for we had been a few minutes late and lunch was ready. The dining room was apiece with the sitting room, with framed drawings and pictures covering the walls. After our host had muttered grace as we stood by our chairs, we sat down to a first course of pasta served with cheese, and a white wine. Then came asparagus, with Hollandaise sauce, to be eaten of course with the fingers. Next a soufflé, of an exemplary lightness and fluffiness, was served, accompanied with Colman's mustard. Miss Rudge remarked that Count Chigi (her employer at the Accademia Chigiana in Siena) had come around to Father Chute's idea that mustard and soufflé do go together, and Father Chute commented: "Yes, this is the only use for Colman's mustard." The final course was fruit, including the nessoli about which I had earlier asked Miss Rudge. And again, at the end of the meal, as we stood beside our chairs, Father Chute gave thanks.

Desmond Chute. Ezra Pound (1929). *Pencil on paper. Whereabouts unknown.*

The conversation during lunch had been about pictures and people. Most of the drawings on the walls were by Father Chute himself and, thinking that one subject bore some resemblance to T. E. Lawrence, I asked if Father Chute had known him. But the drawing proved to be of his good friend Tegetmaier, grandson of the man who wrote the book on pigeons (I had said pheasants!). He later showed me some of Tegetmaier's work—an alphabet and a crucifix.

Father Chute had planned to be a sculptor, but, his eyes failing him, he eventually turned to the priesthood. In the early days he had known and worked with Eric Gill, and his friends had included both Stanley and Gilbert Spencer, David Jones, and Henry Tonks. He had a handsome boxwood virgin-and-child, carved—actually engraved—by Jones in 1924, and a number of Gill's drawings and engravings. Gilbert Spencer's painting of the elevation of the cross hung by itself in the stairwell. The figures of the raisers of the cross resembled Mexicans, and the picture had something of the harshness and strength of color of the Mexican muralists; but the Christ was the little old man of the Norman shrines. Father Chute said he had always felt that the figure of Our Lord was not quite right and the artist had agreed with him.

We talked of course of Ezra Pound, and Miss Rudge was asked to interpret a letter Father Chute had just received from him (he was then still at St. Elizabeths Hospital, just outside Washington, D.C.). The most urgent problem seemed to be whether the orphans in Rapallo could bind for him his set of the Beaumarchais *Voltaire* and how much it would cost. We spoke of the Rapallo concerts that Pound had organized, and Miss Rudge and Father Chute agreed that they had not been generally very well attended.

In the course of our conversation it became apparent that Father Chute was deeply worried about the changes that were taking place around him. As we walked through the garden he remarked that the large apartment houses and hotels jutting out in their newness from the green slopes above the main section of Rapallo were not too bad, but he showed us a screen of cypresses that he had had planted to shut the house next door away from his view.

Later we had tea on a terrace overlooking the garden. It was no simple operation to get Father Chute installed there in his *chaise longue*. A large umbrella was fixed in place for shade; a satchel containing several sweaters was deposited close beside him; and he donned various wraps. As he sat down he spread a shawl over his feet and replaced his visor with a white panama hat. The tea was a very high one indeed to follow so soon after such a lunch: Scotch pancakes, bread and butter, and delicious *petits fours* from the local Rapallo pastry shop.

Our host walked with us a little way up the path when we left. As we shook hands to say goodbye, he seemed to me rather pitiful—a relic of more civilized days being all too rapidly swallowed up by the new, the cheap, and the vulgar.

I saw Miss Rudge again the following day, stopping at Brugo and again climbing the hill on my return from Chiavari, where I had gone to examine the file of *Il Mare* at the Biblioteca della Società Economica. We had a simple tea and then said goodbye. I walked back down to Rapallo by the path Ezra Pound had so often travelled.

THE SEARCH FOR MRS. WOOD'S
CONCERT PROGRAM
1956–1961

I had first heard of Mrs. Wood's program in the fall of 1956. In going over the carbon copies at Yale of some of Pound's letters, I had come across two references:

Mrs. Wood wants me to translate some french & Italian songs for her concert program & as I only have till dinner time to do five mss, perhaps I'd better attend to it. (*Pound to his mother, 19 February 1910*)

I send along Mrs. Wood's concert program. The translations are not particularly valuable, having been scribbled off, the lot of them, in one day. All but the first Verlaine, which I had done, more or less, some time ago. (*Pound to his father, 2 March 1910*)

There hadn't seemed to be much point even in looking for a copy of this ephemeron in the United States, and I had filed the references away among problems to investigate in Italy and England during the following summer.

But in 1957, at Sant' Ambrogio, Olga Rudge and I had not found the program among the printed materials then in her custody; and later, at Brunnenburg, Mary de Rachewiltz could not locate the early scrapbooks kept by Homer Pound, in which the copy her father had sent to his parents in 1910 might well have been placed. A few weeks later, in London, I had had no better luck; but Agnes Bedford—who had arranged the music for Pound's *Five Troubadour Songs* (1920) and selected the passages from his music criticism in the *New Age* for his *Antheil and The Treatise on Harmony* (1924)—had very kindly interested herself in the search. After I returned to the United States, she reported to me that Mrs. Wood was still alive and residing in North Cornwall. I wrote her and received this answer:

Dear Mr. Gallup,

Your letter was a strange reminder of the past. Memories of poor Ezra Pound. I well remember the translations he kindly did for me of the French-Italian words of my recital programme. Alas! two World Wars have sadly disrupted my life & possessions & I no longer have them. It is strange to recall those days when Ezra would "intone" his poems to us of an evening. I fear we used to think his recital of them somewhat unusual if not eccentric & we little thought then that his works would be held in such esteem in future years. He gave me a copy of his first book of poems with an inscription that also I no longer possess. It must have been about 1912 [*i.e.,* 1910] when he brought D. H. Lawrence to our house. We were always "at home" on a Saturday evening to friends & their friends & one of these [evenings] Ezra was dining with us & near the end of dinner he mentioned he had asked a friend to come in, a school teacher from Croydon called Lawrence. Hardly had he said so when the maid ushered in a strange man & in greeting him I asked casually if he had had dinner & he said No. My maid then brought him in the previous courses & we continued with the meal. He certainly was not at all prepossessing looking—a scruffy moustache & unruly hair. During the evening he sat on a stool at my feet & positively charmed me & I fear I neglected my other guests. Next day he wrote me a delightful letter saying how much he had enjoyed himself. This was of course before he had any of his books published. I never saw him again but had another letter regretting he could not come to my recital as he was ill in bed with a bad cold & was watching the window blind cord tap endlessly on the pane. Forgive these reminiscences—a sign of old age—but your letter has conjured up such memories. So sorry I cannot help you.

Yrs sincerely

Florence Derwent Wood

Mrs. Wood and I exchanged other letters, and in December 1957, she wrote that she had heard from her old accompanist, who thought that she might find the concert program among her records and would look for it. "If successful I will send you the results." But if the search was made, it was apparently unproductive, for I heard nothing more. Agnes Bedford had written Pound himself but, although he remembered the occasion, he had no idea as to where a copy of the program might be found. And there the matter rested, more or less, for three years.

In August 1961, just before I left the United States for England, I had written again to Mrs. Wood. It had occurred to me that she might possibly remember the name of the printers of the program and, if the firm still existed, I might be able to see their file copy. But she had answered—not at all surprisingly after fifty years—that she could not recall the name. She had as a last resort written once again to her old accompanist, but the answer was discouraging. She enclosed the first two pages of the reply, which explained that, although the program might well be in a cabin trunk in her kitchen, the trunk was buried under suitcases and boxes, and she could not possibly pull it out since her arthritis made it impossible for her to bend; in short, she could do nothing.

But here was at least some hope that a copy of the program did actually exist. I had received Mrs. Wood's letter in London and, although I did not at the time know the name of the accompanist, her address appeared at the head of her letter: 35 Holbein House, S.W.1. I promptly took a bus to Knightsbridge. Holbein House is a large apartment building and 35 turned out to be on the sixth floor. There was no lift, but I soon arrived before the door, breathless from effort and anticipation, and knocked. After a long pause, I heard footsteps accompanied by the tap of a cane and the door was opened by an old, well-preserved lady of somewhat forbidding mien, wearing a large hat trimmed with feathers. Not knowing her name, I could only wave Mrs. Wood's letter by way of introduction, as I tried to convey the importance to me of the program and to offer my help in pulling out the trunk for her so that she could examine its contents. Yes, Mrs. Wood had written her, but no, it was quite impossible for her to look for the program, and equally impossible for me to be of any assistance. Besides, the songs in the program had only been translated by Mr. Pound and they could hardly be of any importance to anyone. In any case, she repeated, it was quite impossible for her to do anything to help me. There was nothing for me to do but smile wanly and amble dejectedly back down all those stairs.

I told the sad story to Agnes Bedford when I saw her the next afternoon, and she agreed to do what she could to find some friend of Daisy Bucktrout's—for Daisy Bucktrout was indeed the accompanist's name—who might intercede with her on my behalf. A few days afterward, she wrote me saying that the friend she had approached didn't feel that she knew Miss Bucktrout well enough to intervene.

In desperation, just before leaving London for a few days in Cambridge, I wrote Miss Bucktrout, explaining again how important the program was to me, once more volunteering to haul out the trunk, depart, and return whenever she wished me to, to put everything back in order. As if in afterthought, I added that I would gladly pay for the program if a copy was found. I enclosed a stamped self-addressed envelope for her reply. When I returned from Cambridge, the envelope was awaiting me at my hotel. But the letter it contained merely reiterated that Miss Bucktrout could not under any circumstances help Mr. Gallup in his search.

I had not really allowed myself much hope of persuading Daisy Bucktrout to relent and had written another letter to Mrs. Wood in Cornwall, asking her where the recital had been given. I had a prompt reply: she had sung at the Bechstein Hall on Wigmore Street, under her maiden name, Florence Schmidt. Now the obvious question was, what had become of Bechstein Hall? It was certainly not listed in the telephone directory and the piano-manufacturing firm equally seemed not to be listed in London. After numerous inquiries, I appealed once more to Agnes Bedford. When I telephoned her, she was not surprised to hear that Mrs. Wood had sung as Florence Schmidt, for she herself had discovered this in 1957, although she had not mentioned it to me. She was able to tell me at once that Bechstein Hall had during World War I been rechristened Wigmore

Hall. This was excellent news, for even I knew that Wigmore Hall still existed. Miss Bedford added that the present manager had been connected with the hall for many years, and thought it quite likely that he would know of at least some old programs.

I passed an almost sleepless night and with difficulty restrained myself from going to Wigmore Street before I could be reasonably sure that the manager would be there. But at last the time arrived. The ticket sellers at the box office were hardly optimistic about my chances, but they did grudgingly consent to call the manager. I explained to him briefly what it was I wanted. "But, my dear fellow," he replied, "do you realize how many programs we would have if we kept them all? We'd need a separate storehouse!" I admitted that this was indeed true, but ventured even so to hope that some of the early ones might have been kept in more leisurely, roomier days. At last he agreed to see what he could do, promising nothing, and I began to write out the details to leave with him.

As I wrote he seemed to go into a kind of trance: almost as if to himself he chanted slowly: "Now let me see, don't I remember some old volumes downstairs somewhere—?" This had me on the edge of my seat. "Yes? Yes?" I cried excitedly. "Come along," he said. "Mind you, I'm not promising anything, and I warn you it'll be dusty work, but we'll see what we can find."

I followed him down the stairs to the basement of the hall and we came to a small room where a man was at work mounting posters. There against the far wall were three shelves, their contents hidden by curtains. The manager lifted the top curtain to reveal a row of perhaps ten to fifteen folio volumes uniformly bound in a kind of buckram. Excitedly I examined the dates taped on their spines: alas! they were mostly of the thirties. But I had already grasped at the curtain hanging below; here the stamped dates were of the twenties. I dropped to my knees and pulled at the curtain covering the remaining, lowest row: here were 1912–13, 1911–12, 1910–11, and, at last, 1909–10! I seized the volume, pulled it out, and placed it unceremoniously on the floor. "There's probably an index," the manager said, "why don't you look there?" But, knowing the approximate date, I had already turned to the proper section. Sure enough, a flier announced the joint recital of Florence Schmidt and Elsie Hall on Tuesday, 1 March. And there, underneath, was the actual program, securely pasted in. A glance revealed that two of the English texts were signed Ezra Pound, and I knew that I had found what I was looking for. I jumped up and clapped the manager on the shoulder, and he seemed himself to have caught some of my excitement.

The pamphlet was of seven quarto pages, containing a group each of Italian, French, and English, and a second group of French songs, as sung by Miss Schmidt, with English versions of the Italian and French songs. (These were separated by three groups of titles of "Pianoforte Soli" performed by Miss Hall.) Except for a "Chanson Provençal" in the final group, of which only an English version was printed, the texts were in a left-hand column, with the English versions on the right. Only the English versions of the first two French songs had printed attribution to Pound, but his letters to his parents implied that he had translated at least four others and probably all the French and Italian songs. There were three arias, "Cantata Spirituale," by Leonardo Leo, "Non so più cosa son" from Mozart's *Le Nozze di Figaro,* and "Manon" by Massenet; a Siciliana, "Tre giorni son che Nina" by Pergolesi; and seven songs: "Clair de Lune," by Gabriel Fauré, the text by Paul Verlaine; "Lied Maritime" by Vincent d'Indy, the text by the composer; "Ariettes Oubliées (No. 3)," "Aquarelles (Green)," and "Fêtes Galantes—Fantoches," all by Debussy, with texts by Verlaine; "Lisette (Bergerette)," an eighteenth-century setting of an Old French text, and the "Chanson Provençal."

Now came the problem of how I was to copy the document. The manager and I lifted the volume to a table and he, to my astonishment, began to tear the program from the sheet of heavier paper to which its last leaf was fastened. I protested, and had little difficulty in accomplishing its removal without damage to the pamphlet itself. To my further amazement the manager agreed to let me take it away to be photographed on my promise to have it back that afternoon. I thanked him profusely and walked out of Wigmore Hall treading the red carpets very lightly indeed.

Mrs. Wood's Program (1910). Beinecke Library, gift of Donald Gallup.

The Times Book Club is next door to Wigmore Hall and several days earlier I had purchased a few books there, asking that they be sent to New Haven. When I gave my name, the assistant said, "Oh, Mr. Eliot's bibliographer?" and I, very much flattered, acknowledged the identification. It occurred to me that possibly this agreeable young man (whom I later identified as Timothy d'Arch Smith) might know where I could have photographs of the program made on short order, and I stopped to ask him. It turned out that there was a duplicating machine in the shop and in a matter of minutes I had some very good copies of the seven printed pages. Waving them in one hand, and clutching the original program in the other, I returned to Wigmore Hall and handed it to the somewhat astonished manager. I offered to paste it back into the proper volume, but he insisted upon doing this himself. All I could do was take his name: H. T. C. Brickell, Manager, Wigmore Hall; promise to acknowledge my indebtedness to him; and thank him again for his kindness.

Thus, on my last day in London before leaving for France and Italy, 27 September 1961, the search for Mrs. Wood's concert program came to a successful end.

(There was a postscript three years later when Agnes Bedford wrote me that Daisy Bucktrout had died at an advanced age. Resolved to make a final attempt to locate her copy of the program, if she had indeed kept one, I wrote to the executor of her estate, using the Holbein House address, explaining my eagerness to find the copy, describing it and enclosing a small check in payment should the pamphlet turn up among Miss Bucktrout's effects. A month or two later the program arrived in the mail, along with a very pleasant note from Miss Bucktrout's niece, saying how happy she was that a long and careful search through her aunt's accumulated papers had finally located the item. Few additions to my Ezra Pound collection★ have given me greater satisfaction.)

★I gave the entire collection, including the copy of Mrs. Wood's program, to Yale between 1985 and 1992.

I Buy a Fake Gaudier-Brzeska
1961

That last day in England was only a little more than half over when I returned the original of Mrs. Wood's program to the manager of Wigmore Hall and walked out into Wigmore Street carrying my set of photographs. The Hanover Gallery was not far off, and since I hadn't been around to see Erica Brausen, the owner-manager, I decided to drop by and ask if she might be free for lunch. For years she had been sending me announcements of the exhibitions at her gallery, and although I had once written her to inquire about a drawing by David Jones, I had never actually bought anything from her since the war years when she had been with the Redfern Gallery.

At the gallery I was shown down to the inner sanctum, where Erica greeted me and we sat and talked. The conversation soon turned to Henri Gaudier-Brzeska and to the *Portrait of Ezra Pound,* a wood carving that Andrew Ritchie had purchased from her for the Yale Art Gallery. I said that if she had shown that to me, I might have had the chance to buy something from her. In reply, she reached into a side-drawer of her desk and placing a small ivory carving on the table before me said, "Well, what about this?" "This" was a nude female three-quarter-length figure, headless and armless, mounted on a circular black wooden block and standing, with the pedestal, not more than about seven inches. The neck had a curious hole bored into its center, and at the bottom one side was cut off on a slant. But the figure had a great deal of charm and was not at all merely a conventional nude. Its resemblance to some of Norman Pearson's primitive Esquimaux carvings struck me at once. Erica explained that the object had come from the collection of H. S. ("Jim") Ede via a young man to whom he had given it, and that a certificate of authenticity would be furnished. I knew the price would be high, but the appeal of a small figure actually carved by Gaudier-Brzeska, whose work had been so important to Ezra Pound, made me extremely eager to have it. And at last I should be buying something from the Hanover Gallery and Erica's long years of mailing announcements and catalogues would have yielded some return.

The price was (for me) high indeed: one hundred fifty pounds—
at that time four hundred twenty dollars. I gulped inwardly and was
also a little nervous for fear that the payment on my Guggenheim
fellowship due the first of October might not have arrived at the
bank in New Haven; but I tried not to betray my doubts as I wrote
out the check. The little figure was ceremoniously wrapped in tissue
paper and placed in the small cardboard box in which the gallery had
received it, and Erica Brausen took *me* to lunch.

From London I flew to Paris and at the Bibliothèque Nationale
worked especially on Pound's contributions to French periodicals
and French translations of his work. I then continued by train to
Milan, where I went to see Vanni Scheiwiller, Pound's principal
Italian publisher. I showed the ivory to him and his father and brother. They admired it, and Vanni asked for a photograph so that he
might publish it. I told him I thought that could be arranged.

I displayed the statuette again on the evening of my arrival at
Brunnenburg. I had had dinner with Mary and Boris de Rachewiltz
and Mrs. Pound, and had told them about my purchase. After dinner
I brought the carving up for them to see. Mrs. Pound pointed out
that the ivory was almost certainly from an umbrella handle, which
accounted for the curious hole in the top and the slanting cut of the
bottom, and commented upon the back that Gaudier's figures
always had beautiful backs. Mary promised to mention the figure to
her father, who was in the clinic at Martinsbrunn, to find out if he
happened to remember it. This she did the following afternoon,
with rather disappointing results: Pound declared flatly that Gaudier
had never carved anything from ivory and that the figure must be a
fake.

It chanced that on either that day or the following I received from
the Hanover Gallery, forwarded from New Haven, a letter enclosing the promised certificate of authenticity. It read:

Re: The Gaudier Brzeska

This small ivory carving was given to me in April 1959 by Mr. H. S.
(Jim) Ede of Kettles Yard, Cambridge. He knew Brzeska well and bought
the statue from him shortly before he was killed. He tells me that the statue was carved from an umbrella handle.

[*Signed*] Roger Grounds

Although I had no reason to doubt Grounds's statement, it seemed to me advisable, in view of Ezra Pound's skepticism, to get confirmation from Ede himself, especially since Grounds had so thoughtfully provided me with his address. I wrote asking if he would confirm Grounds's statement and at the same time wrote to the Hanover Gallery thanking them for the certificate and explaining why I was writing to Ede.

I was so convinced that the carving was Gaudier's work that I suggested to Mary that she take it to the hospital to show to her father. She was reluctant to do this for fear that he might grab the figure and put it into a drawer, and I didn't press her further. But when she suggested toward the end of my visit that I go down to say goodbye to Pound, I told her I thought I would take the carving in my pocket and show it to him. She agreed that this would be safe enough.

Young Walter de Rachewiltz took me in to his grandfather's room and I held the box in my hands for some time before mentioning it to Pound. I could see that his attention was attracted by it. Finally, I explained that I had brought it along for him to see. He changed his glasses and took the little figure into his hands. After he had examined it carefully, he said slowly, "Yes, this is quite possible, quite possible." I pointed out the evidence of its having been carved from an umbrella handle—by way of answering his original objection that Gaudier would have had no money to buy ivory—and he agreed. I came away from seeing him, exulting in his confirmation of my instinctive feeling that the carving was indeed Gaudier's work.

I didn't have anyone else to show the carving to until I got back to New Haven in November. When I went to Norman Pearson's office to return the Olivetti portable typewriter that I had borrowed, I took the carving along in my pocket. He agreed that it was reminiscent of primitive Esquimaux work and thought it very handsome. At the library I was showing it to Marjorie Wynne, who was rather shocked at my having a nude female figure in my possession, when Fritz Liebert came in. He praised it highly and said that even if it weren't by Gaudier-Brzeska, it would be a very charming carving. I took it back to my apartment and began to think how I should protect it against the onslaught of the college cleaning women.

I had placed the ivory on my desk and had begun to examine my accumulated mail. One of the first letters had come by air from the Hanover Gallery in London. It was from Erica Brausen. I read it with stupefied incredulity. She was extremely sorry to tell me that she had just heard from Jim Ede that the ivory carving I had purchased from her as by Gaudier-Brzeska is not by him, in spite of the statement she had obtained from Grounds. Either he sold it to her dishonestly, knowing that it was not by Gaudier-Brzeska, or he completely misunderstood what Ede had told him about it at the time he made the gift.

She was angry with Grounds, and sorry, and begged my forgiveness. She asked me to return the carving to her, at her expense. She would instruct her bankers to send me a refund of $420.

As I dazedly riffled through my other mail, I came upon the stamped, addressed envelope I had enclosed in my letter to Ede. His answer gave me more information.

He was distressed about the ivory, because of course it was not carved by Gaudier-Brzeska, but by Vivian Cole, an art student of between wars, of whom he had now lost trace. Ede certainly did not tell Grounds that the carving was by Gaudier-Brzeska; indeed he remembered telling him about Cole. He was surprised that the Hanover Gallery should have thought the ivory the work of Gaudier-Brzeska. Grounds's statement that Ede "bought the little ivory from Brzeska shortly before he was killed" was pure fabrication: he had not even heard of Gaudier-Brzeska until about 1929. He thought everyone ought to hand everything back and start over!

For a while, I was too numb to do anything; but then I wrote to Erica explaining that I had really become attached to the figure and asking her if possibly I could arrange to buy it for perhaps ten to fifteen pounds. At the same time I wrote to Ede. A few days later, the Hanover Gallery's refund of my money arrived. Rather than complicate matters further, I wrapped the figure carefully and sent it, at my own expense (I felt that I had received at least that much pleasure from my brief possession of it) by airmail to Erica. I heard nothing from her and wrote to ask whether it had arrived safely. She replied that it had, but that Grounds was maintaining that the gallery had bought the figure at its own risk. I heard nothing more for several months and wrote again to ask what had happened. Erica replied that she had got her money back and that Grounds had got his sculpture back and if I wanted it I would have to write to him. I did write, on 25 January 1963:

Dear Mr. Grounds:

In September 1961, I purchased from the Hanover Gallery in London a small ivory statue that they said was by Gaudier-Brzeska. When they notified me shortly after my return to the United States that the carving was not after all by Gaudier-Brzeska, I sent it back to them and my money was refunded. I understand from Mrs. Brausen that the statue was returned by the Gallery to you.

I became attached to the carving while it was in my possession and wonder if you would care to sell it to me? I haven't the slightest idea what a fair price would be, but should be glad to pay ten pounds for it.

I never had any reply.

(Four years later, my desire to own an original—and genuine—Gaudier-Brzeska was at last satisfied. In London in July 1965, I had gone to see Anthony Rota at the new quarters of Bertram Rota Ltd. in Savile Row, only a few yards from the building where his late father had conducted the business so successfully for so many years. As I approached the handsome entrance, I was surprised to see on display in the shop's window a portrait of Pound that I knew must have been drawn by Henri Gaudier-Brzeska. I soon found out from Arthur Uphill, Anthony Rota's righthand man, that the drawing was indeed by Gaudier—one of the many hurried sketches done with a brush in Japanese ink as studies for the hieratic head (Pound refers to some hundred of them, the one Gaudier gave him, which he reproduced in a number of his books and even on his stationery, being the best known). Like the Cole ivory nude, it stemmed from the H. S. Ede collection, having been given or sold by him to Mervyn Levy, from whom the firm had purchased it. Fortunately, it was for sale and since the price was not prohibitive, I purchased it. It has been reproduced on a number of occasions and was used as a titlepage vignette in the second edition of my Pound *Bibliography*.)

The Files of the Little Review
1961–1965

I HEARD IN 1961 of the discovery, in a garage on Long Island, of several large crates containing archives of the *Little Review*. This was the magazine devoted to literature, music, and art, founded in Chicago in March 1914 by Margaret C. Anderson, later moved to New York and, finally, to Paris, where, from autumn 1921 until publication ceased in May 1929, Jane Heap served as joint editor. In April 1917, Ezra Pound took over the foreign editorship, and he became largely responsible for the magazine's printing a considerable portion of James Joyce's *Ulysses,* as well as poems by T. S. Eliot and W. B. Yeats, and prose by Wyndham Lewis and Pound himself. During its Paris years it appeared irregularly, devoting special issues to Constantin Brancusi, Francis Picabia, Joseph Stella, and Juan Gris.

I knew that Erica Brausen, whom I had seen frequently at the Redfern Gallery during the war years and who was now running in London her own Hanover Gallery, was a friend of Jane Heap. I talked with Erica about the *Little Review* papers and learned that they had been shipped to London and placed in storage, where it seemed likely they would remain for the foreseeable future: Jane Heap was particularly concerned about getting from the various correspondents permission to dispose of their letters. Erica promised to let me know if and when there seemed to be any chance that the papers would become available for inspection.

In January 1964, Gorham Munson reported to Norman Pearson that Carol Robinson, who had been at one time a close associate of Jane Heap and Margaret Anderson, had shown him a number of folders of letters "salvaged from the *Little Review* storage files," including correspondence from both Gertrude Stein and Ezra Pound. Munson said that Miss Robinson "hasn't much idea of what to do about these letters"; she had agreed to his suggestion that he write Norman about them.

Norman was on leave of absence in Japan until early March, but his secretary sent me a copy of Munson's letter. I telephoned Miss Robinson, of whom I had often heard from Frances Steloff, and told her that we should like very much to acquire the papers for Yale. She said she would write to London to be certain that she had permission from Miss Heap and Miss Anderson to dispose of them.

It turned out that what Miss Robinson had was the contents of a single carton, overlooked when the rest of the *Little Review* files had been sent to London in 1961. On 3 February she reported to me that she had mailed all the material she had found to Jane Heap. She suggested that when I next visited London I might be able to secure permission to examine it, but added that "It will take ... months and [perhaps even] years to convince Miss Heap of this."

I wrote to Erica Brausen on 10 February:

I have been so involved since 1961 with the Pound bibliography that I haven't been able to attack the problem of the *Little Review* correspondence ... . Now the recent flurry concerning the forgotten carton at Carol Robinson's drives me to write you, hoping that you will discuss my letter with Miss Heap.

We are ... eager to secure these papers for the Yale Library ... and very much hope that something can be worked out. (I think that Miss Heap knows that we already have the *Dial* correspondence—and Alyse Gregory has given some of her own papers and promised to bequeath the rest; a vast amount of Ezra Pound—including the letters he wrote to Miss Anderson from St. Elizabeths [Hospital], which we purchased from her several years ago; William Carlos Williams; James Joyce; D.H. Lawrence; and T.S. Eliot; all the manuscripts and correspondence of Gertrude Stein—including letters to her from both Miss Heap and Miss Anderson; the *Hound & Horn* correspondence, the Stieglitz Archive, papers of Lachaise, Hartley, Mabel Dodge Luhan, and Muriel Draper, with a great number of less closely related groups of manuscripts and correspondence of twentieth-century writers like Eugene O'Neill, Sinclair Lewis, Edmund Wilson, Philip Barry, and such institutions as the Theatre Guild and the Société Anonyme. Thus there is plenty of material at Yale to complement and supplement the *Little Review* papers and, of course, we have the printed material as well, including an extensive collection of little magazines and practically complete collections of first editions of many of the writers.)

As for the authors' permissions, I know that Mary de Rachewiltz (Ezra Pound's daughter) would be happy to write Miss Heap to assure her that her father would be glad to see his letters go to Yale, and I am sure that Mr. Eliot would also have no objection. Certainly Alice Toklas would be delighted to have Gertrude Stein's letters here. Of course we should be quite prepared to ask that any scholar wishing to see the letters should first have the permission of their writers.

Now, if Miss Heap is agreeable in principle to the material's coming to Yale, how can this be accomplished? If there is still no detailed listing ..., Miss Heap would probably not be able to set a price and it would be impossible for us to approach a possible donor. In this case, I suggest that, if arrangements can be worked out with Miss Heap, I ... come to London early this summer to list the material under the supervision of either Miss Heap herself or ... whomever she may designate. I should be glad to donate my services in listing the papers (the trip would be my vacation) if Miss Heap would agree to give Yale first refusal of the material once the price is established. ... it may be that Miss Heap already has enough of an idea of the contents to have made up her mind what she would want for the archive. In that case, we could approach our possible donor before I left for London and if when I saw the material I was convinced that our donor would agree that it was worth the price, I could arrange for at least a down payment and could oversee the shipment of the papers to New Haven. Of course we would keep the papers together as the *Little Review* Collection and would be willing to consider any other conditions that Miss Heap felt should be imposed.

Please assure her again, Erica, that we are eager to have the material here and feel very strongly that this is the most appropriate depository for it.

Erica replied on 9 March that she had given my letter to Jane Heap, who would decide whether or not I could come to London. The papers were still in their big packing-cases and it would take quite a lot of time to unpack them all. Erica would advise Jane to let me come. I answered on the 16th, repeating my offer to fly over.

I had already had some correspondence with Margaret Anderson, first, in 1952, about my use of some of her letters in *The Flowers of Friendship,* and then, in 1955, about our purchase of the letters she had received from Ezra Pound at the time of her editing *The Little Review Anthology*. Deciding that it would be well to enlist her support, I wrote her on 7 May 1964, enclosing a carbon of my letter to Erica Brausen:

You have been so kind to me on several occasions that I venture to ask if you would be willing to help in another matter. When I was in London in 1961, my friend Erica Brausen told me that all the *Little Review* files were being sent to Miss Heap for storage and eventual disposition. Miss Brausen knew how eager I was to secure the material for Yale if we could raise the necessary money, and talked with Miss Heap about it. Miss Heap said that of course she would have to get Ezra Pound's permission before she could sell us the Pound letters for instance and I assured her that EP had already steered a number of collections of his letters in our direction, including Paige's carbon copies of all the letters gathered for the *Selected Letters*. ... early this year the forgotten carton at Carol Robinson's gave me the push that resulted in the enclosed letter to Erica. Erica replied that she would show the letter to Miss Heap and that Miss Heap would probably get in touch with me. Since then nothing.

Now I wonder if you might possibly be willing to give Miss Heap a little "push." I see certain favorable signs here that we might be able to raise the money for such a purpose and am not certain that the atmosphere will be so propitious a year from now. And of course the market for this kind of material is very high now and may not continue so indefinitely. I know that the easiest thing for Miss Heap ... is to do nothing, and if you felt that you could influence her into making a decision now and were willing to exert the influence, I should be even more greatly in your debt.

Miss Anderson answered on the 13th, promising to do her best to help with the papers. Jane Heap had been ill for years with diabetes, etc., and was now almost completely blind, and terribly over-worked, but Miss Anderson would write to both Jane and Elspeth Champcommunal, who now lived with her, helping her run her shop, "The Rocking-Horse." She suggested that the next time I was in London I might simply drop in to the shop unannounced. I replied on 19 May, saying that I expected to be there the following summer and would follow her advice.

But in only a matter of weeks Jane Heap was dead. I wrote Erica Brausen as soon as I saw the *New York Times* obituary, on 2 July. She replied on 17 August, but apparently forgot to mail the letter. In it she thanked me for my note about Jane and told me not to worry about the papers. They had been given away years ago, but the person to whom they had been given was not well enough to see about selling them. Erica would let me know as soon as they became available: whatever happened, Yale would get the first refusal through her.

I had not received this reply when Jackson Bryer, who had come to Yale to work with our *Little Review*-related materials, informed me that Michael Currer-Briggs was acting on behalf of Jane Heap's estate, especially in connection with the *Little Review* papers. I wrote him on 12 September:

For some two years before the death of Miss Heap I was in communi-

cation with her through our mutual friend Miss Brausen concerning the
Little Review archives. I had suggested that I would be willing to come to
London and, under Miss Heap's supervision, put the papers in order and
list them with the idea that Yale University would be given the opportunity to purchase them if and when Miss Heap decided that they should be
sold. Miss Brausen had written me that Miss Heap was considering my
suggestion but I had received no answer from her when her death was
reported in the papers. I wrote Miss Brausen, asking her to let me know
what disposition of the archive was planned, but I have not heard from her
and it may be that no decision has yet been made.

Certainly the Yale University Library continues to be very much interested in acquiring the *Little Review* papers. ...

I hope that you will excuse the liberty I take in writing to you, but I am
most eager that the *Little Review* papers should come to Yale.

Currer-Briggs replied that Erica Brausen had already written me.
Since her letter had still not arrived, I wrote again to her on 22
September:

Happening to hear from a scholar who was here working on our *Little
Review* materials that he had had a note since Jane Heap's death from Mr.
Currer-Briggs on the subject of the *Little Review* papers, I wrote to him.
He has very kindly written to say that you had already written me several
weeks ago; but, alas, your letter has never arrived and must have been lost.
Perhaps by now it has been returned to you? In any case, I wanted you to
know why I had not thanked you for your letter.

I do very much hope that, somehow, the *Little Review* papers may come
to Yale. I feel so strongly that this is the most appropriate place for them. If
there is anything I can do, personally, to help in London in organizing the
papers prior to their disposition, I should be only too happy to be of service. Since I took only six days off this summer, the University could hardly object to my playing hookey for a couple of weeks and I sha'n't be
teaching my course [in Bibliography] this term.

On the same day, Erica apparently discovered that she had not
mailed the letter she had written me in August, and finally sent it off
(the envelope bears the postmark, 22 September). I acknowledged
its receipt on the 26th:

It was very good of you to take the trouble to write me ... , and I am
relieved that the letter eventually turned up. (It crossed my recent letter to
you, written after Mr. Currer-Briggs had communicated with me.)

I am of course delighted that Yale can count on having first refusal on
the *Little Review* papers when the owner gets around to making arrangements for their sale, and I shall keep still and not do a thing—except hope!

Erica kept her word and mailed me (from New York) in December 1964 a twenty-nine-page typed list of "The *Little Review* Papers in London." There were more manuscripts and typescripts of contributions but far fewer letters from contributors than I had expected, but the archive was still obviously an important one, with extensive groups of letters from Elsa Freytag von Loringhoven, Robert McAlmon, Moholy-Nagy, Nicolaus Pevsner, Ezra Pound (134 letters and a postcard), John Quinn, Tristan Tzara, and Ossip Zadkine. In an accompanying letter Erica explained that she had handed the Gertrude Stein letters to Alice B. Toklas in Paris, in accordance with Jane Heap's instructions. (In spite of her statement to me in her letter of 17 August that the files had been given away, she seemed to treat them as part of Jane Heap's estate, subject to the decisions of Miss Heap's executors.) Subsequently, Margie Cohn of the House of Books Ltd in New York telephoned, and on 18 December, wrote me, formally offering the *Little Review* papers, as agent for the owner, at $55,000. She asked if I thought the library would be interested. If not, she would offer the papers elsewhere. The owner would like to have an early decision.

I replied on the 21st:

Many thanks for your letter. I am working on the *Little Review* material and we shall try to make our decision on the basis of the list that we have; the executors will, understandably, not wish to be bothered with questions as to details.

But I have had one disappointment already and it may take longer than I had expected. I can assure you, however, that the Library is very definite-ly interested (after all, I have been on the trail of this material since 1961) and I very much hope that it will be possible for us somehow to find the money with which to pay for it.

The "one disappointment" I had already had was from my old English instructor, Ted Hilles, who had been so helpful in con-nection with the Ezra Pound archive. I had drafted a letter to send to him; but when I discussed the *Little Review* papers with James Tanis, now the Yale Librarian, he showed me a letter from Ted, explaining that his financial help to the library would in future have to be lim-ited to his most immediate interest, the Boswell papers. I altered my draft letter slightly and addressed it to John Ecklund, the University Treasurer, with whom I had been dealing on matters pertaining to the Pound archive. I raised with him the possibility that money might be borrowed from the fund established by anonymous gift for the purchase of the Pound papers. When this idea too, proved not to be feasible, I wrote to John Slocum, whose James Joyce collection the library had acquired, asking him if he had any suggestions as to how we might proceed. Apparently, he could think of nothing for I never had a reply.

Paul Mellon, Yale 1929, was then, with Jock Whitney, Yale 1926, the library's most likely source for funding of such materials (the Beinecke brothers had turned us down in our appeal to them for funds for the Pound papers). I telephoned Jackson Mathews, with whom I had had some dealings in connection with the Bollingen Prize, thinking he might be willing to raise the matter with Bollingen Foundation or even Paul Mellon himself, and wrote him on 27 January:

Confirming our telephone conversation, I am enclosing my "selective index" digested from the 29-page mimeographed list of "The *Little Review* Papers in London," compiled by Michael Currer-Briggs, one of the executors of Jane Heap's estate. These papers are being offered to Yale—in consequence of a promise made to me by an executrix of the estate, Erica Brausen—through the House of Books Ltd. in New York at $55,000. Miss Brausen has assured me that if Yale decides not to acquire the papers, they will then be offered elsewhere at a "substantially higher" price. Yale definitely has first refusal.

As I explained over the 'phone, we are extremely eager to secure this material because it fits in so well with other collections that we now have or hope to acquire in the future. We have been negotiating for more than a year to secure the Ezra Pound Archive and funds ($250,000) have been given the University specifically for this purpose. We have had the papers of the *Dial* on deposit for more than ten years, and the presence here of the *Little Review* papers will, I am certain, influence the executors of Scofield Thayer's estate when, after his death, the question of the ultimate disposition of the *Dial* papers (of which he is the owner) comes up. Lincoln Kirstein several years ago gave us the papers of the *Hound & Horn*. Cleanth Brooks and Robert Penn Warren have given us the files of the *Southern Review*. We have, of course, the *Yale Review* papers, and a number of other, smaller archives, such as those of *Furioso, Blues, View, Yale Poetry Review,* and *Chimera*.

Of the three most important American literary periodicals publishing "advanced" material in the twenties and thirties, the files of one, *Poetry, A Magazine of Verse,* are forever out of reach in the Harriet Monroe collection in the University of Chicago Library*; the files of the *Dial* are, as I have said, on deposit here at Yale; the files of the *Little Review*—insofar as they exist—are now being offered.

I very much hope that Bollingen Foundation may feel that the acquisition of these papers is something that it can help us with. I'll be glad to send down the complete list if you'd like to have it.

Unfortunately, Bollingen Foundation was just then cutting down on grants of this type and could not help. Jack Mathews said that the Old Dominion Foundation was a possibility, but the directors would not meet until March. Meanwhile, he was obliged to leave for Paris and had to postpone any further action until he returned to New York.

I had nothing concrete to report to Mrs. Cohn when, a month after her original letter, she telephoned me. I wrote her on 17 January that we would give her a definite answer by the end of the month. The very next day I was shocked to receive a cable from Erica Brausen in London: an offer for the *Little Review* papers of $75,000 had been received; would we let her know at once whether we would pay more, otherwise the offer would be accepted. Jack Mathews was still in Paris, but I telephoned Ernest Brooks at Bollingen Foundation. He was willing to approach Paul Mellon directly, but that would take at least a day or two.

I telephoned Erica Brausen in London and pointed out that, through the House of Books as her authorized agent, she had made us a firm offer of the *Little Review* material at $55,000. She replied that she had not regarded Mrs. Cohn as her exclusive agent; in any case, someone else (a representative of the University of Wisconsin) had seen the papers and had offered $75,000. The other executors would not allow her to sell to Yale at $55,000. I explained that it was against our policy to enter into competitive bidding with another

*More of the *Poetry* archive did actually exist—in the possession of the daughter of Alice Corbin Henderson, the assistant editor, but I knew nothing of it at that time. Those papers are now at the University of Texas, Austin.

institution. She answered that she had no choice but to accept the higher offer. I telephoned Margie Cohn, who was understandably annoyed at what seemed to her a blatant violation of business ethics. I also called Ernest Brooks to let him know of Erica Brausen's decision and that it would not be necessary for him to bother Paul Mellon. And so the long effort to acquire the *Little Review* papers ended at last in ignominious failure.

Carlotta Monterey (1928?). Photograph given by her to Eugene O'Neill, inscribed in lower right corner: "I love you/Carlotta/'28." (The O'Neills sailed for Europe on the SS Berengaria, 10 Feb. 1928 and were married in a civil ceremony in Paris on 22 July 1929.) Collection of Donald Gallup.

Pursuing O'Neill in Elm City
and Manhattan

Administering the Collection
1947–1980

DEALING WITH Carlotta Monterey O'Neill in the months just after her husband's death increased substantially both the interest and the challenge of my curator's job. Physically she was at a low ebb, and in no condition to withstand the cruel blow that came in the spring when Boston University purchased the Hotel Shelton in order to convert it to a dormitory. She was obliged at short notice to leave the two rooms where she had nursed O'Neill through his terminal illness. Eager to insure that some of the objects that had meant a great deal to him would be safe after she was no longer around to take care of them, she sent a good many to Yale for the collection, explaining their significance in letters to me.

One was a cigarette case that she had given to her husband:

in 1927, when I had begun to believe that all "artists" needed honest, unselfish friendship more than anything else, . . . I asked him if he had ever wanted something, that was quite unnecessary, but he just *wanted* it! He looked at me & smiled that charming smile of his, & said, "Have you?" I said I had!

Then, with a pause, & another *sweet* smile, he answered, "I always envied a man who could reach into his pocket & nonchalantly pull forth a long, thin, plain, solid gold cigarette case!" And, he laughed—& almost blushed when he said this. And, I laughed. And, that was that. I got him the case—&, he was flabbergasted!—It seems he had never been given presents before!—But he enjoyed the case—& asked me to have it engraved as it is engraved—"To Gene from Carlotta"!—★

★The engraving reproduces Carlotta's handwriting.

Only five days later, it was O'Neill's "'writing desk' so to speak."

He could never write at a table or desk! I bought him various styles of each—but it was simply wasting money—He always had a particular chair (we tried various chairs, too!) in which he sat with his feet on a footstool. And, the leather blotting-pad was on his knees & he wrote for hours at a time like this—in pencil! He used this particular pad—since May 1928!

On 24 July 1954, she wrote me about books that she had sent:

Did you not once ask me about the "Wolfville" books? "Wolfville Days" & "Wolfville Nights"? It appears that when Gene was a boy (10 to 15?) he adored these books written by Alfred Henry Lewis. And, during his years with me (Feb. 10, *1928* to Nov. 27, *1953)* whenever he was fed-up with writing plays, the business of living, or was not well,—he would re-read the "Wolfville" stories over, & over & over again!

When we had given up house-keeping—& our books were in storage—& he was so ill (1951—'52—'53) he asked me to get him the "Wolfville" books—. Of course I had to advertise for them & pay collector's prices! But, he had what he wanted. He also asked for Kipling's verse—Mark Twain's Works, "Alice in Wonderland"—& wanted James Whitcomb Riley's verse—to be able to read "An Old Sweetheart of Mine"! But, at the very last, it was Lindbergh's book [*The Spirit of St. Louis* (1953)] that he enjoyed so much. It was, to him, so well written—& had the *poet's* insight—He was reading it for the *second* time—when he died!

In an earlier letter, she had told me the story of another of O'Neill's treasured possessions, already sent to Yale:

Having so much to do—I stupidly thought if I let my hair grow I wouldn't have to waste time going to the hair-dresser! So, I let it grow— (It grows very fast—I always had heavy, long hair.) It was a most horrible nuisance! I loved working in the garden—had taught Gene to prune—& to cut shrubs in various forms. As, by nature, he was meticulous & neat— he became a very good gardener!

One hot day we were working in the patio, & my long hair kept annoying me by falling over my face. I pulled it down & made it into a braid—& the braid kept falling into my face! I was *so* annoyed I took the garden shears and *sawed* my braid off close to my head! I was a *sight!* And Gene was *furious!* He flew at me & grabbed what was left of the poor braid. And he did not speak to me for twenty-four hours!—And, then, in no uncertain terms, he informed me that I had *no right* to do such a thing without asking *my husband!* He had always loved my long hair! He always kept this braid among his "treasures"—in a Chinese lacquer box—with letters, etc—I found it after his death—bless him!

Rejoicing in all the information that Carlotta was sending, I thanked her, and commented that her letters would become "an important part of the Eugene O'Neill Collection." Her reaction left me dumfounded:

Surely, you can't mean to add them to Gene's things—this being able to be frank, honest and to pour out my heart to you in black, sad hours,—*can't* be used for *strangers,* the cold-blooded mentality of to-day ... ,—oh, *no*—it would be too cruel! I can't have my love for Gene ... made into something that is "just too comic"!—

Even re-doing the diaries has started me thinking maybe it will seem to others there is too much of *me* in them! But, they are *my* diaries! Gene *did* use them for reference—& often asked me to put *this* or *that* in them!

Life has become hideous! I can't figure out, from any standards (for there are *NO* standards today!) what is best for Gene's Collection without placing myself in a false position!

There is *NO ONE* who knows what O'Neill was but me! No one mourns him,—*but me!* No one loved him, *but me!* ...

I hastened to reassure her:

It always bothers me that volumes which have meant a great deal to some person or persons lose so much of this significance when they become part of a large library like Yale's. Take, for example, the Lindbergh book: it has the O'Neill (Gene & Carlotta) bookplate, but if it weren't for the things which you have told me and written me about it, no one would know that it was at all different. That is what I meant by saying that your letters to me would be valuable: because they explain so many things. No, those letters will never be seen by strangers, but it would be selfish—indeed reprehensible—of me not to pass them on to my successor as curator of the American Literature and O'Neill Collections. I shall of course see that a typed note of explanation is placed with any book or other object which needs explanation; but I shall have to give my authority, and there may, eventually, be some reason to look up the authority, in these cases, and see exactly what you have said about them. A curator has to take this objective view even concerning things which should be considered subjectively, as warm, human things alive, because, after all, we hope that the Yale Library and the O'Neill Collection will be here long, long after we both are dead. And although the individuals who look at these books and manuscripts— at your diaries, for instance—a hundred years from now will be strangers, yes, to O'Neill and you and me, still there will certainly, we hope, be some among them who will be helped by these personal things better to understand the man Eugene O'Neill and the woman Carlotta Monterey. And no one can write well and enduringly of O'Neill and his work without this understanding.

It is a wonderful thing that you are doing and please do not doubt it.

Her reply relieved my concern:

I like the manner in which you impressed upon me how objective the work I am doing really is. If *no one* is to see these things for 25 Years from Gene's death that *does* make a difference. That will be Nov. 27, 1978! ...
And thank you for your amazing patience and understanding!

The twenty-five year restriction on the bulk of the manuscript collection was enforced even more strictly in the years just after Eugene O'Neill's death. His "Work Diary" and Carlotta's own diary were included, along with notes, drafts, and all original *pencil* manuscripts. Mrs. O'Neill felt that her husband had *published* plays enough to keep scholars occupied for at least twenty-five years. On one occasion, she even had her New York counsel make a special trip to New Haven to be sure that the restriction was being carried out. One of the few times when I had to pacify an angry Carlotta on the telephone was when an article by Arthur and Barbara Gelb published in the Sunday *New York Times* seemed to indicate that we at Yale had allowed her diary to be seen. Fortunately, I was able to prove to her that the quotation in question had come from an earlier interview she had given to Seymour Peck, in the course of which she herself had read to him a particular passage.

In June 1954, we received a request from a representative of one of the British papers, whom I shall call "X," explaining that he had Mrs. O'Neill's permission to read anything he wanted to in the Yale collection. I wrote Carlotta to ask whether we were to make an exception in this man's favor, and promptly received a telegram. Dated Saturday the 19th at 10:00 A.M., it was addressed to me at Jonathan Edwards College:

YOUR LETTER JUST RECEIVED PLEASE TELL [X] ... NO ONE CAN EVEN SMELL THE O'NEILL COLLECTION WITHOUT A WRITTEN ORDER FROM ME AND LOOK OUT FOR THAT YOUNG MAN HE IS NOT TO BE TRUSTED IN ANY WAY ... AM WRITING AT LENGTH

Her letter was delivered to the library on Monday morning:

The ... news almost brought on a stroke! That dreadful little *liar!* I wouldn't allow him to see even what there is to see about Blemie [*the O'Neills' Dalmatian*].

Having read your letter 3 times—to be certain I had seen correctly—I got a taxi & drove down to the main office of Western Union (Congress Street) & sent you a wire ... .

[X] ... does work in [the] office of the [British paper] ... He does not write—he cuts certain items out of papers & magazines—I presume to send to [Britain] ... He snoops, he does not tell the truth—... . My real feeling about him I can't put on paper—... .

More details followed on the 24th:

I received such an insulting letter from the "young man" relative to not being allowed to go over the O'Neill Collection that I asked my lawyer to come up and read it. He did & told me to ignore it—but, if I received any further letter to bring it to him immediately & he would take over. He took the letter with him. It (the letter) smelled of blackmail! Briefly, if I refused to tell him of details of my husband's private life "up to the time of his death" he would be forced to get his information where best he could—& how he could! I nearly passed out when I read it! You see he is not interested in O'Neill's works but in gossip—scandal! ...

I had already written her on the 21st:

I'm sorry that you went to all the trouble of telegraphing as well as writing. ... [X]'s letter made me suspicious, and my suspicions were, I see, well founded. But again I apologize for causing you all that bother.

We aren't letting anyone see anything in the Collection unless we hear from you that it is all right; this policy has been in effect since about last December when you telephoned Jim [Babb] to that effect.

Mrs. O'Neill let me know that the restrictions she had imposed on the O'Neill manuscripts did not permit us to lend them for exhibition elsewhere. When the American Academy of Arts and Letters asked to borrow items for an O'Neill exhibition they were planning in 1956, soon after the publication of *Long Day's Journey,* I had to inform my friend, Mrs. Matthew Josephson, the librarian, accordingly. When the academy applied to the Princeton Library (which had been given the same instructions by Mrs. O'Neill), they received a different reply. The Princeton librarian explained to Carlotta that after his telephone conversation with her he had checked with his staff to determine whether any of them had promised the Academy of Arts and Letters to lend material for its O'Neill exhibition. He found that the curator of the Theater Collection had indeed made an implied commitment to cooperate.

Although the librarian was of course eager to honor all of Mrs. O'Neill's wishes, she would appreciate that he was obliged to follow the spirit at least of any agreements made on the library's behalf. But he assured her that Princeton would never lend any important materials to anyone under conditions that might result in their damage.

Mrs. O'Neill sent the letter to me with a comment:

> The enclosed rather startled me—I could hardly believe one in such a position could be so tactless! (To put it mildly!) If Gene were here he'd ask to see the manuscripts—& tear them up! So life goes!

It was not always clear exactly how restrictions were to be applied to the manuscript materials. In an article, "The Eugene O'Neill Collection at Yale," contributed to the *O'Neill Newsletter* in 1985, I referred to this early era:

> The period during which some of this [restricted] material had been used gave rise to rumors that we were playing favorites, allowing some scholars to see things denied to others. The charge was made in print by Tom Olsson in his book on O'Neill and the Royal Swedish Theatre,* but it didn't particularly bother me: we did our best to carry out to the letter Mrs. O'Neill's current instructions as long as she lived.

A response from Olsson was printed in a subsequent issue of the periodical:

> The statement which Dr. Gallup refers to must be a note ... in Chapter Five of my book ... , which ... reads as follows [*in English translation*]:
>
>> L. Josephson did, late in the summer of 1952, research at Yale, and was one of the first scholars outside the USA given permission to study the O'Neill Work Diary. But when it came to taking notes from this object the rules were very rigorous: such notes were not permitted to leave the Library. <The O'Neill Collection was at that time in the Main Library of Yale, i.e., the Sterling Library; the Beinecke Library was opened only some ten years later.> L. Josephson got the privilege, through Dr. Gallup, to make notes from his own notes.

Dr. Lennart Josephson himself told me about this incident ... . [He] ... is, unfortunately, unable to write a statement for the Newsletter himself; for many years he has been in the hospital with an incurable brain tumor and is incapable of any mental action. He told me, when I was still at work

---

*Tom J. A. Olsson, *O'Neill och Dramaten* ([Stockholm]Akademilitteratur [1977]).

on my dissertation [*in December 1977*] that he found the rigorous rules a bit peculiar. That is all.

When I did research at Yale's Beinecke Library, I was received in a very friendly manner and was given all the help possible by Dr. Gallup and his staff. I worked there for a total of six months ... in 1974 and 1975. I still consider the Beinecke Library as the foremost source of O'Neill material and Dr. Gallup a personal friend from those years.

My explanation followed in the same issue of the *Newsletter:*

The passage I was referring to in Tom Olsson's book was not the one he cites but another in the "English Summary" on page 169:

> This work <Martin Lamm's *Det moderna dramat*> was published in a new, revised edition in 1964, edited by another important O'Neill critic in Sweden, Lennart Josephson, who was one of the first *outside of Gallup's circle at Yale* to gain access to O'Neill's Work Diary of 1924–1943 ... (*italics mine*)

I took this to mean that Olsson was accusing me of making the "Work Diary" available to an inner group of my Yale friends, while I was keeping it from most other non-Yale O'Neill scholars.

The "Work Diary" *was* seen, as Olsson explains, by Josephson, but only after Mrs. O'Neill had given her permission. She explained that we were to allow Josephson to take notes but not to copy O'Neill's actual words. On the day preceding Josephson's departure from New Haven, he showed me his notes and I was surprised to find that they included extensive quotations, especially from drafts of the Cycle plays. I telephoned Mrs. O'Neill to report that Josephson had apparently misunderstood her instructions. She insisted that we not allow him to take the notes away with him in their then present form. Josephson's landlady here in New Haven [*Mrs. J. W. D. Ingersoll, who had been my landlady when I was in Graduate School at Yale*] later told me that he had stayed up most of the night before his departure making notes on his notes so that he could obey the letter of Mrs. O'Neill's directive. This explains Olsson's phrase "to make notes from his own notes" and probably accounts for Josephson's finding "the rigorous rules <of Carlotta Monterey O'Neill> a bit peculiar."

It is highly ironic that Olsson should have imagined a circle of my friends at Yale as having access to restricted O'Neill material. It was a source of great disappointment to me during my 33 years as Curator of the Yale Collection of American Literature that, except for Norman Holmes Pearson, who served as conduit for the early O'Neill gifts to Yale and had no need of permission from me to examine manuscript material, outside scholars invariably showed far more interest in the archives of contemporary writers than members of the Yale faculty. Indeed, in all those years, I can recall only one Yale scholar who worked at all extensively with the O'Neill manuscripts, and he certainly never saw the "Work Diary."

Although the most important unpublished material in the O'Neill collection at Yale was not available for use by scholars during the twenty-five-year restricted period, 1953–78, our resources for research were still substantial and certainly extensive enough to satisfy the requirements of most students of the dramatist's achievement. The O'Neills, between them, had preserved typescripts and proofs, with manuscript annotations *in ink,* documenting the changes made in the course of a particular play's production and publication. Besides all this material relating to the later plays given to Yale by the O'Neills, the plays that had been produced by the Theatre Guild were represented in that archive, also at Yale, by various scripts, often containing variant annotations. In that collection too was one of the most important of the O'Neill correspondences. The Guild's albums of clippings covered not only the early production history of each O'Neill play, but also the later tours and revivals. Because the O'Neills also subscribed to a clipping agency, the performance history of most of the O'Neill plays was well documented at Yale. Both the O'Neill and the Theatre Guild collections contained extensive selections of photographs. Over the years, friends and associates like Harry Weinberger, Dudley Nichols, and Robert Sisk gave their O'Neill letters (those to the firm of Richard Madden, O'Neill's agent, were included in the O'Neill gift), and additional letters and manuscript items were purchased—and not just on the Eugene O'Neill Fund. A great deal of important O'Neill material was thus not only available during the years 1953–78, but also widely used by scholars from all over the world.

THE EUGENE O'NEILL FUND
1956–1980

In one of her early letters to me, on 4 July 1954, Mrs. O'Neill had written:

my dream is *(somehow)* to create a Eugene O'Neill Fund for the furtherance of the plays … . But, I do have to live to be able to do it!

Her dream played an important part in her decision, less than a year later, to give to the Yale Library publication rights in *Long Day's Journey into Night*. In *Pigeons on the Granite* I discussed her reasons for turning away from Random House as publisher of the play. Even after forty years, there is still an anti–Carlotta faction that holds her guilty of having violated her husband's instructions in permitting Yale University to arrange with its press for publication of a play that he had originally intended not be made public until twenty-five years after his death. I see no reason to doubt the truth of Carlotta's statements (reported in *Pigeons*) that

After Gene, Jr.'s suicide, O'Neill told ... [her] that it had really been out of consideration for his son that he had set the twenty-five-year restriction on publication of the play and there was no longer any reason for withholding it.

and

When she worried about their financial future, he comforted her by saying that *Long Day's Journey* was their "ace in the hole" and could be counted on as a last resort.

It is abundantly clear that Eugene O'Neill was not the most considerate of husbands: he could easily have altered his instructions to Random House concerning the typescript of the play he had entrusted to them. In any case, even Carlotta's enemies agree that the release of *Long Day's Journey into Night* for publication in 1956 and its production in that same year, first in Sweden, and then in the United States, played a significant part in the revival of O'Neill's reputation and in the world's recognition of him as America's most important playwright.

In June 1955 Jim Babb and I had drafted an announcement of Mrs. O'Neill's gift to the Yale Library. It was read and approved by her, and released for the morning papers of 21 June:

New Haven, Conn., June 20:—Yale University announced today that Carlotta Monterey O'Neill, widow of the Nobel-Prize-winning playwright Eugene O'Neill, has given to the University the American and Canadian publication rights of Mr. O'Neill's unpublished play "Long Day's Journey Into Night."

The Yale University Press will publish the new play next February 20, 1956.

It was from Yale that Eugene O'Neill received an honorary Doctor of

Letters degree in 1926, the only honorary degree he ever accepted. He received the Nobel Prize for Literature in 1936, and the Pulitzer Prize three times, first in 1920 for his first long play "Beyond the Horizon," again in 1922 for "Anna Christie," and the third time in 1928 for "Strange Interlude."

The Yale Library has owned for several years the original manuscript and a number of later typewritten drafts of "Long Day's Journey Into Night," given also by Carlotta Monterey O'Neill as part of a large collection of manuscripts, photographs, and printed material relating to Eugene O'Neill's plays and their production in America and abroad.

The deed of gift by which the rights become Yale's provides that income from the publication of the play is to be used for the upkeep of the Eugene O'Neill Collection in the Library, for the purchase of books on the drama, and for Eugene O'Neill scholarships in the Yale Drama School.

The fund was actually set up less than a year later. The Yale University Press, on 8 May 1956, forwarded to the library its share of the advance payment from the Book of the Month Club for use of *Long Day's Journey into Night* as an alternate choice, and informed us that the club's sales of its edition already totaled 17,000 copies. In his letter of acknowledgment to the press, Jim Babb gave some further details, agreed upon with Mrs. O'Neill, of the purposes for which the fund would be used:

"First: For the maintenance and preservation of the Eugene O'Neill Collection, now lodged in the Yale University Library, and for the addition to that collection and to the Library of the Yale School of Drama of important books and manuscripts in the field of dramatic literature, in the discretion of the Librarian of the Yale University Library, as available, up to $4,000.00 annually.

"Second: For the granting of scholarships to be known as 'Eugene O'Neill Scholarships' to worthy students of playwriting; and

"Third: For such other purposes connected with Yale University Library or the Yale School of Drama as Yale may determine."

Mrs. O'Neill subsequently gave to the library publication rights in the remaining unpublished plays: *A Touch of the Poet,* published by Yale University Press in 1957; *Hughie* (the only completed unit of the one-act play series, "By Way of Obit."), published in 1959; and *More Stately Mansions,* published in the version shortened from O'Neill's partly revised script by Karl Ragnar Gierow, in 1964. Royalties from all these plays also were added to the principal of the Eugene O'Neill Fund.

There was no problem about the handling of the fund in the office of the university treasurer so long as Jim Babb was around to keep an eagle eye on the monthly reports. But not long after his retirement and subsequent early death, we discovered that the royalties being paid by the Yale Press on *Long Day's Journey* and the other O'Neill plays were being reported not as additions to the principal but as ordinary income. To treat them in this way would obviously mean that the memorial fund would cease to grow beyond its current amount and the O'Neill scholarships in the School of Drama, for instance, would never provide the substantial aid that had been intended. We protested to the treasurer's office. Because the accountants there much preferred not to have to handle a constantly changing principal, they obstinately argued against the procedure outlined in the original establishment of the fund. Eventually it became necessary to appeal to the provost of the university to direct the office of the treasurer to treat the Yale Press royalties as additions to principal.

One of our first important purchases on the income from the Eugene O'Neill Fund came in 1959. Although under the terms of the divorce settlement, Agnes Boulton was required to return to O'Neill all manuscript material relating to his work, she held back a good many items. Gradually, even with Carlotta very much alive, Agnes began quietly to sell some of this material. Her third husband. "Mack" Kaufman, had a friendly relationship with the Seven Gables Bookshop in New York, and it was through its agency for the most part that the O'Neill items were sold. Although some of them went to C. Waller Barrett for the University of Virginia Library, those that obviously belonged in the Yale collection were offered to us. And by this means we were able to acquire what was actually the original manuscript of O'Neill's dramatic adaptation of Coleridge's "The Ancient Mariner." He had prepared it for the Provincetown Playhouse in New York, where it opened on 6 April 1924 and was given a total of twenty-nine performances. Although he apparently thought well enough of the experiment to consider allowing it to be revived under the auspices of the Federal Theater in 1937, there seem to be no later references to the play and, save for some brief excerpts in the *New York Times* ("Coleridge and O'Neill," 13 April 1924), the text was not printed during O'Neill's lifetime.

In 1960, Mrs. O'Neill kindly allowed us to publish the Coleridge adaptation in the *Yale University Library Gazette*. The manuscript was described in an introductory note:

Using a copy of *The Rime of the Ancient Mariner and Christabel* (New York and London, G. P. Putnam's Sons, The Knickerbocker Press [n.d.]) purchased from the Gotham Book Mart, O'Neill pasted in at the beginning two blank leaves and on them in red ink wrote his opening stage directions. In the text of the poem he added further directions in the margins in red, underlined occasional passages for use as supplementary stage directions, indicated speakers' initials in blue or red, and cancelled in red the passages of the poem to be omitted. He apparently intended the prose glosses to be ignored except when, as in a number of instances, he underlined parts of these in red. The excerpts printed in the *Times* are prefaced by a statement that "O'Neill has added no spoken word to 'The Ancient Mariner' in making his 'dramatic arrangement' of that poem." Although this is not strictly true, the additional dialogue amounts altogether to fewer than a dozen words, plus an occasional repetition of a phrase from the poem, and O'Neill's writing may be said to have been confined to stage directions.

Another acquisition facilitated in part by the fund was the correspondence between O'Neill and theater critic and producer Kenneth Macgowan. The two men had formed a partnership with stage designer Robert Edmond Jones in 1923 to run the Experimental Theatre at the Provincetown Playhouse. Although their professional association in this venture lasted less than three years, Macgowan and O'Neill remained close friends. Macgowan was one of the few links O'Neill maintained with the outside world during the months after he left his wife and two young children in Bermuda in November 1927 and until he and Carlotta Monterey were married in Paris in July 1929. Their joint correspondence with Macgowan continued until 1951. Fortunately he kept the letters, preserved carbons of some of his own, and, in 1962, through Jake Zeitlin of the firm of Zeitlin & Ver Brugge in Los Angeles, offered to sell us the collection. There were some ninety-five letters and eleven telegrams from O'Neill, dating from 1921 to about 1950; twenty-one letters and a telegram from Carlotta, and a single letter from Agnes Boulton; along with thirty-one carbons of Macgowan's own letters and telegrams. This was material that obviously belonged at Yale, and the O'Neill Fund, with some supplementary help from other sources, made the purchase possible. (Some weeks later, Jake Zeitlin wrote to ask our frank opinion as to whether the price had been fair: Macgowan's friends had apparently assured him—as friends occasionally do in such cases—that he could have got a better price elsewhere.)

Carlotta was delighted that Macgowan had offered the letters to us and that the O'Neill Fund had been instrumental in enabling us to buy them. She agreed at once to our proposal that the library publish the correspondence, any income from the publication to be added to the fund. I typed transcripts of all the O'Neill letters, but could not find time to do the editorial research necessary to ready them for publication. When Jackson Bryer, an industrious young English professor at the University of Maryland, came to New Haven seeking some O'Neill project to work on, I turned over to him my copies of the letters and secured from Travis Bogard, professor of dramatic art at the University of California, Berkeley, his promise to write a series of introductory essays. The Yale Press published the resulting book in 1982 as *"The Theatre We Worked For": The Letters of Eugene O'Neill to Kenneth Macgowan*. It contained this much too generous statement:

The editors wish to acknowledge their gratitude to Dr. Donald Gallup, former Curator of the Collection of American Literature at the Beinecke Rare Book and Manuscript Library of Yale University. This book was his conception, and he has been a faithful collaborator at every step. The Library graciously gave permission to publish the manuscript materials.

It was the Eugene O'Neill Fund that provided a major part of the support for the purchase of one of the important author's archives added to the Yale Collection of American Literature during the period of my curatorship—that of Barrett H. Clark. He had written the first biography of O'Neill, published in 1926, and could claim the rare distinction of having received the cooperation of his subject: O'Neill corresponded with him over a number of years, and even read a set of proofs for the book, making extensive manuscript annotations for his benefit.

It was Croswell Bowen, Yale 1929, who brought the papers to our attention. He had had numerous meetings with Clark's widow while he was doing research—with the nominal assistance of Shane O'Neill—for *The Curse of the Misbegotten; a Tale of the House of O'Neill* (1959). Bowen persuaded Mrs. Clark that she should sell her husband's archive to Yale. He informed us in mid-December 1960 that she was willing to let us have the collection. She was then living in Briarcliff Manor, New York, but was on the point of moving; prompt action would be necessary.

I got in touch with her at once, and on 23 December picked up the papers, along with a good many books, mostly presentation copies from their authors. I warned Mrs. Clark that it would be difficult to arrive at a fair price for these manuscripts and letters: they were of course unique, and worth what the highest bidder felt he or she could afford to pay. Yale did not have sufficient funds to compete on the open market at current retail prices for such items. Because of the special treatment that we were willing to give the collection, she agreed to offer it to us at its wholesale value, understanding that this was roughly half the price at which she could reasonably expect to sell it at retail. She and I signed a formal agreement to this effect.

In order that there should be no undignified haggling about the actual price, our agreement specified that the entire collection would be appraised by an impartial bookseller acceptable to us both. Yale would either pay the amount established by him as the wholesale value of the archive or return it to her. The university would of course insure the materials while they were on deposit in New Haven.

I knew that the appraisal would be enormously facilitated by a detailed listing, and spent my entire Christmas vacation that year in compiling a catalogue. This extended to thirty-four typed double-spaced pages. John Kohn of the Seven Gables Bookshop in New York had been agreed upon as appraiser, and he did his customary prompt and efficient job. The amount he arrived at as the wholesale value seemed to us a fair one. Finding the money was made less difficult because of Mrs. Clark's wish that our payments be spread over three years. Relying upon income from the O'Neill Fund during that period, plus miscellaneous amounts from other sources, the library committed itself to the purchase.

Negotiations, complicated by Mrs. Clark's ill health, dragged on for six and a half years. In 1963, the boxes containing the Clark materials were transferred along with the Yale Collection of American Literature to their new home in the Beinecke Rare Book and Manuscript Library. Bowen had taken upon himself the role of Mrs. Clark's agent in the sale, and my detailed listing of the contents of the archive made it easy for him to approach two other libraries—those of the University of North Carolina at Chapel Hill, and the University of Virginia. Each offered some five thousand dollars more than the price arrived at with Yale.

Finally, on 5 June 1967, Mrs. Clark, now living in Hagerstown, Maryland, decided that, in spite of the two higher bids, she wanted her husband's collection to stay at Yale. But she asked us to raise our "final" offer by two thousand dollars and to secure specific permission from Paul Green to make his 292 letters and 23 telegrams, included in the collection, available to our readers.

Quick conferences with Fritz Liebert, the Beinecke head, and James Tanis, the university librarian, confirmed that we would pay the new amount. (In the years during which the Clark materials had been here on deposit, similar items had been increasing in value on the auction market.) My letter to Paul Green brought forth a welcome response:

I am delighted that Mrs. Barrett H. Clark has sent the papers of her husband to your university. As to my letters in the collection, ... I have no objection whatever to anyone's consulting them. No doubt there are personal matters in them, but what the heck!—all of us make our records on earth such as they are and they are irrevocable anyway and why try to control them after the fact. So, so far as I am concerned they are wide open.

With best greetings and regards.

The transaction was at last completed to the satisfaction of all parties in July 1967, and the first payment, half from the O'Neill Fund and half from Beinecke funds, was made that month. A second payment came a year later, and the final payment in July 1969. (Sadly,

Mrs. Clark did not live to receive that last instalment, and it was turned over to her children.) Thanks to the O'Neill Fund, the importance of the Yale Collection of American Literature for research in the field of the drama had been substantially increased. Besides the materials by O'Neill (54 letters, 5 telegrams, a typescript, and corrected proofs) and Green, the Clark papers included extensive correspondences and miscellaneous manuscript materials of such other American dramatists as Maxwell Anderson (17 letters), Rachel Field (20 letters), Sidney Howard (86 letters and 8 telegrams), Elmer Rice (42 letters), and Lynn Riggs (163 letters, 19 telegrams, and 12 original manuscripts and typescripts, including "Green Grow the Lilacs," on which the musical "Oklahoma!" was based). And there were important papers of British and European dramatists, like George Moore (24 letters) and Ernst Toller (38 letters), as well as an extensive collection of autographs of theater personalities.

By good luck, one of my students in bibliography at that time was very much interested in the American theater. When I suggested that he write a paper on the Clark collection, he welcomed the assignment. "The Barrett H. Clark Collection," by Richard Stoddard, appeared in the *Yale University Library Gazette* for January 1971.

At about this same time, we acquired, also on the O'Neill Fund, additional material formerly held by Agnes Boulton, who had died in 1968. By an odd coincidence, the news of Carlotta O'Neill's death reached me on 18 November 1970 while I was at the Waldorf-Astoria in New York collecting this final group of O'Neill manuscript materials being sold to Yale by Agnes's executors. There were some 270 letters to her and O'Neill from various writers, including John Peale Bishop, Hart Crane, Lord Dunsany, St. John Ervine, and Waldo Frank, along with a single letter to O'Neill from his brother James, and another from his mother. (Although, after he left Agnes, O'Neill continued to keep important incoming letters—in his *Work Diary* he refers now and then to filing such correspondence—they seem to have disappeared. I asked Carlotta more than once what had happened to them, but she never gave me a satisfactory explanation.) That final group of manuscripts from Agnes

Boulton's estate contained, most importantly, the "Scribbling" diary O'Neill had kept in 1925—the only one that has survived. It was incorporated as an appendix to the O'Neill *Work Diary, 1924–1943,* published by the library in 1981.

THE O'NEILL PROPERTIES
1972–1980

Carlotta's will provided for the establishment of the Eugene O'Neill Trust—its assets the O'Neill writings—operated by her lawyers, Cadwalader, Wickersham & Taft, for the eventual benefit of Yale University. Inasmuch as changes in the tax laws in 1969 had made the income of such private trusts taxable, Cadwalader dissolved the trust and turned the O'Neill properties over to Yale effective 31 December 1971.

Eugene O'Neill in his will had left all of his "right, title, and interest" in his writings to Carlotta; with the dissolution of the trust, the writings became Yale's property. But the situation was not quite that simple. In 1956, the U. S. Supreme Court had decided that a widow and any surviving children share in the copyright renewal term of a literary work as a group, the children only receiving the renewal term if the widow dies prior to its commencement. Eugene O'Neill, Jr. had committed suicide in 1950. Inasmuch as Shane O'Neill and Oona O'Neill Chaplin outlived their father, they began in 1956 to share with their stepmother in some of the O'Neill plays; because they survived her, they would become sole owners of two plays in 1973 and 1974.

In summary, the situation was this:

(1) The plays that had been copyrighted by O'Neill and had had their copyrights renewed during his lifetime passed to Mrs. O'Neill under his will, belonged to her exclusively, and now belonged to Yale. (Most of the plays were in this group.)

(2) The plays copyrighted by O'Neill but copyrights of which had been renewed after his death were owned, after the Supreme Court decision in 1956, jointly by Mrs. O'Neill and her step-children and were now owned jointly by Yale and the children. (These plays

were *Ah, Wilderness!*, *Days Without End*, *Dynamo*, *Mourning Becomes Electra*, *Strange Interlude*, and *The Iceman Cometh*.)

(3) The plays copyrighted by O'Neill as unpublished dramatic compositions in 1945 and 1946 respectively were owned by Mrs. O'Neill exclusively and controlled by Yale from 1972, but would become the property of the O'Neill children when their copyrights were renewed on 3 August 1973 and 4 January 1974 respectively. (These plays were *A Moon for the Misbegotten* and *A Touch of the Poet*.)

(4) The plays copyrighted by Mrs. O'Neill were hers and became Yale's exclusively. (These plays were *Hughie*, *Long Day's Journey into Night*, and *More Stately Mansions*.)

As of 17 November 1970 (the date of Carlotta's death), her executors and testamentary trustees had entered into an agreement with the O'Neill children concerning the six plays they had owned jointly with their stepmother. Essentially a reaffirmation of a similar agreement drawn up as a result of the Supreme Court decision in 1956, this provided that Herbert F. Jacoby of the firm of Schwartz, Burns, Mermelstein, Lesser & Jacoby should act as attorney-in-fact for the O'Neill children; that neither they nor Carlotta would enter into an agreement affecting any of the six plays without the written consent of the others; and that proceeds derived from exploitation of any of those six plays should be divided equally. (This agreement, which affected Yale from 1972, applied only to the United States. Rights to the six plays—and to *A Moon for the Misbegotten* and *A Touch of the Poet*—as to territories outside the United States, and income from those plays as to those territories belonged to Mrs. O'Neill alone and now belonged to Yale.)

Inasmuch as I had been one of Mrs. O'Neill's three administrators during her last years and was thoroughly familiar with her views, the librarian, Jim Babb, and the treasurer, John Ecklund, asked me to continue to make decisions concerning O'Neill matters for Yale, in consultation with Spencer Miller (a classmate) in the treasurer's office, where all O'Neill contracts were signed.

We at once considered selecting a literary agent to handle the complications that would inevitably arise in dealing with the O'Neill properties. A meeting was arranged with the firm of Brandt & Brandt and their subsidiary, the Robert A. Freedman Dramatic Agency, who had long served as literary and dramatic agents for the Thornton Wilder writings. Carol Brandt and William Koppelman of that firm met with Jacquelyn Swords of Cadwalader, Wickersham and Taft, Judson Pearl of Simpson, Thacher and Bartlett (Yale's counsel in New York), and me on 25 January 1972. Because royalties from the late plays published by the Yale Press would of course continue to be paid directly to the Yale Library and would therefore generate no income for an agent, Carol Brandt said that Brandt & Brandt would not be interested in the appointment; and because all the O'Neill plays were subject to "specific long-term contractual encumbrances" so far as their development for moving-pictures and television was concerned, Bill Koppelman felt that, for the time being, the Freedman Dramatic Agency would also not wish to act. It was consequently agreed that Cadwalader, Wickersham and Taft would continue as agent for Yale, as they had been for Mrs. O'Neill and her estate ever since the retirement of Jane Rubin of the Richard Madden firm, O'Neill's agent for many years,

On 15 February 1972, I outlined for Spencer Miller the procedure proposed for future operations:

Inasmuch as Brandt & Brandt ... have declined to take over ... the handling of the Eugene O'Neill properties at least until certain outstanding legal complications concerning them are cleared up, and since any other literary/dramatic agents would presumably make the same decision, we have asked Cadwalader, Wickersham & Taft to continue to act on Yale's behalf ... . Decisions concerning policy will be made by the Curator, Yale Collection of American Literature (in accordance with principles established by Mrs. O'Neill and after consultation with the appropriate individuals at Yale). Cadwalader, Wickersham & Taft have been urged to press for the earliest possible solution to the various legal problems now encumbering the O'Neill properties. Simpson, Thacher & Bartlett as Yale's legal representatives in New York will act as liaison between Yale and Cadwalader, Wickersham & Taft on technical legal matters. Legal documents will be prepared by Cadwalader, Wickersham & Taft for the signature of the Associate Treasurer, Yale University, and forwarded through Simpson, Thacher & Bartlett to the Curator, Yale Collection of American Literature.

Cadwalader, Wickersham & Taft will remit to the Curator, Yale Collection of American Literature, all royalties received on outstanding contracts for the O'Neill properties and on contracts subsequently negotiated by them with notation of any amounts in which the O'Neill children have a two-thirds interest ... and Yale will pay to Herbert Jacoby as attorney the amounts representing this interest. After any such payments have been made, sums so received by Yale will be credited to the principal of the Carlotta Monterey and Eugene Gladstone O'Neill Memorial Fund. ...

It is considered appropriate in accordance with the terms of Mrs. O'Neill's will that the income from the Carlotta Monterey and Eugene Gladstone O'Neill Memorial Fund be apportioned as follows:

(1) One third for the maintenance and preservation of and for additions to the Eugene O'Neill collection in the Collection of American Literature, Beinecke Rare Book and Manuscript Library, and for subsidizing projects for publication of O'Neill materials that may not be commercially feasible.

(2) One third for the granting of scholarships, to be known as the Eugene O'Neill Scholarships, to worthy students of playwriting in the Yale School of Drama.

(3) One third for the addition of important books and manuscripts in the field of dramatic literature to the Library of the School of Drama and to the Yale University Library (including the Beinecke Rare Book and Manuscript Library).

Royalties received from the Yale University Press for the Eugene O'Neill plays published by the Press will continue to be paid directly to Yale and credited to the principal of the Eugene O'Neill Memorial Fund established in 1956. ...

Our failure to interest an agent in handling the O'Neill properties was chiefly due to separate contractual agreements that had been entered into, the first by Mrs. O'Neill herself in June 1961; the second, five years later, by the then agent for the plays, Jane Rubin of the Richard Madden firm.

In 1961 Mrs. O'Neill had signed a contract with Ely Landau, a producer, for moving-picture and television productions of all the plays, beginning with *Long Day's Journey into Night*. She had high hopes for the enterprise by which, according to Landau, versions of the plays would be available for use at colleges and other educational institutions throughout the world. The grandiose project was to be guided by a committee, consisting of Landau, his righthand man, and Mrs. O'Neill herself.

The plan came to grief in its very early stages. The committee met in Carlotta's apartment at Carlton House to discuss the casting of *Long Day's Journey* for moving-picture production. She was very decidedly opposed to Landau's idea that Katharine Hepburn should be engaged to play the part of Mary Tyrone. Whereupon, Landau called for a vote of the committee and ruled that because Mrs. O'Neill's was the only negative vote, the ayes had it. Disillusioned with Landau, Carlotta attempted to have the contract cancelled, but to no avail. The moving-picture, directed by Sidney Lumet, with musical score by André Previn, was made the following year with Miss Hepburn in the role of Mary, Sir Ralph Richardson as James Tyrone, Jason Robards, Jr., as James, Jr., and Dean Stockwell as Edmund. For various complicated reasons, the entire project later faltered, and Landau's interests in all the plays except *Long Day's Journey* and *The Iceman Cometh* were reassigned to Mrs. O'Neill in 1967. (The two excepted plays came under Yale's control twelve years later.)

In spite of Mrs. O'Neill's difficulties with Landau, Jane Rubin, acting as agent for the O'Neill interests (but without consulting Mrs. O'Neill's lawyers) on 12 July 1966 signed a letter agreement with Dan Curtis Productions, granting an exclusive sixty-day option to acquire television rights to any O'Neill play that Curtis might choose. Once he exercised his option, all the plays were to be kept off the market until his rights expired, "four years after the date of first telecast of any play hereunder." Because there was no indication of when that first telecast had to take place, the effect was completely to frustrate exploitation of the plays for television for an indefinite period.

In ways too tedious and unimportant to detail here, one Santangelo wound up as the ultimate assignee of the Curtis letter. Cadwalader, Wickersham and Taft were at last able to arrange a settlement with him in May 1973. This granted him Yale's right, title, and interest in *A Moon for the Misbegotten* for the balance of the original term of United States copyright (which expired in August of that year). The play then became, in the United States, the exclusive property of the O'Neill children. Outside the United States, the play remained Yale's property, thus enabling Yale to share in any arrangements affecting television rights to that play in foreign countries.

The other play involved in the Santangelo settlement was *The Hairy Ape,* then in its copyright renewal term, which expired in 1977. Thus Yale became free at last, in 1973, to exploit all its O'Neill plays for television except—for the final four years of its term of copyright—*The Hairy Ape,* and except *Long Day's Journey* and *The Iceman Cometh,* which came under Yale's control six years later.

Cadwalader, Wickersham and Taft continued to act as agent throughout the remainder of my term as curator. We relied upon that firm to make all contracts, distinguish between our and the children's interests in the plays, take responsibility for any requisite consultation with their counsel, and indicate, when they forwarded payments to us, the correct amounts, if any, to be paid to Jacoby for the children.

It wasn't always just the plays that concerned us. In February 1974, Jack Swords, of the Cadwalader firm, forwarded to me a bill from Forest Hills Cemetery in Jamaica Plain, Massachusetts, for the maintenance of the grave of Eugene and Carlotta Monterey O'Neill, explaining that it had been passed back and forth in their office for some time. He assumed that Yale University would wish to consider taking on "a good part" of this charge, with any balance coming, perhaps, from Mrs. O'Neill's grandson, Gerald Stram. He didn't know where else they could turn except to Yale.

I made a recommendation in April, but the treasurer resisted taking on a commitment without a time limit, like this one, and I wrote Jack:

> Before I pursue the matter further here, I'd like to sound you out on one point: why wouldn't it be appropriate, especially now that Oona and Shane are getting substantial income from both *[A] Moon for the Misbegotten* and *A Touch of the Poet,* to turn to them through … Jacoby as a source for part of the charge for the upkeep of their father's and step-mother's grave? I daresay Mr. Jacoby would want to consult Oona [Lady Chaplin] before he gave you an answer.

Jacoby did consult Oona, who was acting as guardian for her brother Shane, and she promptly agreed to assume the entire cost of the upkeep of the grave.

O'Neill's completed, but only partly revised Cycle play, *More Stately Mansions*, had been published in the shortened version prepared by Karl Ragnar Gierow in 1964. Although Mrs. O'Neill had allowed Jose Quintero to make his own version of the play for his 1967 production, starring Ingrid Bergman and Colleen Dewhurst, I felt that in fairness to Gierow and the time and effort he had expended on it, this play should exist only in his version, at least until the end of the 25-year restricted period in 1978. But another adaptation of it was proposed in mid-1974 by the great Austrian actress Elisabeth Bergner. She wrote me from London on 15 July, explaining that she had been acting the role of Deborah Harford in Germany over a period of three years, making cuts, especially in the first three scenes of the Gierow version, in an attempt to improve its effectiveness on the stage. Peter Diamond, manager of the Edinburgh Festival, had commissioned Jim Sanders to prepare a revised English version in time to present a production starring Ms. Bergner. But the script was not ready in time, and Ms. Bergner decided to try it out in Greenwich, where it would be directed by Vivian Matalon. The script finally delivered by Sanders proved a disappointment to both Ms. Bergner and Mr. Matalon. They proposed to use instead another version based on the German text that Ms. Bergner had used, but with further drastic cuts in the second half of the play, and sent a copy to Yale for our approval.

I answered Ms. Bergner's letter on the 18th:

The script of "More Stately Mansions" arrived ... yesterday and I read it last night. I certainly found nothing to object to in your first three scenes, but was very much disappointed to find that the last half of the Gierow version had been so drastically—and so obviously—cut. Now from your letter I know the circumstances and realize that you understand that such drastic amputation is not a solution fair to O'Neill and what he was trying to do in the play. (The play as presented in New York suffered of course from the same harsh treatment of the second half, compounded by Quintero's use of the linking scene with "A Touch of the Poet" as opening of the play—in order to build up the part of Sara—and the consequent necessity to condense even more radically.)

We at Yale have the greatest respect for you as an artist and particularly as interpreter of the role of Deborah and wish to cooperate with you in your attempt to make O'Neill's unfinished script into a play that "works" on the modern stage. ... Obviously the trial-and-error method is essential to the eventual realization of a play that will be worthy of O'Neill's name. My only suggestion is that you might write or telephone Karl Ragnar Gierow at the Swedish Academy in Stockholm. He, too, is devoted to the play, worked with it over a period of several years, and would, I know, have sympathy for what you are trying to do. (The version we actually used for our publication was merely the most successful of several that he had experimented with for the Royal Swedish Theatre.)

It seems to us that if it is not possible to find a solution that will preserve O'Neill's own words, however cut down, then the adaptation must await the expiration of the copyright period and a complete reworking of O'Neill's materials by someone who will take full responsibility for whatever he [or she] does with O'Neill's text. ...

With all best wishes to you and for the eventual success of your production.

Unfortunately, differences between Elisabeth Bergner and Vivian Matalon led to the cancellation of plans to present the play at the Greenwich Theatre. (In 1988, Martha Bower published the full typescript, and that was the text printed in that same year in the O'Neill *Complete Plays,* three volumes edited by Travis Bogard for the Library of America.)

Later in 1974, problems arose in connection with the one-act play *Hughie.* Yale had contracted for a production of the play in Chicago with Ben Gazzara in the principal role. When it met with success, the producer asked Yale to allow him to bring his production into New York. This conflicted with plans by Jason Robards and Jose Quintero (who had been responsible, the former as actor, the latter as director, for the original production of the play) to revive *Hughie* on Broadway. Robards was then acting in a successful revival in New York of *A Moon for the Misbegotten,* and had moving-picture commitments which meant that the Quintero-Robards production of *Hughie* could not be ready for at least two years. A good deal of pressure from both sides was brought to bear, with the eventual result that the play was revived in New York with Gazzara—to the bitter disappointment of both Quintero and Robards.

On 14 August 1974, while I was on vacation in Europe, Cadwalader, Wickersham and Taft telephoned William Feeney (who was now handling O'Neill matters in the office of the treasurer) to report that they had only just been informed of a plan to present *Hughie* in California in October for sixteen performances, with Jason Robards, for the benefit of a fund being raised for the purchase of Tao House, the O'Neills' residence in Contra Costa County from 1937 to 1944. Mr. Feeney said that Yale would not waive royalties on these performances. At the end of the month, after I had returned to my desk, Cadwalader telephoned to say that pressure to persuade Yale to change its mind on the royalty matter was continuing. They advised making some gesture in this direction. I agreed that Yale would waive its royalties on the opening-night performance (for which considerably higher prices were being charged). This decision was passed on by Cadwalader to the Robards group. Subsequently the firm telephoned to relay an inquiry from *Mrs.* Robards as to whether it would do any good for her to telephone Yale. I asked Cadwalader to inform her that it would not. On 29 September, Jason Robards himself addressed a one-and-a-half-page, single-spaced mailgram to President Kingman Brewster. This was a protest against the self-serving stinginess of Yale in refusing to cooperate with the campaign to save Tao House from the developers. Robards explained that all services that could legally be obtained through solicitation and volunteers (including hardened Hollywood press agents) had been donated so that the total profits from the production would be used for the sole purpose of purchasing the house. He and his group were merely asking that Yale forgo royalties for this benefit, but, he said, the request had fallen on deaf ears.

Considering Yale's refusal a personal insult and grossly unfair to those dedicated to the project, Robards would in future refuse to have anything to do with the O'Neill plays from which Yale derived royalties. He was sorry that he felt obliged to send this letter. Up to now he had regretted not having graduated from an excellent academic institution like Yale instead of the U. S. Navy, but not so much any more.

I prepared an argument for the information of the president:

It seems to us that the decision to waive royalties on only the first of the sixteen performances of "Hughie" is the correct one in view of these considerations:

(1) Waiving royalties on the opening-night performance is an entirely adequate gesture from Yale in cooperating with a worthy project.

(2) Waiving royalties on more than one and especially on so many as sixteen performances would establish a dangerous precedent. Yale would find it almost impossible to refuse subsequent similar requests from several other equally worthy O'Neill projects:

(a) The O'Neill Memorial Theater in Waterford, Conn. It is quite possible that the theater, although it is designed to present works by apprentice playwrights, might wish to give benefit productions of O'Neill plays if it could do so without payment of royalties.

(b) The O'Neill family home on Pequot Avenue in New London, Conn. This property was acquired a few years ago, the previous owner being given life tenancy. He has now died and a project is under way to restore and furnish the house as a museum. Benefits of some kind are almost inevitable.

(c) The O'Neill home "Casa Genotta" at Sea Island, Georgia. The O'Neills built this house and lived in it from 1932 to 1936. There Eugene O'Neill wrote "Ah, Wilderness!," "Days without End," and other plays. The movement on the West coast for Tao House may very well be met by an East coast movement for Casa Genotta. If so, benefits would again be almost inevitable.

(d) Several other O'Neill houses still exist, especially the Château Le Plessis near Tours in France, where "Mourning Becomes Electra" was written. European interest in O'Neill has always been strong and it is quite possible that the Château might be made into a shrine.

(3) Yale has an obligation to both O'Neills to do everything possible to support the O'Neill endowment funds, most of the growth of the principals of which may be expected to cease with the expiration of copyrights. This will occur in not more than twenty-eight years. Since the O'Neill funds are themselves used for charitable purposes at Yale, to waive all royalties for the California production of "Hughie" would be robbing Peter to pay Paul.

(4) Robards' threat to refuse to be associated with future productions of plays owned by Yale—including of course "Long Day's Journey into Night"—is probably not to be taken too seriously. It is consistent with the exaggerated, angry tone of his letter, which dismisses Yale's agreement to waive royalties on the opening-night performance as "lending a deaf ear" to his request.

President Brewster replied to Jason Robards on 7 November 1975:

Dear Mr. Robards:

I needed more information on "Hughie" before I was able to answer your mailgram. As I have been out of town a good deal my reply has been further delayed. I apologize.

I cannot change our agent's statement to you that Yale would waive royalty rights for the opening night performance of "Hughie." The terms of the O'Neill will charge Yale with the responsibility for maintaining the endowment funds, which obviously depend on royalty fees, and to use those funds for student aid in the Drama School, as well as maintenance of the O'Neill library collection. To forego fees for all performances would be inconsistent with our trusteeship of the O'Neill gift.

Since I am an admirer of your very great contributions to the theatre of the nation, I regret your resentment of Yale's position; but we cannot put other worthy O'Neill enterprises ahead of the purposes for which we were entrusted.

In 1977, Edward Albee acted in the role of whistle-blower for Yale. He had seen one of the performances of *Long Day's Journey* by the Center Theater Group at the Ahmanson Theatre in Los Angeles and had been so outraged at the "butcher shop cuts" made in the play that he reported them to Robert Brustein, dean of the School of Drama. Brustein alerted Cadwalader, Wickersham & Taft to what had happened. Although the final performance had already taken place, Sean Connor at Cadwalader wrote to Charles Mooney of the Center Theater Group on 5 May. He asked Mooney to supply a copy of the stage production script so that the extent of the deletions made by the group could be determined. Edward Albee had reported that the cuts had reduced the running time by approximately an hour and thirty minutes. Had Cadwalader known that such extensive deletions were being planned, permission to stage the O'Neill play would not have been granted.

There was apparently no response at all from the Center Theater Group for almost a year. A telephone call then elicited an answer, on 4 May 1978. Because the agreement with Cadwalader to produce *Long Day's Journey* did not contain a "no cut" provision, the group felt that they were at liberty to make deletions. Because they no longer had a copy of their prompt script, they could not accurately determine the exact extent of the cuts that were made. But they assured Cadwalader that, as they remembered their production, the deletions were not nearly so substantial as Mr. Albee had reported. The letter was signed by the "production coordinator" for the group, Michael Grossman.

The ultimate outcome of the matter was reflected in Sean Connor's report of 24 May:

> As you so correctly said, this serves as an unfortunate lesson for all of us to be careful of even what appears to be a first class theater group. Certainly none of us would have expected a responsible group to make substantial cuts without permission. Although the Center Theater Group should undoubtedly not be dealt with again, I do believe any benefits which might be derived from legal action against it would be outweighed by the expense involved. Let us hope, at least, that Mr. Grossman is correct in his assertion that the cuts were not as substantial as had been reported to us by Mr. Albee, although I see no reason to question the keenness of Mr. Albee's powers of observation.

In that same year, 1977, I had reluctantly consented to the request of the Franklin Library to include four O'Neill plays in its series, The Great Books of the Twentieth Century, because the plays were, for the most part, controlled by Lady Chaplin (Shane O'Neill had died in June). Some months afterward, Franklin Library demanded additional distribution rights for its edition. Although I initially refused Yale's permission, the pressures became so great that I did finally yield. But I indulged in a (lengthy) protest to Sean Connor at Cadwalader's:

> Yale's refusal to allow the Franklin Library to publish an edition of O'Neill plays controlled by Yale had nothing to do with impairment of O'Neill's reputation and image and little to do with possible competition between the Franklin Library ... and ... Random House. Our objection was to the Franklin Library, its ... advertising (describing as "rare" and "limited", editions of many thousands of copies), and its harmful effect upon collectors and booklovers generally. The pressure brought to bear upon us to authorize the original edition requested was extremely distasteful (I received personal telephone calls from three people at Random House, including [*the Vice-President*] Mr. Klopfer himself—and I believe that you were bothered with at least that many 'phone calls; I had long letters also from Klopfer, from my friend Carlos Baker, an adviser to the Franklin Library editions, and even from the U.S. Bicentennial Commission on the grounds that the Franklin Library had cooperated so admirably with the Commission—I assume in producing medals, another snare for the unwary buyer). The current threat to remove the O'Neill

volume from their series unless they are allowed to distribute to countries specifically excluded from the original agreement is, to me, another instance of this high-pressure campaign. Inasmuch as Yale gave its consent to the O'Neill volume only because two of the plays were, for the U.S., entirely controlled by Mr. Jacoby's client and the two others chiefly controlled by her, I am most reluctant to yield to the Franklin Library's demand. I don't think there is the slightest possibility that the Franklin Library having printed the books will withdraw the O'Neill volume from the series. But since Mr. Jacoby is so worried about Mrs. Chaplin's $10,000 and since his Miss McGuirt assures him that she will undertake the necessary clearances so that Yale will not be put to any additional expense, Yale will go along with the proposal. You may communicate to Mr. Jacoby the gist of this letter but you are not to give him a copy of it or quote my actual words. (I don't want to receive any more angry 'phone calls from the Franklin Library accusing me of libel!)

One of my most welcome gifts on 12 May 1988 was a copy of the Yale University Press paperback edition of *Long Day's Journey into Night* with this inscription:

Drawn from the 57th printing, this is paperbound copy #934,036 of this remarkable autobiographical play first published in February 1956 by the Yale University Press. Added to the sale of the clothbound edition, the sale of the millionth copy is expected to occur early next year.

Signed by Colleen Dewhurst and Jason Robards, currently appearing in the tandem production of "Ah, Wilderness" and "Long Day's Journey into Night" in New Haven under the joint auspices of the Yale Repertory Theater and the Long Wharf Theater, this copy is presented to Donald Gallup on the occasion of his 75th birthday, with the respect and affection of its publisher.

Chester Kerr

Chester had persuaded both actors not just to sign their names in the copy, but to write warmly flattering inscriptions.

One of the reasons for *Long Day's Journey*'s first place among the Yale University Press's bestsellers was that Mrs. O'Neill had refused to allow the play to be reprinted in any of the innumerable anthologies of American plays. Many of them put together by instructors in the history of the drama in colleges and universities across the country, these compilations, bound usually in paper, were "adopted" as textbooks in college classes, mostly taught by those same instructors, and their sale provided a welcome—and sometimes very much needed—supplement to salaries. Carlotta felt that to allow O'Neill's best and most personal play to be included in any anthology would be to cheapen it. (For some time she refused to permit the press to make the play available in a less expensive paperbound issue.)

One of the first of the anthology appearances, proposed in December of the play's publication year, involved the *Best Plays* annual, originated by Burns Mantle and then being edited by Louis Kronenberger. Following Mrs. O'Neill's instructions, the Yale Press turned down the request; but the publishers protested the decision, pointing out that the ten best plays included were not condensed or cut versions, but, rather, samplings of the plays and good advertising for prospective readers of the full texts. They also reminded the press that nine O'Neill plays had been represented in earlier volumes of the series. They added that Louis Kronenberger was "very keen indeed about *Long Day's Journey*," and declared that omission of the play from this standard reference annual would be a great pity: it would certainly be conspicuous by its absence.

Chester Kerr merely forwarded the letter to Mrs. O'Neill, explaining to her on 7 December 1956 that in refusing permission the press had acted in what they believed to be accord with her wishes. She replied on the 10th:

Dear Mr. Kerr:

You "believed" right. "Long Day's Journey Into Night" can neither be published nor produced with one comma changed or omitted. ...

I hope you won't suggest I let *Reader's Digest* have it—some day.

There was another special request in March 1960, and Chester suggested that the publishers address their plea directly to Mrs. O'Neill. She sent me a copy of their two-page letter, marking certain sections for my especial attention. The proposal was for a two-volume anthology of American literature that would "bring it into sharper focus than has obtained in the past"; only O'Neill of all American playwrights from the 18th century forward could be thought to have the power and continuous importance to place him in such a book, and with *Long Day's Journey* included, more space would have to be allotted to him than to any other writer; the inclusion of the play was particularly important to Eric Bentley, editor of the O'Neill section. The publishers could not resist putting their case to Mrs. O'Neill personally because they expected their anthology to be standard for a generation, defining the corpus of American literature for many years to come and, without *Long Day's Journey*, that definition would be radically incomplete.

Carlotta forwarded the letter to me on 12 March 1960, commenting:

> One thing that amused me, no end, was to learn that Mr. Eric Bentley "is concerned to represent the characteristic achievement of Eugene O'Neill's genius in all major stages of its development." This sentence made me laugh. I have read several of Eric Bentley's books which laid down the law concerning O'Neill's lack of genius and trying to prove that he was of no importance whatsoever.

Needless to say, permission was not given.

The Yale University Press followed Carlotta's wishes in anthology matters until she died. When I became responsible for making such decisions with regard to O'Neill plays published by the press, I felt that Yale should continue to observe Carlotta's policy with regard to *Long Day's Journey,* and the sales of clothbound and paperback copies continued to prosper. (After my retirement, the committee that took over responsibility for publication decisions succumbed to pressure and allowed *Long Day's Journey* to be anthologized—and the Yale Press was of course happy to collect in each instance its fifty per cent. of the established fee.)

In September 1980, when I retired as curator of the Yale Collection of American Literature, the principal of the Eugene O'Neill Memorial Fund stood at just under one hundred twenty-five thousand dollars; that of the Carlotta Monterey and Eugene Gladstone O'Neill Memorial Fund amounted to just over a million.

Publishing the Restricted O'Neill
1979–1996

I

IN 1963, YALE'S HOLDINGS OF O'Neill's verse were substantially enlarged by the acquisition, among manuscripts purchased from Agnes Boulton on the O'Neill Fund, of ten poems, nine of them O'Neill's retained copies, typed and sent in 1914 and 1915 to a girlfriend in New London, Beatrice Ashe. Mrs. O'Neill relaxed the twenty-five year restriction to allow William H. Davenport of Harvey Mudd College, Claremont, California, to read all the poems in the collection, "allude to their nature, describe them, and quote occasionally in order to fill out the portrait of their author." He was especially interested in the late poems, of which we had published two, written for Carlotta, in *Inscriptions* (1960).* The resulting article, "The Published and Unpublished Poems of Eugene O'Neill," was printed in the *Yale University Library Gazette* for October 1963. At the end of his essay, Davenport ventured to suggest that "Someday, perhaps, a collected edition of the materials ... may yet see the light."

When the restriction on the unpublished manuscripts ended on 27 November 1978, the poems became the first of a series of "preliminary" editions of O'Neill material issued by the Yale University Library. An introductory note provided background information:

> Beyond the appearance of individual poems in periodicals and newspapers, the only considerable prior publication of O'Neill's verse was in the Sanborn and Clark *Bibliography* in 1931. There thirty of the poems were reprinted—twenty six of them from the *New London Telegraph* [Aug.-Dec. 1912]—prefaced by "An Explanation":

> > The reader is requested to remember that the following poems are examples of Mr. O'Neill's earliest work and that he was extremely

---

*The poems were "Quiet Song in Time of Chaos," for Carlotta's birthday, 28 December 1940, and "Song in Chaos," for another birthday, in 1942.

reluctant to have them reprinted. However, he has graciously given his consent in order that this record might be complete.

There is further documentation of Eugene O'Neill's attitude toward the *Telegraph* poems in the proofs—now at Yale <in the Clark Collection>— of Barrett Clark's *Eugene O'Neill,* which Clark submitted to O'Neill for his approval. Besides reprinting "It's Great When You Get In" (from the *Telegraph)* in its entirety, Clark had, in the proofs, written at greater length than in the book as published about the poems, quoting a stanza each of "Nocturne" and "Only You." Deleting these passages, O'Neill wrote in the margin:

> I wish you would leave all this out. ... The seriousness with which you take it, the amount of space you give it, all serve to cre-ate a wrong impression of my own opinion of it—now and in those days. ... To me it seems this stuff had no bearing on my later development. I never submitted a verse that was really close to me, that I had felt, to the Telegraph. I couldn't—and unless you under-stand this about me at that time—as now—you've got me wrong!
>
> ... I was trying to write popular humorous journalistic verse for a small town paper and the stuff should be judged—nearly all of it—by that intent.

We planned our edition to include all the known published poems and as many unpublished ones as could easily be located. (Other early love poems, addressed to Maibelle Scott, another New London girlfriend, are known to exist.) The Berg Collection of the New York Public Library owned a poem written in 1914 for Katherine Murray, a nurse at the Gaylord Farm Sanatorium, Wallingford, and, among O'Neill's letters to Beatrice Ashe, other poems written to her in 1914 and 1915. The Clifton Waller Barrett Collection of the University of Virginia Library held three poems written in 1925 in Bermuda for a young woman with whom O'Neill used to swim. Those libraries kindly allowed their texts to be included in our edition. In the O'Neill papers there was a clip-ping of an additional *New London Telegraph* poem. Even with the excellent cooperation of the New London Public Library, we were unable to discover the issue of the newspaper in which that poem was printed and could give its date only as "sometime before the Waterways Convention in New London, 3–4 September 1912."

It was a simple matter to supply the necessary annotation. O'Neill himself had indicated the sources of his inspiration for some of the verse: Kipling, Longfellow, Riley, Burns, and Milton. Clark and Sanborn added others: Villon (via D. G. Rossetti), Walt Mason, and Robert W. Service. I suggested additional influences—Shelley and Masefield—and supplied bibliographical details. The typescript from which our edition was reproduced was prepared professionally and its printing was subsidized, in 1979, by a welcome grant from the Witter Bynner Memorial Foundation for Poetry. Copies of the finished "preliminary" edition, paperbound, entitled *Eugene O'Neill Poems 1912–1942*, were—and continue to be—distributed gratis to O'Neill scholars and to libraries all over the world.

Chester Kerr, recently retired as director of the Yale University Press, had been persuaded to become head of Ticknor & Fields, the newly created division of Houghton Mifflin Company, in New Haven and New York. He and I had lunch at the Graduate Club; I handed him a copy of the library's edition of the *Poems,* and he agreed on the spot to include the title in the very first list of his new firm. *Eugene O'Neill Poems 1912–1944* (the title change reflected the extensive revision in 1944 of the 1942 "Fragments") appeared, clothbound, on 2 June 1980. It was published in London four months later by O'Neill's English publisher, Jonathan Cape Limited. Both the American and English issues were "Dedicated to the Memory of Carlotta Monterey O'Neill (28 December 1888–17 November 1970)."

In her notice of the book in the *New York Times Book Review*, Barbara Gelb echoed O'Neill himself in deploring the " 'general awfulness' of his formal poetry." She observed that although I apparently had felt no qualms about braving Eugene O'Neill's ghost in this way, I had at least taken the precaution of propitiating the possibly even more formidable shade of Carlotta Monterey O'Neill by dedicating the volume to her memory. Other reviewers agreed with Mrs. Gelb in finding the poems unworthy of America's foremost dramatist, but the *Library Journal* pointed out that "This volume completes our picture of O'Neill and, thus, belongs in collections of American Literature."

The picture we had presented proved to be, after all, incomplete. The Ticknor & Fields edition had already been printed in May 1980, when Winifred Frazer of the University of Florida called our attention to an additional poem that should have been included (where it would have required another change in our title). "The 'American Sovereign' (With Apologies to the Literary Executors of O. Khayyam)," had been printed anonymously in Emma Goldman's anarchist monthly, *Mother Earth*, in May 1911. Frazer had contributed to the *Eugene O'Neill Newsletter* for May 1979 an article offering "persuasive evidence for attributing the poem to O'Neill, thus moving back the date of his first publication from 1912 to 1911."

II

The twenty-five year restriction imposed by Carlotta Monterey O'Neill on the bulk of the unpublished O'Neill manuscript material at Yale had denied would-be biographers and other scholars access to documents of vastly greater importance to their research than the poems. Perhaps the most essential of all was the "Work Diary," in four volumes, covering the period from January 1924 to 4 May 1943. The first two of these leather-bound five-year diaries had apparently been given by Carlotta to her husband in 1931 (the second volume has an inscription from her dated Sept. 1931) and he seems to have begun this record in that year by transcribing the pertinent data from old "Scribbling" diaries that he had been in the habit of keeping since at least 1924. One of these earlier volumes was not returned to him, along with other manuscript materials, by Agnes Boulton at the time of their divorce in 1929. Although O'Neill charges her, in the "Work Diary," with having sold that volume, it was still in her possession when she died in 1968, and we acquired it for the Yale collection in 1970. Because O'Neill destroyed all the other "Scribbling" diaries after he had copied from them the data he wished to transfer to the "Work Diary," this 1925 volume provides the only evidence known to exist as to what these more detailed diaries were like. Since O'Neill was obliged to reconstruct the "Work Diary" for 1925 "from memory & few records," the volume also makes it possible to correct the errors that he made—almost inevitably—six or more years after the fact.

Even after 1931, O'Neill, like most diarists, did not invariably bring his "Work Diary" up to date at the close of each day's activities. There are indications that he was obliged now and then to refer to his wife's journal in order to refresh his memory.

I had transcribed the O'Neill diary in connection with work on the Cycle plays during 1968–69. Its publication became possible when the twenty-five year restriction ended in November 1978; and I retired from Yale in September 1980, a year or so before retirement would have been obligatory, primarily in order to complete the necessary editorial work. The volumes of her own journal that Carlotta kept from 10 February 1928 through 1944, at Yale as her gift, helped to establish identities of persons O'Neill referred to by initials, and were an aid in deciphering his sometimes difficult handwriting. We decided to publish our edition in two paperbound volumes and to print the 1925 "Scribbling" diary at the end of the second volume so that the reader could, if he or she wished, compare easily the entries reconstructed in 1931 with those actually set down in 1925. I rented an IBM Selectric typewriter and typed out the text, which was then reproduced by the Yale Printing Service. *Eugene O'Neill Work Diary 1924–1943* was published by the Yale University Library in 1981 on the Carlotta Monterey and Eugene Gladstone O'Neill Memorial Fund.

Chester Kerr had hoped that this might be another O'Neill title for which Ticknor & Fields would become publishers of the final edition. I doubted that the material was of sufficient general interest to make its commercial publication feasible, in spite of its obviously great value for all students of O'Neill's work; but I did submit the typescript for the firm's consideration. On 3 April 1981, Chester communicated the decision:

Alas, I'm afraid you're right. We have now had a chance to weigh the trade market for O'Neill's WORK DIARY in full discussion with our Boston colleagues and the conclusion is not favorable to its chances as an investment for a trade house. We simply don't think we could sell enough copies.

III

Other essential manuscript material for research in the Yale collection was a series of three notebooks, dated 1918–20, 1921–31, and 1931–38, containing O'Neill's notes of ideas for plays. Virginia Floyd, of Bryant College in Smithfield, Rhode Island, had often used the Beinecke collection and had impressed us all as a highly qualified scholar who worked thoroughly and expeditiously. We entrusted the editing of the notebooks to her. At the end of a mere two years, she had a manuscript ready for publication and had found a publisher for it. Her *Eugene O'Neill at Work: Newly Released Ideas for Plays* was published in 1981 in New York by the Frederick Ungar Publishing Company. She went on to publish, also with Ungar, a "new assessment" of *The Plays of Eugene O'Neill* in 1985. In 1988 she followed this up with O'Neill's notes for *The Unfinished Plays* ("The Visit of Malatesta," "The Last Conquest," and "Blind Alley Guy"). All this she achieved in spite of an heroic struggle against illness that she eventually lost—to the deep regret of her friends and all students of the work of Eugene O'Neill.

Jack Bryer and Travis Bogard had done an excellent job with the O'Neill letters to Macgowan, published by the Yale University Press in 1983. They continued their work with the O'Neill correspondence and the press published their most useful edition of his *Selected Letters* in 1988. In the same year the press issued also a collection, edited by Bogard, of various unpublished or uncollected items (many of them drawn from the Yale collection) under the title *The Unknown O'Neill*. And so, gradually over a number of years, much of the important unpublished material was made available.

IV

Carlotta had given me permission, in 1967, to work with the various notes and drafts for the "Cycle." This was the vast project, eventually titled "A Tale of Possessors Self-Dispossessed," to which O'Neill had devoted most of his time, thought, and creative energy from 1935 to 1939, a period that should have been his most productive

and mature. Only one play of the planned eleven was ever completed to his satisfaction. The notes were sent to Yale, along with a mass
of miscellaneous manuscript material, including the typescripts of
Long Day's Journey into Night and an unfinished Cycle play, *More
Stately Mansions,* in 1951, when the O'Neills were moving from
their Marblehead cottage, their last home together. The typescript of
Long Day's Journey was sealed, not to be read until twenty-five years
after the author's death, and the *More Stately Mansions* typescript was
marked to be destroyed when O'Neill died; but there was no indication that the Cycle Papers were not to be preserved permanently
as part of the O'Neill collection. The dramatist spent his last days at
the Hotel Shelton in Boston, being nursed by Carlotta. Explaining
to her that no one must be allowed to finish the unfinished plays, he
asked her help in destroying original manuscripts still in his files of *A
Touch of the Poet* (an early version that he had drastically rewritten),
and *More Stately Mansions,* along with the outlines and notes for two
earlier Cycle plays of which he had destroyed first drafts in 1944.

O'Neill died in 1953, and Mrs. O'Neill subsequently asked that
none of the pencil manuscripts be made available for readers until
1978, twenty-five years after her husband's death. During 1954 and
1955, there was no reason to raise with her the question of the
destruction of *More Stately Mansions.* In *Pigeons on the Granite* I
explained that when I returned the typescript to Carlotta at her
request in 1956, I quite deliberately removed the leaf bearing
O'Neill's direction that the script be destroyed. Karl Ragnar Gierow,
director of the Royal Swedish Theatre, was successful in persuading
her that the typescript could be reduced to a producible play. His
version was presented in Swedish at the Dramaten, and in due
course, the original O'Neill equivalent of the Gierow version, edited by me, was published by the Yale University Press.

Pleased with the work I had done on this, the sixth play of the
projected eleven-play Cycle, Carlotta herself and Karl Ragnar
Gierow endorsed my successful application to the Guggenheim
Foundation for a grant that enabled me to spend the academic year
1968–69 free of my teaching and curatorial duties. Attempting to do

anything at all with the fascinating Cycle materials without violating the dramatist's injunction against anyone's finishing his plays seemed from the outset doomed to failure. At least these hundreds of pages of his almost microscopic handwriting could be transcribed, and that I set about doing. The library allowed me to borrow not only the standard Royal typewriter that I normally used, but also, much more importantly, the original manuscripts, since I would be working on them in my resident fellow's apartment in Jonathan Edwards College, in university property of stone and steel construction, with minimal chance of fire or theft. Working with a magnifying glass, I spent the greater part of the year in making the transcripts. But at the end of my leave in June 1969, I had little beside some fifteen hundred pages of typed copies to show for my effort. I still had no clear idea of exactly what I should do with the material.

In the following year, when my usual month's vacation from work at the library gave me at last the free time again to mull over the problem, I began to experiment with the full-length scenario for *The Calms of Capricorn,* planned to follow *More Stately Mansions* in the eleven-play Cycle. O'Neill's dramatic imagination was so vivid and his knowledge of the theater so great that the scenario turned again and again into actual dialogue. I wondered whether something approaching the play he had visualized might not be put together from his own words with a minimum of tampering. During that summer of 1970, I occupied myself with "developing" the scenario and found that the result was surprisingly complete. When I had finished a script, I let Norman Pearson read it, and was pleased to have him comment that "It is by no means O'Neill's worst play."

At just this time, Louis Martz, Sterling Professor of English, who had been in the Yale Graduate School with me at the outset of our academic careers, was appointed director of the Beinecke Library. I was overjoyed at his accepting the appointment—although I did not in the least understand his motives for doing so—and, early on in the period of his all too brief administration of the library, I discussed with him possible publication of the O'Neill play. We agreed that the transcription of the scenario, exactly as written, must be part of any printing, and that the project should be submitted first to the Yale University Press, already the publisher for the library of *A Long Day's Journey into Night, A Touch of the Poet, Hughie,* and *More Stately Mansions.*

Edward Tripp was then editor at the press for books relating to the theater and it became his responsibility to deal with *The Calms of Capricorn.* To me, he seemed lacking in enthusiasm, with a tendency—born doubtless of caution bred of past experience—almost always to take the pessimistic view. Obviously there were plenty of arguments against this particular proposal: O'Neill's scenario was only the bare bones of a dramatic work, without the appeal of flesh and muscle; it was melodramatic, even sometimes ridiculous; and yet the play was the original starting point for the entire Cycle.

The Yale Press had neither the imagination nor the courage to rise to the challenge: a doleful delegation headed by Chester Kerr waited on me in my office at the Beinecke to communicate the decision, based on Tripp's recommendation, that the press could not accept the library's offer that it publish this play. And there the matter rested for a decade, because I was determined to do nothing further about it until I had rechecked my transcription against the original manuscript, and attempted to improve the play's faithfulness to O'Neill's intentions, insofar as they could be determined.

The first year of my retirement, 1980–81, gave me the time to do this. And then, in spite of my vow after I had typed the setting copy for the O'Neill *Work Diary* on the IBM Selectric typewriter never again to have anything to do with that infernal machine, I undertook the much less formidable job of producing with it copy of the *Calms of Capricorn* material for reproduction by offset. Greer Allen, now printer to the university, provided models and papers, and I managed to prepare finished pages for printing. We decided to bind the scenario as a separate first volume in order to facilitate comparison between the original text and its development. Because a few at least of O'Neill's own set designs demanded inclusion, the Yale Printing Service printed from type the first four pages for each of the two volumes, incorporating reproductions of the drawings, along with the opening page of the manuscript.

The paperbound edition was ready in July 1981, just a day or so before I was to leave for Switzerland, and we sent out a few copies. One went to Travis Bogard, professor of dramatic art at the University of California, Berkeley, for I was especially eager to have his opinion. When Chester Kerr had regretfully turned down the *Work Diary* as a possible publication for Ticknor & Fields, he had indicated that he would welcome some other O'Neill title for his firm's list. And so, in spite of the Yale Press's having declined in 1970 to publish *The Calms of Capricorn,* we left a copy at Chester's office for him to consider. I doubted that he, as director of the press, had done much more than glance at the manuscript, and thought that, with circumstances altered, he, already publisher of the O'Neill *Poems,* might be rather more sympathetic to our project. This proved to be the case: the play, in a single clothbound volume with the scenario now an appendix, was published by Ticknor & Fields— with the enthusiastic approval of Travis Bogard—on 24 May 1982.

Oddly enough, its first production had already taken place. One of the principal reasons for rushing the library's edition into print was that Esther Jackson and John Ezell, producers of *More Stately Mansions* at the University of Wisconsin in 1980, had read a type-script and had requested permission to present the new play. They and their students needed copies of the script, and it seemed best not to allow the play to circulate in unpublished, uncopyrighted form. Several sets of our two-volume paperback went off to Madison in July, and the Jackson-Ezell staged readings took place in December 1981 and January 1982. We were highly gratified at the subsequent report that the Wisconsin students involved in work with the play had found it even more interesting and meaningful than *More Stately Mansions,* and ventured to hope that we had not disturbed too roughly Eugene O'Neill's sleep in the quiet earth of Forest Hills.

But fears of antagonizing the dramatist's ghost continued to make it difficult for me to fix upon some scheme for utilizing the tran-scribed Cycle notes, and I extemporized, again, by dealing with two particular documents.

The scenario for *A Touch of the Poet,* then the first unit of a *six-*play Cycle, had been completed on 24 February 1935. As outlined at that time, the play, tentatively titled "The Hair of the Dog," differed radically from its final version. In this early plan, Simon Harford's mother—here Abigail, later Deborah—and her daughter-in-law, Sara Melody, meet only in an epilogue that takes place after the Harford-Melody marriage. Completely sketched, this scene contains little that was salvaged by O'Neill for either *A Touch of the Poet* or *More Stately Mansions*. Although some of the exposition is rather awkwardly handled, the epilogue as a whole shows O'Neill in excellent form. I prepared an introductory note, and submitted the transcript to the *Eugene O'Neill Review*. Fred Wilkins, the editor, agreed that this was writing of which neither O'Neill nor his ghost had any reason to be ashamed, and as "O'Neill's Original 'Epilogue' for *A Touch of the Poet*," it was printed in the Fall 1991 issue of the periodical—distributed in April 1992.

The second document I dealt with was another scenario. Completed on 9 November 1935, this was for the first act of "Greed of the Meek," the play planned to precede *A Touch of the Poet* in an *eight*-play Cycle. O'Neill went on, in September 1936, to write a first draft of all three acts, but, in the process, concluded, reluctantly, that he needed still another play, "Give Me Death," which would then become the first of a *nine*-play Cycle. That, too, he completed in first draft, in December 1937, having decided on 9 August to call it "Greed of the Meek" and to change the title of the second play to "And Give Me Death." He was far from satisfied with the two plays, finding them much too long and complicated; but he could see no way of condensing either one without ruining it. When, more than two years later, in October 1940, he came to restudy them, he decided that the only possible solution was to replace them with four plays in what would become an *eleven*-play Cycle. In order not to be too much influenced by the old two when he came to write the new four plays, he destroyed the two first drafts on 21 February 1944, just before he and Carlotta left Tao House. (The outlines for the two plays were apparently burned in 1953.)

The first-act scenario for the second of the old two plays had been written in a special morocco-bound notebook that Carlotta had given her husband, thus saving the manuscript from destruction. I wrote a brief introduction, and submitted the transcript to the *Eugene O'Neill Review*. Fred Wilkins found the material of great interest for the light it shed on the destroyed play, and printed " 'Greed of the Meek,' O'Neill's Scenario for Act One of the First Play of His Eight-Play Cycle," in the *Review* for Fall 1992—mailed in March 1994.

Publishing these two documents had brought me no closer to a solution of the problem of what to do with the Cycle material as a whole. I decided eventually that I must find answers to three basic questions: What had O'Neill tried to do? How had he set about doing it? and Why had he failed? I must then put together an account of the undertaking, telling the story insofar as possible in the dramatist's own words. The entries in O'Neill's *Work Diary,* along with the dates inscribed on many of the notes, provided a basic, chronological outline. In the closing years of his life, after he had given up hope of being able to complete the Cycle, O'Neill had talked about the project with three individuals: George Jean Nathan, Elizabeth Shepley Sergeant, and Hamilton Basso. Nathan and Basso published accounts of their conversations with him; Miss Sergeant made elaborate notes which she carefully preserved with her papers (and bequeathed to the Yale Collection of American Literature). And O'Neill made invaluable references to his plans for the Cycle in letters to various friends.

The Cycle Papers in the O'Neill archive at Yale supplied the flesh for the skeleton, but there was at once too little and too much of it. Too little remained of the first two plays of the nine-play Cycle after the destructions of 1944 and 1953 to make possible a reconstruction of their action in any detail. Although O'Neill had made the decision in August 1935 to use the much reworked material for his "Bessie Bowen" play as part of the final unit in what was then a *seven*-play Cycle, he never worked out fully the plot of that final play, eventually titled "The Hair of the Dog." He had prepared scenarios only for *The Calms of Capricorn, A Touch of the Poet,* and *More Stately Mansions,* explaining to his friend Richard Dana Skinner in June 1939 why even the outlines of the later ones were never completed: he felt it was better not to try to finish them until he had gone on much farther with the whole thing, "A matter of keeping them in their right place so they won't anticipate too much of what must appear again when the curve completes its circle."

And yet, in the scenarios and outlines, there is at the same time a characteristic excess of detail. At an early stage in his work on the Cycle, on 7 April 1936, O'Neill had warned Theresa Helburn of the Theatre Guild that his drafts were "intolerably long and wordy," because he put everything in them and relied on subsequent revision and rewriting, after a lapse of time with better perspective on them, "to concentrate on the essential and eliminate the overweight." It was easy for me to cut passages of dialogue that did not further the action; but when I attempted additional condensation, I found myself forced to substitute my own words for O'Neill's. I opted for retaining, wherever possible, the author's phrasing even when this meant a somewhat overlong summary.

And there was too much material in the way of character analyses and possible plot complications. O'Neill's attempt to portray the involved motivation, both conscious and subconscious, of his characters became eventually self-defeating, as he himself later acknowledged.

Once having established as best I could exactly how the project developed and what was to happen in each of the plays, I still had to determine why O'Neill had eventually been able to complete to his own satisfaction only one play. Had he, after working out the detailed scenario for *The Calms of Capricorn,* gone on to write similar outlines for the following three plays in what was then just a four-play Cycle, he might well have been able to "pull it off." After all, *Mourning Becomes Electra* is a *trilogy.* But, having written the outline for the first of the four plays, each having as central character one of the Harford sons, he began to feel the need to know much more about their parents. Incorporating the story of the courtship and marriage of Simon and Sara Harford, the Cycle quickly grew to five and then six plays. O'Neill explained to Elizabeth Shepley Sergeant, in 1946, that he "could never be sure of [the] place where he ought to begin. Everything derived from everything else." And so the series gradually expanded to eleven. Travis Bogard suggests that his long-continuing involvement with the Harfords may have been, at least subconsciously, his way of putting off the confrontation with his own family that he wanted to write about but knew would have to be set down in blood—as indeed it was—in *Long Day's Journey into Night*.

There was an additional obvious reason for O'Neill's failure: ill health. He had explained to his lawyer, then Harry Weinberger, on 5 March 1938, that he only had to tear up the stuff he forced himself to write when he was under the weather. It just wouldn't come right unless he felt reasonably fit. Reading the *Work Diary*'s record of the illnesses that afflicted him through the entire five-year period during which his principal creative effort was devoted to the Cycle, one wonders how he could possibly have managed to produce so much, however abortive some of the writing may have been.

As the years passed and the number of plays continued to grow, the war in Europe, too, came to have its effect. Writing to Sean O'Casey on 5 August 1943, O'Neill explained that of the four Cycle plays that he had written only *A Touch of the Poet* "approached final form." The others would have to be entirely recreated—if he ever got around to it—because he no longer saw them as he did in the pre-war 1939 days in which they were written. In August 1949, O'Neill confessed to his old friend George Jean Nathan that any writing was out of the question: he just felt that there was nothing more he wanted to say.

Both Elizabeth Shepley Sergeant and George Jean Nathan report O'Neill as having become convinced that the "dramaturgical plan" of his Cycle was faulty. Nathan quotes him as saying that the Cycle "should deal with one family and not two ... ." Both Nathan and Miss Sergeant imply that his dissatisfaction was limited to the first two plays of the nine-play Cycle as written and was, in part, the reason for the destruction of their first drafts in 1944. But the Cycle notes indicate that the flaw was in the plans outlined in November and December 1940 for the first four plays of the eleven-play Cycle. There, indeed, O'Neill had assigned even more prominent roles to the "Three Sisters," who were no longer blood-members of the Harford family. In the two destroyed plays the women had been daughters of the first Harford—then named Evan—by his first wife. In the plan for the four plays to replace them, the Harford progenitor—now named Jonathan—became the much younger *step*-father of the three daughters. It is probable that the major reconstruction of his plans for those first four plays that would have been required to correct this flaw became a final, telling reason why O'Neill, his energies at a low point because of ill health and depression at the state of the world, failed to do any major new work on the Cycle during the last years of his life.

By the spring of 1986, I had completed a rough draft of my narrative, beginning with O'Neill's initial idea, set down in his notebook in 1927, for a play—at first called "Billionaire," then "It Cannot Be Mad?," and eventually "The Life (Career) of Bessie Bowen"—on the corrupting power of material possessions. Although I became dissatisfied with this plan, Ellen Graham, senior editor at the Yale University Press, with whom I had worked on a number of projects, read my manuscript and, in May, made some very helpful suggestions, almost all of which I eventually followed. She told me that the press would be glad to look at a revised version of the manuscript when it was ready.

I rewrote it drastically, now beginning in 1931 with the original idea for *The Calms of Capricorn*, soon to become the first of a four-play Cycle. This scheme made possible a more coherent account. I continued to work on it until October 1992, when it seemed to me sufficiently well developed to show again to the Yale Press. In the interim, Jonathan Brent had succeeded Ellen Graham as editor. He read my manuscript promptly and reported to me on the same day, asking a number of questions. I attempted as best I could to reply in a fifteen-page letter, delivered to the press on 26 October. But Brent was the editor in charge of the vast Russo-American project for publishing the secret archives of the USSR, which obviously had to take precedence over Gallup on O'Neill. When, after a full year, I had heard nothing, on 8 October 1993 I requested—and received—the return of my manuscript.

But I never approached any other publisher, the Yale Press being for me so obviously the ideal one: (1) with Random House's refusal, in 1955, to issue *Long Day's Journey into Night,* Yale University Press had become O'Neill's primary American publisher; (2) that play had been the press's all-time bestseller, and (3) the original Cycle material with which my manuscript was concerned was in the Yale Collection of American Literature, of which I had been curator for thirty-three years.

Travis Bogard had on a number of occasions asked to read my manuscript. In September 1995 I sent it to him. His enthusiastic reaction gave me new confidence in what I had written. I reported his letter to my old friend Ulla Dydo, who had worked on her [*Gertrude*] *Stein Reader* with Jonathan Brent while he was at the Northwestern University Press, and who was working with him at Yale on the publication of the Stein-Thornton Wilder correspondence. She learned from Brent that the press had returned my manuscript to me while he was away from New Haven on one of his Russian trips. Through Ulla Dydo, he asked that I resubmit it, and I did so—on 3 June 1996.

In November, I was informed that the press's publications committee would be considering my manuscript at its meeting on the 18th. By an odd coincidence, the *New York Times* that very day featured on its front page a story by Peter Applebome, reporting that American university presses were having to cut back on publishing such specialized monographs as mine. But even though the committee could hardly have expected that my book would become a bestseller, they voted to accept it for publication. Jonathan Brent telephoned the welcome news. Eugene O'Neill's involvement with his self-dispossessors had continued for some twenty years; mine with his notes had lasted twenty-eight!

T.S. Eliot, Randolph, New Hampshire, June 1933. Photograph by Henry Ware Eliot, Jr. Collection of Donald Gallup.

Pursuing Eliot in New Haven, Cambridge, and New York

The Eliots, and the T. S. Eliot Collection at Harvard
1936–1988

I

T. S. ELIOT, especially in his late essays and lectures, was often careful to state his qualifications for dealing with a particular subject. Following his example, I must explain my presumption in venturing to write about one of the important collections of Harvard University, where unique resources are offered for research in so many fields of knowledge. The Eliot collection is, in its entirety, the most important available gathering of manuscripts, letters, and printed material by and about the man whose achievement was honored all over the world in his centenary year, 1988. And if a single individual may be said to have been responsible for the presence of this collection at Harvard, that person is certainly Henry Ware Eliot, Jr. I first met both Henry and T. S. Eliot in Wellesley on 29 September 1936. From that time until I was drafted into the United States Army in 1941, and for the few months from the end of the war until Henry died of leukemia in 1947, he and I corresponded intensively. We were both building up Eliot collections—he for Harvard, I for my own use in compiling a bibliography and eventually, of course, for gift or bequest to Yale.

Nine years his brother's senior, Henry Eliot had gone from Smith Academy to Washington University in St. Louis for two years, and then to Harvard, where he graduated in 1902. His gift for light verse was displayed in *Harvard Celebrities, A Book of Caricatures,* published at the end of his junior year, in 1901. He went on to law school at

Harvard, and then pursued careers in printing and publishing. From 1917 to 1929, he was a partner in a Chicago advertising agency. In 1926 he had met and married the artist Theresa Garrett, who had been associated with the Chicago Arts Club. It was a marriage blessed by the happiness that comes from deep mutual devotion. They moved to New York in 1930, and in 1932 Henry's detective novel, *The Rumble Murders,* was published (under the pseudonym Mason Deal) by Houghton Mifflin. Its dust wrapper featured a collage of newspaper headlines. In the copy of the book that he gave me, Henry Eliot wrote a characteristic inscription: "The jacket, done with infinite labor by me, is the only part of which I am proud." T.S. Eliot's letter to his brother about the novel is preserved in the Harvard collection; it includes this comment:

It was very satisfactory to receive your Rumble Murders (the title puzzled me at first until I found out that a rumble is the same thing as a dickey). ...

I read any detective story with enjoyment, but I think yours is a very good one; I am simply amazed at any human mind being able to think out all those details. I am quite sure that I could never write a detective story myself; my only possible resource for adding to my income would be to write children's verses or stories, having had a little success in writing letters to children (and illustrating them of course). But apart from my astonishment at your skill in plot, I was especially interested by the book as a social document—I guessed that it was probably Winnetka. The picture of that society is extremely interesting to me; there is nothing like it in England. For one thing, you would never get that combination of wealth, crudity and intellectual activity. "County people", who form the stupidest, most intolerant and most intolerable part of society in England, would never collect incunabula or mention Proust; intellectual activity, and interest in art and letters, is found in isolated individuals all over the country, but otherwise is confined to a limited society, drawn from various natural classes, and most of the individuals composing which, I probably know.

In 1936, Henry and Theresa Eliot moved to Cambridge, where Henry at last found his true profession as lecturer and research fellow in anthropology at the Peabody Museum. The fruit of his studies was a series of graphic analyses of *Excavations in Mesopotamia and Western Iran: Sites of 4000–500 B.C.,* published by the museum three years after his death.

Henry suffered all through his life from deafness, the result of scarlet fever in childhood, and this strengthened a natural tendency toward diffidence. It was with Henry in mind, Valerie Eliot tells us in her edition of the *Letters*, that T.S. Eliot wrote in the fourth of the "Preludes," of "some infinitely gentle / Infinitely suffering thing." The brothers were devoted to each other, and Henry documented Tom's career photographically whenever opportunity offered; reproductions of his early snapshots add a great deal to the first volume of the *Letters*.

II

Not long after he settled in Cambridge, Henry and his sisters established the collection of their brother's work by gift to the library of Eliot House. President Eliot was not a close relative (he was a third cousin once removed of their grandfather); but their cousin Henry Eliot Scott was then an undergraduate in Eliot House. It was through him that the initial gift was made. When Eliot House was taken over by the Navy during World War II, the Eliot collection was transferred temporarily to the Houghton Library. Returned briefly to Eliot House in 1948, it was permanently redeposited in Houghton three years later.

In retrospect, it may seem strange that the collection was not presented to Widener. Henry Eliot later wrote me that, had the Houghton Library been in existence in 1936, he might well have been tempted to give the Eliot materials there, where they would be more accessible than at Eliot House, in the care of a permanent librarian, and housed in air-conditioned quarters. But Henry, at the time of the gift, was thinking primarily of making available to students everything that his brother had written. It was to be a working library, and only incidentally a gathering of rare items. He described it in a letter of December 1936 as

quite a collection of T.S. Eliotana, including many English periodicals such as the London Times [Literary] Supplement, New Statesman, Athenaeum, etc., in which his essays first appeared. Some articles are included which have not appeared in book form since. With these are a number of his books, (which formed part of his library in college) and a great many reviews, critiques, etc., of his works. Perhaps the more valuable part of this collection was owned by my mother, who preserved them as sent her by T. S. Eliot from time to time.

It was an essential part of Henry Eliot's intention that the collection was to grow and be kept up to date, and he devoted much of his time to adding items and to making a detailed catalogue of its contents. Eliot House made him a fellow; and he was, of course, allowed access to the collection at all reasonable times. Two years later he spoke of the additions he had made, describing them to me as

for the most part books of commentary, and critiques and reviews, to get which I have spent perhaps too much money, in buying back numbers of periodicals. Yet I think myself that these reviews, many of them by eminent writers, are of great interest as giving an idea of what TSE's contemporaries thought of him. I have spent infinite labor in pasting [some 400 or so of these] . . . neatly on large cards, and the longer articles have been bound in cloth boards.

In 1936, when the collection was established, T.S. Eliot's first editions were only just beginning to be sought after, and it is not surprising that Henry Eliot thought of his gift primarily as a reading library. Because he expected the materials to be used especially by undergraduates, he had many of the paperbound volumes, including his brother's first book, *Prufrock and Other Observations* (1917), put into cloth boards for preservation and ease of handling. But the question of binding versus use of slipcases became a bothersome one. In April 1946, T. S. Eliot had given to his brother for the collection a copy of the rare *Noctes Binanianae*. These "poetical effusions"—in English, French, German, and Latin—had been written mostly in 1937 and 1938 by Geoffrey Faber, T. S. Eliot, F. V. Morley—all partners in the Faber publishing firm—and the distinguished bibliographer John Hayward, their friend. He resided during this period at 22 Bina Gardens, Earls Court, London, and the group of friends met usually at his flat—hence the title ("Binanian Evenings"). The verses, signed only with the pseudonyms Whale, Possum, Elephant, Coot, and Spider, circulating at first in manuscript, had been printed privately in 1939 in an edition limited to twenty-five copies. When I suggested to Henry that the pamphlet ought to be preserved in a slipcase, keeping its original paper wrappers intact, he agreed; but only a few months later he wrote me about some foreign translations:

Do you think that paper-bound volumes (such as so many of these translations) should be bound? It protects them but rather spoils them for exhibition purposes. What is the approved practice?

Henry Eliot's substantial expenditures in building up the collection and in binding items for inclusion were made at some financial sacrifice for him and his wife. He had written me in March 1937:

I have been spending some money filling in gaps in the E[liot]. H[ouse]. collection; I'm now trying to bum some free copies off of TSE of Faber books. Just figured my income tax, and have to pay in N.Y., Mass., and U.S.A. (on top of moving expense here) and am gnashing [my] teeth (which will probably need dental attention soon anyway.)

And in the following May:

I wonder whether you could delicately hint to your Alma Mater that she may, if she feels the urge, pay me for her set [of photostats of the manuscript of *Murder in the Cathedral*]? I have blown in about $75.00 on books and magazines for this collection just this year, and God knows I can't afford it … . The prints cost 20 cents apiece, or $3.60 for Yale Library's set.

In 1941 Henry was able to report some good fortune:

I have had a break—received a grant, for which I had applied in Jan., of $500 for cost of materials and implements for making graphic exhibits of archaeological sites. . . . It is pleasant to be able to blow myself on T-squares, stencils, pens, paper of the best grade, etc., in a care-free manner. … The exhibits are 30 x 40 in. and I reduce them by photostat to about half size, and I believe the intention is to publish an edition of 100 or so photostatically, to sell to libraries, colleges, etc. There is no money in it, of course.

(Finances continued to be a problem for Theresa Eliot after Henry's death. She was appointed honorary curator of the collection, and tried to see that its growth continued as Henry had wished, keeping his catalogue up to date. But she lived at first on a very limited budget and on several occasions was obliged to sell items, including at least one—Tom's copy of Alfred Weber's *History of Philosophy* (New York, Scribner's, 1907)—that Henry had originally intended for inclusion in the Harvard collection. Eventually, through Phil Hofer and other Harvard friends, she secured commissions, and life became somewhat easier. Her deep, active interest in the Eliot collection continued right up until her death at well over ninety.)

It was not to be expected that T. S. Eliot would share unreservedly his brother's determination to make the Harvard collection complete. He wrote me in December 1942:

I don't really take any interest in my own early editions and indeed I never even want to read anything I have written six months after publication, except under the occasional necessity of giving poetry readings.

A man of genuine humility, he felt that searching out and preserving minor periodical contributions tended to give to these casual productions an importance out of proportion to their merits. (He would have preferred that the *Noctes Binanianae* not even be listed in his bibliography, feeling that the verses were much too inconsequential for such attention.) As for manuscript materials, of course he recognized, after 1936, that he was under some obligation to give items to a collection of his work established at his alma mater by his brother and sisters in memory of their mother; but even here his feelings were equivocal. He had already, in 1934, presented to the Bodleian Library at Oxford (where he had been a graduate student at Merton College), the manuscript of his Ariel poem *Marina,* along with most of the drafts pertaining to the pageant play *The Rock* and his translation of the *Anabase* of St. John Perse. Furthermore, after 1933, when he and his first wife, Vivien Haigh-Wood, separated and half of his income began to go to her, he seems to have tended to use the sale of his manuscript materials as a way of raising funds for charitable purposes. Early in 1936, just before the establishment of the Eliot House collection, he had been approached by an enterprising individual acting for a bookseller's client interested in purchasing poetry manuscripts. Eliot explained that since he composed mostly on the typewriter after making preliminary pencil notes, he seldom had any substantial amount of manuscript. At that time there were only some fourteen pages of drafts for *Murder in the Cathedral.* These he would be willing to dispose of at a price, but would ask that the amount be paid to a particular charity that he had in mind (in this case it was the Lord Victor Seymour Memorial). Fortunately for Harvard, the sum seems to have been more than the bookseller's client could afford, for nothing came of the proposal. Within a few months, the Eliot House collection had been established, and the manuscript pages relating to *Murder* became T. S. Eliot's first important gift to his university. Three years later, when *The Family Reunion* was published, he also gave a scenario for and three drafts of that play to Eliot House. (Another draft that he had sent to his old friend Emily Hale was subsequently given by her to the collection.) But when, in 1941, after the periodical publication of the third of the *Four Quartets, The Dry Salvages,* Henry asked his brother about the manuscript of that poem, Tom replied:

I have thought I ought to give it to Magdalene [*he had become a fellow of that college in Cambridge*]: Eliot House already has a good deal of stuff, and the Bodleian has "The Rock" and "Anabase." . . .

He added that the manuscript of *East Coker* had been split up: he had responded to an appeal from Hugh Walpole for material to be auctioned for the benefit of the Red Cross by handing over to him the pencil notes relating to that poem. (Bob Barry was successful in buying them for me.) He subsequently contributed for another Red Cross sale the typescript of three lectures he had given at Johns Hopkins. That was purchased by the Houghton Library and became part of the Harvard Eliot collection.* From 1946, when T.S. Eliot and John Hayward began to share a flat in Carlyle Mansions (the apartment house beside the Thames in which Henry James had once lived), much of his manuscript material, including the various drafts of *The Cocktail Party* (1949), was given to Hayward, who bequeathed his entire Eliot collection to King's College, Cambridge.

T.S. Eliot's attitude toward bibliography was also equivocal. He acknowledged the importance of dates of composition of individual essays in titling his major collection, published in 1932, *Selected Essays 1917–1932.* But in 1948, when I ventured to point out to him that the years given for seven of the essays seemed to be incorrect, he replied:

---

*Edited by Ronald Schuchard, it was published in 1993 as part of *The Varieties of Metaphysical Poetry.*

I am afraid that my answer . . . will be so brief as to shock you. It is simply to say that I have not the slightest doubt that you are entirely right in every instance. I think the explanation is that I dated the essays entirely by guess-work when I prepared the volume in 1932, and never bothered to look up the exact dates of first periodical publication. So now you have just stirred up trouble and we shall have to notify both Faber and Faber and Harcourt, Brace and Company for the benefit of future reprints.

(In subsequent editions, the dates were dropped from the title and the book became simply *Selected Essays.)*

And yet, T. S. Eliot had a phenomenal memory for many other details concerning his work and was extremely helpful in supplying information both to his brother and to me. In the December 1917 issue of *The Egoist*, a paper that he was then editing, the correspondence columns were extended—to fill up space—with extracts from letters purporting to be written by J. A. D. Spence, Thridlingston Grammar School; Helen B. Trundlett, Batton, Kent; Charles James Grimble, The Vicarage, Leays; Charles Augustus Conybeare, The Carlton Club, Liverpool; and Muriel A. Schwarz, 60 Alexandra Gardens, Hampstead, N.W. Thirty years later, on our way from New Haven to Cambridge, T. S. Eliot recalled the occasion and, from memory, gave me the names and addresses of, as I remember, all five of the fictitious correspondents. (The extracts are reprinted in the first volume of the Eliot *Letters.)*

III

Henry was a careful—and occasionally critical—reader of his brother's writing and, over the years, he also gave me many helpful suggestions for the bibliography. When I sent him an advance copy of the first Eliot *Catalogue* in February 1937, he responded:

I have typed off (enclosed) some items of reviews, by T. S. E., which you have not listed. . . . I shall examine our copies, however, with care once more to make sure that they are by T. S. E. In most cases the evidence is that they are initialled by him in blue pencil; these were copies that he sent my mother at the time of their appearance.

He returned to the subject a few days later:

As for the Times [Literary] Supplements, I have gone over all that Eliot

House has . . . to check evidence of authorship. Curiously I find . . . that the first nine issues . . . are marked in blue pencil at the head of the article, "T. S. E." I could not swear that this is his handwriting, as it is in Roman initials; it might be the writing of Miss Pearl Fassett, his then secretary, who, I believe, was thoroughly efficient (and plain). But the [later] issues . . . , though blue-pencil-marked, are not initialed. The reviews sound like T. S. E., and I cannot conceive of his sending a review of a translation of Ovid (to take an example) to his mother, marked, unless it was by him; for though my mother was very well read, there are many articles in these Timeses of more interest to her than a new Ovid. I suppose the only sure way is to write the Times (T. S. E. himself might not be infallible). . . .

(Henry did write to the *Times,* only to be informed that "they did not themselves now know the authorship of the articles ... .")*

On 7 April 1937 he reported to me:

I was highly gratified this morning to receive from my London book-seller, [F.J.] Ward, a complete file of the *Listener [the organ of the B.B.C.],* as concerns contributions (broadcasts) by T.S. Eliot. I had given a "blanket order" but was astonished to find that he had made so many broadcasts that I did not know anything about. (In one of his letters recently he referred merely to one made last fall.)

. . . although I have of course not read this new bunch yet, the articles appear to me both interesting and important. And one thing that I like about these radio addresses is that the necessity for oral delivery, to a general audience, imposes the duty of being highly explicit instead of (sometimes obscurely) allusive. I enclose a carbon of the complete list ... .

A few weeks earlier Henry had given me details concerning the manuscript of *Murder in the Cathedral:*

I have now to confess to a very stupid error of mine. I received from TSE two pages of typed MS which I could not identify, though I was certain (until I looked through my copy of *Murder*) that they were from that play. Not finding the passage in *Murder,* I asked my brother what it was; and he replied in his letter of yesterday that it was the chorus at the beginning of Part II of *Murder.* That was the first that I knew that this chorus was not printed in the first edition, either the Canterbury or the F[aber] & F[aber] one. Which seems very strange, and I have asked him why.

Still more information came in April:

---

*A change of ownership—and policy—now allows scholars access to the *TLS* records. In *Notes and Queries* (June 1995), David Bradshaw of Worcester College, Oxford, lists eleven additions to the canon of T. S. Eliot's contributions to the *TLS.*

You will be interested to know that I received from my brother the other day another page of pencil MS of *Murder*. It was pinned to a letter from the Sunday Times, London thanking TSE for the loan of it for some exhibit. On this TSE had typed (to me) "Another scrap of M[urder] in [the] C[athedral]." I read the first few lines and then combed both editions for them but could not find them—despite the fact that they were familiar. Finally I found that these first lines had been taken by TSE and used in a short poem called "Bellegarde" which he never finished or published. The rest of the MS *was* from Murder—a speech of the Second Tempter ... . I then examined the "Bellegarde" MS (which is typed, not handwritten) again, and noted that the four lines on p. 2 of it sounded very much as if meant for Becket. So this Bellegarde is evidently discarded material from Murder.

In other letters I had further evidence of Henry Eliot's intense interest in the texts of his brother's poems. Early in our correspondence he had pointed out "how T. S. E. shuffles his verses around," and had suggested that it might be of interest to me to study especially the evolution of "The Hollow Men," comparing

its final form with that in which it appeared in the *Dial* for March 1925. Also you will find in the Chapbook for 1924, p. 36, *Doris's Dream Songs*, by TSE. The last section of this was later incorporated by TSE into The Hollow Men. The first two sections you will find in Collected Poems, 1909–1935 (Faber, 1936), pages 143 and 144; and you will notice the similarity of that on p. 143 to The Hollow Men.

In 1944 he wrote me about the Faber edition of *Four Quartets:*

in *Burnt Norton* (p. 8): the line "And reconciles forgotten wars" [is] changed to "Appeasing long forgotten wars," which may make [TSE's] ... meaning clearer, but the word "appease" has been so overworked lately that I am tired of it. In two other places blanks between sections have been closed up, which does not seem to me an improvement, as there is a definite change of mood or rhythm indicated.

Henry Eliot often, as he did here, voiced his own opinions. About an early poem, "The Death of Saint Narcissus," he wrote that

evidently TSE does not want [it] published, or he would have done so himself. I had never heard of the poem till you told me of it. Do you know the date of it? It has some good lines, but to me it seems that the bizarrerie is rather strained, and as you say, doesn't quite "come off."

In March 1940, Henry reported that he had received "a while ago" from his brother two typed letters from Ezra Pound . . . in re Waste Land. It seems that at first they discussed the advisability of prefixing Gerontion ... . Does that not now seem incredible? However, they agreed against it. Unfortunately EP's letter is so peppered with obscene phrases that it won't do for general exhibition. In fact, TSE prohibited its inclusion in the Collection; but I think some kind of limbo might be instituted for such items.

(It is an indication of the astonishing advance in permissiveness in the past half century that Pound's "obscene phrases" have not only been made part of the Harvard collection, but have now been printed, without remark, in the first volume of the Eliot *Letters*.)

When I admitted to Henry in 1939 that I had had some difficulty in reviewing his brother's *The Idea of a Christian Society* for the *Dallas News,* Henry replied:

The Xn Socy. . . . seems to have baffled them all. It certainly baffles me, and I can only ask "So what?" after reading it.

In 1940 Henry wrote me about the recent production of *The Family Reunion* at Harvard:

It was given twice, and we saw it both times. It seemed to me very well done, despite the too evident youth of the actors in a few minor parts. The problem of the Eumenides was evaded rather than solved, but I think wisely. Their apparition was indicated merely by a light in the window. After all, these are subjective and not physical images, and to have them there, with most of the actors pretending not to see them, is running the risk of a laugh in the most seriously intense moments.

The summary of the play in the programme, which I think was written by Prof. Theodore Spencer, states that Harry actually did murder his wife. I do not agree with this, and I hope to have word on that point from TSE, to whom I have written a description of the performance. Spencer's notion seems to me to detract greatly from the merit of the play, and makes it flat and melodramatic. It is not consistent with TSE's predilection for subjective conflict (cf. *Murder in the Cathedral*).

It was to be expected that Henry Eliot would make an attempt to solve the mystery of the disappearance of the *Waste Land* manuscript, given by T. S. Eliot in 1922 to the lawyer-patron-collector John Quinn and untraced after his death in 1924. Henry informed me in April 1940 that the well-known bookseller-collector "Dr. [A. S. W.] Rosenbach . . . doesn't know where it is," and wondered "whether one would get anything by writing the Query

Department of the N. Y. Times SUP. [*i.e.*, *Book Review*], or perhaps to some bibliophile periodical." In December 1945 he had written to the famous editor and collector of Horace Walpole, Wilmarth Lewis, who had had an article in the *Atlantic* on manuscript chasing, "to ask him whether he had ever heard of the whereabouts of the MS ... . He had not, but he asked Mr. [Archibald] MacLeish [then Librarian of Congress] and the Librarian of Yale University to be on the watch for it." Some nine months later he had written to John D. Gordan, curator of the Berg Collection in the New York Public Library. Gordan referred him to Jacob Blanck, who was then writing a column on rare books in *Publishers' Weekly*. Henry wrote to Jake, who promised to print a note of inquiry in *PW*. Two years after Henry's death a typescript of the poem that had belonged to Quinn was actually given to Harvard by Jeanne Robert Foster, his devoted friend, and Bill Jackson hoped at first that this was the long-lost manuscript. Its whereabouts became known to the public only after Bill, John Gordan, and T. S. Eliot were dead.

IV

Henry Eliot's letters revealed now and then the kind of private person he was. In February 1937, in discussing items that he might possibly offer me in exchange for things I had sent him, he wrote:

I have negatives of early snap-shots of TSE, some of them quite charming ... . I have given some to Eliot House, but I do not intend to give away any others (except to you) as I do not like to publicize matter of a purely personal nature.

And he returned to the subject of photographs of his brother a few days later. Referring to things that he might lend for the Eliot exhibition I was arranging for the Yale Library, he told me that

the two early snap-shots of T. S. E. . . . are for yourself, but, while I hope you are not disappointed, I have about come to the conclusion that I would prefer that they not be included in the exhibition. . . . In the first place, it seems to me that they do not exactly belong in an exhibit of books, but rather in a collection of relics, of the sort that are usually shown after a man is dead. They are very cute pictures, but I think that in T.S.E.'s place it would make me feel just a shade foolish to have childhood photographs on view to the public. . . . I feel a certain sense of responsibility for the pictures (which I took), and I should think twice about allowing Eliot House to put them on view—though it is perhaps a trifle different here, where quite a number of people knew him as a child. I think the 1933 photograph which I sent you, however, is quite all right to exhibit, if you like. In fact, I should be glad of it, because most of the published photographs of T.S.E. are quite uncharacteristic of him and actually falsify his personality.

(In an earlier letter he had written about this particular photograph of 1933 that

(if I do not seem to praise myself too much as a photographer) I like it better than any professional or other photograph that I have ever seen of TSE in adult life. The photographs used to accompany reviews are all abominable and utterly at variance with his personality; they make of him a sleek broker.)

When, in January 1939, Henry Eliot gave me a letter that his brother had written him, mentioning a copy of *The Family Reunion* inscribed for me, he hedged the gift round with restrictions:

I would ask . . . that you do not exhibit this letter from TSE publicly, as it is so recent; in fact, I might ask you to be rather selective as to whom you show it (for a few years, anyway). . . . I shouldn't want it to get in circulation—not because it is particularly personal, but because I feel a personal responsibility to my brother for it.

And he added in manuscript in the margin of his typed letter: *"Don't photostat it! Nor allow anyone to quote."*

Henry Eliot's feeling about the sanctity of private correspondence never changed. In March 1946, only a year before he died, he wrote me enclosing copies of a letter and a telegram from his father announcing the birth of TSE:

A cousin of mine in Portland Oregon has sent me a bushel of old letters written by my father to his father, who must have saved all his letters since the Civil War. I am not sure that I like the idea of reading private correspondence, even that of my father to his brother. I have, however, read some of the earlier ones. I am glad to have discovered this letter and telegram.

The telegram is dated 26 September 1888 and reads: "Lottie and Little Thomas are well Hurrah for Harrison and Morton". (Benjamin Harrison and Levi P. Morton were the—eventually successful—Republican candidates for president and vice president, respectively, in the national election of 1888.) Henry's comment was: "My father was almost invariably brief ... ."

A minor crisis developed in March 1937 when Henry and Theresa Eliot invited me to visit them in Cambridge and see a production at Harvard of *Murder in the Cathedral:* should we wear evening dress for the occasion? Henry wrote me:

In re dinner coat, I shall make careful investigation. It is my usual ill luck to be wrong at least 85% of the time. I went to a tea in Boston yesterday, all slicked up in cutaway (per order the spouse) and was alone in my glory. Most of the guests were college presidents, or Directors of Museums— including ex-President Lowell of Harvard, dressed as if he'd just got up from an after-dinner nap.

There was another letter a few days later:

I think I told you that Dr. Spencer believed evening clothes would not be in order. I should hate nothing worse than for our party to be the only glad rags contingent in the audience, and I am sure there will be at least a large contingent in day clothes, so I think day clothes are the safest.

Eventually a telegram announced that dinner coats appeared after all to be indicated. At the performance, which was given in the courtyard of the Fogg Museum, there were enough other parties in evening dress so that we were spared any embarrassment. But the Eliots had invited a British graduate student to join us for dinner and hadn't apparently informed him that we'd be dressing: he appeared in rather rumpled tweeds enlivened by a violently red tie.

Henry Eliot almost never in his letters commented on individuals, but he made an exception of J. J. Angleton, who was then editing the magazine *Furioso* at Yale, and was later to achieve notoriety in his career with the C.I.A. In June 1942 he had visited Cambridge to use the collection in order to prepare an article about T. S. Eliot. Henry reported to me:

Angleton is an agreeable fellow, but I think I am justified in calling him a bit singular, inasmuch as, having been invited to tea at 5:00, he stayed till 8:30. We would not have minded asking him to dinner but that there happened not to be much in the house, and we imagined him each moment to be on the point of going. Furthermore, although his views on world trends and currents are original, they seem to me particularly unoriented

and at times self-contradictory. In short, I call him a genuine eccentric. He
. . . claimed that his last issue [of *Furioso*] sold 3000 copies; which is a bit
[much] to swallow, if it is true (as I have been told) that the *Partisan Review*
sold only 700.

V

In the *International Herald Tribune* of 17 August 1988 a dispatch
reprinted from the *New York Times* was headlined "The Lost Letters
of Lucia Joyce: What Price Family Privacy?" The story reported that
at an international symposium on James Joyce, held in Venice in
June, Stephen Joyce, the writer's grandson, announced that he had
destroyed all the letters he had received from his Aunt Lucia, who
spent most of her adult life in mental institutions and who died in
1982. He admitted also that he had destroyed letters written to his
aunt by Samuel Beckett, Joyce's onetime secretary, at Beckett's
request. A member of the audience, Michael Yeats, son of William
Butler Yeats, spoke against such destruction, saying that documents
about great writers belonged to the world. Mary de Rachewiltz,
daughter of Ezra Pound, agreed with Yeats and said that Lucia Joyce
had been harmed by her nephew's action. The *New York Times*
pointed out that Stephen Joyce's decision raises complicated issues:

What are the legal rights and ethical responsibilities of biographers, scholars, and literary heirs? . . . Deciding when private matters have literary relevance is an issue that scholars redefine endlessly.

The redefinition will continue in relation to the T.S. Eliot collection here at Harvard. On 26 August 1938, Henry Eliot wrote me
that

after my mother's death there was in her desk a drawerful of letters to her
from TSE. I asked TSE what about them and he bade me burn them. I did
not do so, but mailed them to him. Whether he destroyed them I do not
know.

In her introduction to the first volume of the collection of her husband's *Letters*, published in the fall of 1988, Valerie Eliot reports that
TSE did indeed burn a good part of his correspondence with his
mother and brother, including much of their side. She points out
that

in his mother's case, there is a gap between 23 August 1921 and 12 January 1926, for which she may be partly responsible, having written to him on 18 March 1924 to say that she had all his letters from the time he went to Milton [Academy], and supposed she ought to destroy half of them.

Those letters of 1921 to 1926, filled as they must have been with details of the disintegration of his marriage, would have seemed to both Charlotte and T.S. Eliot far too personal and painful to risk their ever being seen by strangers. But *The Waste Land* (1922)— probably the most influential poem of the twentieth century—grew directly out of its author's agony, and the hell that he suffered left its mark on much of his later work, especially *Sweeney Agonistes* (written in 1923 and 1924, not published in book form until 1932) and *The Family Reunion* (1939). Every detail that can be recovered therefore becomes important. The first volume of the *Letters* sheds a great deal of light; but in the early 1920s, even such a close friend of the T. S. Eliots as Ezra Pound had only a vague idea of exactly what was wrong with Vivien's health. And now in the *Letters* as published there is no indication of what seems to have been her longstanding addiction to various drugs and chemical substances, especially ether.

It is fortunate that T.S. Eliot could not bring himself to obey completely the instructions he had given to his brother, for the letters to Charlotte Eliot that he preserved were of vital importance to his widow, first in the editing of the *Waste Land* manuscript and then in filling out the biographical outline that she has chosen to present in publishing her husband's correspondence. T.S. Eliot himself deposited the letters to his mother in the Houghton Library, and they are an invaluable part of the Harvard collection.

Unfortunately, wisdom did not prevail for all of the letters between the two brothers. I have indicated their importance in what I have said about Henry's dogged determination to extract from his brother pertinent information about his work. Henry did make some of the letters part of the collection and quoted from them generously in his elaborate catalogue. But Theresa Eliot told me that, after her husband's death, she asked Tom what she should do about the substantial number of the letters that Henry had not, for one reason or another, turned over to Harvard. He replied that he had already destroyed Henry's letters to him.★ Whereupon Theresa felt she must agree, reluctantly, to the destruction of all of Tom's own letters not already placed in the collection. At 84 Prescott Street, she brought them to him, and together they burned them in the living room fireplace. Thus disappeared further evidence of the important role Henry had played in his brother's life and in building up the collection at Harvard.

I can attest to the importance of the letters from my own experience in writing about Eliot and Pound. When my article about their friendship appeared in the *Atlantic* in 1970, Theresa Eliot scolded me for not having given Henry proper credit for his substantial financial assistance to his brother during the troubled early years. But neither I nor anyone else outside the family was aware of the extent of Henry's self-sacrificing support. Tom and Vivien knew, and Theresa had been told; but even their closest friends seem not to have been aware of Henry's generosity. (Ezra Pound made light of the assistance by informing John Quinn that he believed Eliot's family "do send him rent or something.") The dimensions of Henry's help were not revealed until the first volume of the *Letters* appeared in the fall of 1988. Adding up the amounts acknowledged by Tom in just the letters to Henry that Valerie Eliot has printed gives an impressive total, considering that Henry himself was not well off, apparently living economically in boarding houses through most of the period. When he visited his brother in London in 1921, he brought his typewriter and left it in place of the broken-down one that Tom had been using. The succeeding volumes of the Eliot *Letters* will doubtless clarify further the role that Henry played in his brother's career. It is chiefly to help give Henry Eliot the credit he so richly deserves that I have put together this account. *Si monumentum requiris, circumspice.*

★But Valerie Eliot informs me that she has "a fair number" of Henry's letters.

The "Lost" Eliot Manuscripts
1958–1996

I

A RUMOR WAS widely circulated in 1958 that the manuscript of *The Waste Land* had been acquired by "a middle-western university library" for $100,000. T. S. Eliot, when the story was relayed to him, commented that he felt he should be entitled to part of the money because, as he remembered it, he had sold the manuscript to the New York lawyer-collector John Quinn for one thousandth of that amount. (Actually, he had *given* Quinn "The Waste Land" and had at the same time sold him a notebook containing copies of most of his early poems, published and unpublished.) My hunch was that, if the rumor had any basis, the buyer must be the Lilly Library at the University of Indiana; but Dave Randall, the librarian, denied that "The Waste Land" had even been offered to him.

I had always supposed that the manuscript must be in the possession of whoever owned the originals of John Quinn's correspondence. When Grover Smith was still teaching at Yale and working on his first book on Eliot, I understood him to say that he had looked up the will and found that Quinn had bequeathed the papers to Jeanne Robert Foster, his secretary. What he doubtless reported was merely that Mrs. Foster had been authorized to make a selection of the letters and have copies of them typed for deposit in the New York Public Library, a duty that she eventually carried out.

In connection with my work on the Ezra Pound *Bibliography* in 1961, I had gone up to Harvard to look at the typescripts of *The Waste Land* and Eliot's anonymously published early brochure *Ezra Pound His Metric and Poetry* that Mrs. Foster had just given, along with her letters from Pound, to the Houghton Library. I subsequently wrote her to ask about the originals of the Quinn correspondence. She replied that she thought Quinn's niece, Mrs. Thomas Conroy, had already given them to the New York Public Library.

But when I asked Robert Hill, the head of the manuscript division at the library, for more information, he replied that he could not give it to me. I wrote Mrs. Conroy herself, specifically about the letters but mentioning the *Waste Land* manuscript, and her reply was similarly evasive: she could not help me. I gave up trying to defeat such an obvious conspiracy of silence. The manuscript had still not surfaced when T. S. Eliot died on 4 January 1965.

When B. L. Reid, professor of English at Mount Holyoke College, announced a projected book on John Quinn and later received a Guggenheim grant to help him write it, I assumed that at last the whereabouts of the manuscripts would be made public. Valerie Eliot strengthened my assumption by telling me, in London in 1967, that Reid had let her know that they did exist, but he could say nothing further about them. I therefore eagerly awaited the publication of the Quinn biography.

In mid-September 1968, the Yale Library received, among some Book of-the-Month Club galleys, a photocopy of the setting typescript of Reid's book. I went through it hurriedly; much to my disappointment, beyond some additional quotations of letters from Eliot to Quinn relating to the manuscripts, there was no new information about their present location. (Reid did add that Eliot, in an interview, had explained that the passage imitating Pope in the original *Waste Land* draft had been deleted because Pound pointed out that it was a mistake to attempt to copy something that had already been done perfectly.)

On 18 September, a day or two after I had gone through Reid's typescript, I lunched in New York with John Kohn of the Seven Gables Bookshop. When I mentioned to him my disappointment at having found in the Quinn biography no new facts concerning the fate of the Eliot manuscripts, he remarked quietly that he apparently knew more about them than I did. He told me in confidence that in 1958 he had viewed a microfilm of the manuscripts and from it had prepared an appraisal for their sale. He could tell me very little more—indeed he said he had probably already told me more than he should have done—but added that he had been led to understand that the present location of the manuscripts would not be made public until two people were dead (I guessed that they must be T. S. Eliot and Mrs. Conroy).

I now deduced that if, as Mrs. Foster had told me, Mrs. Conroy had given the Quinn correspondence to the New York Public Library, she would have directed that the Eliot materials be offered first to that institution. There, probably only the Berg Collection, richly endowed by the Doctors Berg, would have had the funds for such an important acquisition.

II

At a Jonathan Edwards College fellows' meeting in October 1968, Richard Ellmann, then briefly at Yale as professor of English, mentioned that the John Quinn archive was to be opened to scholars at the time of the publication of the Reid biography. I told Dick a little of what I suspected concerning the Eliot manuscripts. On Thursday, 24 October, he telephoned me that the New York Public Library was holding a press conference that afternoon to announce the acquisition of the manuscript-typescript of *The Waste Land* and a holograph notebook of Eliot's early poems.

I went out earlier than usual the following morning to get my copy of the *New York Times*. Its report of the library press conference included the information that a microfilm of the Eliot materials had been handed to Valerie Eliot in London during the summer by James W. Henderson of the library staff. The manuscripts themselves were to be placed on exhibition, along with examples from the Quinn correspondence given to the library by Mrs. Conroy (who was still alive), beginning Thursday, 7 November—publication date for Reid's *The Man from New York: John Quinn and His Friends.* I recalled having recently been shown a letter from Valerie Eliot stating that she would be in New York on that day for "an important announcement concerning T. S. Eliot's work," and I gathered now that some plan was being prepared for the publication of the *Waste Land* manuscript.

I was glad that I had seen the *Times* rather earlier than usual that morning for, at about nine Arthur Crook, editor of the (London)

Times Literary Supplement, telephoned to ask me to write a report on the Eliot manuscripts. I said that I'd be happy to do it, but inasmuch as Mrs. Eliot had had a microfilm copy for some time and since she was to be in New York in two weeks, she might already have made arrangements for the materials to be edited by some individual, who would be the obvious person to write the account for the *TLS.* Crook said that he would telephone Mrs. Eliot and would let me know the result.

The next Monday morning I was at the Beinecke Library (I was at this time on leave, with a Guggenheim grant to work on Eugene O'Neill's Cycle plays), when Crook telephoned again, reporting Mrs. Eliot as delighted that the *TLS* had asked me to describe the manuscripts. She was going to allow the use of two pages as illustrations. Crook explained that his paper would want to print the story in its issue for 7 November, simultaneously with the opening of the exhibition at the New York Public Library and the publication of Reid's book. This meant that my report must be in his hands not later than eleven o'clock (New York time) on Monday morning, exactly one week from the time we were speaking. I warned him that either he or Mrs. Eliot would have to let the Berg Collection know that I was to be allowed to examine the manuscripts, and agreed to do the best I could to have the "purely descriptive" article he wanted ready in time. He explained that it could be sent via telex in the New York office of the London *Times,* or even telephoned if absolutely necessary. The *TLS* would be willing to devote one or two pages to my report, and he asked me, after I had examined the manuscripts, to cable whether I'd be sending 2,500 or (a maximum of) 4,000 words.

I telephoned Lola Szladits, the acting curator of the Berg Collection, and explained the situation. She thought it would be all right for me to plan to arrive at ten the following morning but wanted to clear the matter with Mr. Henderson. She called me back to say that he felt the library should wait for Mrs. Eliot's authorization and that I had best not come to New York until the confirmation had arrived. I pointed out to her that I must get to work on the manuscripts at the earliest moment possible: I would plan to be at the library and if the cable from London had not been received, I would telephone Mrs. Eliot.

I took the eight o'clock train on Tuesday morning and, at the Berg Collection, was very much relieved when Lola told me that the authorization had come. It was an exciting moment when the assistant brought the two, typical, Quinn Solander cases and placed them before me; but I wasted no time on mere sentiment and began at once to examine the poetry notebook (to which Eliot had given the title "Inventions of the March Hare") and its accompanying loose leaves. From those I proceeded to *The Waste Land*. Having read through everything hastily, I returned to the notebook and began a detailed description of its contents. I completed my rough pencil notes that day and, back at my hotel in the evening, typed them up. On Wednesday I made notes on the loose leaves, and again devoted the evening to typing. I finished a very hurried description in pencil of the *Waste Land* manuscript on Thursday morning, but then had to spend much more time than I had planned with a representative of Harcout Brace Jovanovich (publishers of Eliot's poetry), discussing the manuscript and plans for its publication. At about two, finally, I was free to begin the job of writing. (I had already informed Crook, via the *Times*'s telex, that my report would contain the maximum 4,000 words.)

I had quite deliberately taken down details that I knew I'd not have space for in the final account. These related particularly to the paper used by Eliot—its size, watermarks, folds—which would make it possible to group some of the manuscripts as having been written at about the same time. I had established what I thought was the correct order of the copying of the first poems into the notebook, and began to describe them in that sequence. I had completed a rough draft, and it was already 2:00 A.M., when I had to admit to myself that the scheme I had been following was far too detailed: the report would be more nearly ten times 4,000 words if I carried it through. I was already so tired that I knew I could do nothing more that night and expect it to be any good, and so I forced myself to put the whole thing out of my mind, take a hot bath, and go to bed.

At about five-thirty, I got up, had a nourishing breakfast, and gradually became confident that I might in the next eight or nine hours get something written to show Mrs. Eliot when she visited the library that afternoon. Fortunately, in beginning again, I hit upon a formula that seemed to work, and by noon I had completed my description of the notebook and its loose leaves in what seemed to be just about the right number of pages. I went out for lunch and a breath of air, and then returned to tackle "The Waste Land." When Mrs. Eliot arrived at three, she told me at once that she had given the *TLS* permission to include not two but three photographs, including one showing Ezra Pound's comments. This meant that the article would be even more important than I had expected. I spent some time with her and the Berg Collection staff, going over the materials, but after an hour or so, excused myself, retrieved "The Waste Land," and completed checking my description of it before I left the library. I had dinner and, back at my hotel, began the necessary typing. I finished at about nine o'clock, and was relieved to find that it too came out at about the right length. I immediately took a hot bath and went to bed.

But I could not sleep, my mind continuing to wrestle with problems. After an hour or so, I got up, spent some thirty minutes organizing all my various notes and drafts, then wrote out and typed my letter to Crook. I had followed chronological order, describing the notebook first, but in my letter explained that the two sections could easily be reversed if the *TLS* preferred to begin with *The Waste Land* (from which all three illustrations were taken).

I had already typed out a page or two of an introductory account of the manuscripts when I realized that giving even the essential details would raise the total for my article to well beyond the allotted maximum, and I should be doing little more than summarizing facts contained in Reid's book. And so I decided to refer the reader to the biography for details of how the manuscripts happened to be in John Quinn's possession. When a rough word-count produced 3,920 as the total, I could at last go back to bed.

I awoke shortly after six, and again went out for breakfast—to Horn & Hardart. I had finished my meal and was making some last-minute revisions in my article when I looked up to see a familiar figure approaching. It was Thornton Wilder! (He had told me that when he was in New York, he occasionally ate early breakfast at the 42nd Street cafeteria.) He was returning to New Haven at eight o'clock and I was soon to meet Harvey Simmonds of the Berg Collection—to be admitted an hour early—but for thirty minutes or so Thornton and I had some pleasant talk, most of it, for once, coming from me. Of course he was very much interested to hear about "The Waste Land."

At the Berg Collection I went over my account of the manuscript with the original, and checked the notebook and its leaves. My typing had not been infallible and in two instances I had omitted items. I managed to make the necessary corrections not too illegibly on my typescript and at about 10:30 had it ready for photocopying.

The machine at the library had just broken down and I had to wait nearly a half hour for photographs by another process. Meanwhile Simmonds had discovered more errors, which had to be corrected in all the copies. Even after I had said goodbye to him and was about to take the elevator down to street level, he came rushing out to report yet another mistake; he phoned me a final error a half hour later at the *Times* office.

From the library I walked to the Grand Central Post Office nearby and mailed one copy of the article with my covering letter by airmail special delivery to Arthur Crook. Continuing to the *Times* office on East 42nd Street, I left another copy for transmission by telex to London and then, in a state of almost complete mental and physical exhaustion, took the next train back to New Haven.

It occurred to me en route that since Mrs. Eliot was giving the *TLS* permission to use as an illustration part of the original opening of the fourth section of *The Waste Land*, "Death by Water," a narrative of the voyage of a fishing schooner from the Dry Salvages to the eastern Banks, it would be appropriate to quote in my report the lines which describe the final shipwreck (against an iceberg). The next day, Saturday, I thought again about the passage and decided to telephone Mrs. Eliot. I finally located her on Sunday, in Washington, and she gave me permission at once, only asking me to remind Arthur Crook when I phoned the addition to him the next morning, to include the appropriate copyright notice.

I thought again as well about the original opening of *The Waste Land*'s first section, "The Burial of the Dead." In my report I had summarized its content: "A male speaker tells of a low-life evening on the town in London, with friends, ending at sunrise." On reflection I began to suspect, more and more, that the passage had an American, probably Cambridge and Boston, setting. This impression was reinforced when I recalled Conrad Aiken's description of the "varieties of experience" he and Tom Eliot had shared during their undergraduate and postgraduate years at Harvard. Aiken had written (in his contribution to *T. S. Eliot, A Symposium*, published in 1949 as a tribute to the author on his 60th birthday) that he and Tom had met "at Buckingham and Brattle Hall dances," and that Tom had taken boxing-lessons "at a toughish gymnasium in Boston's South End" from "an ex-pugilist with some such monicker as Steve O'Donnell" (a possible prototype of Sweeney?). In the typescript draft, Eliot had written of "three gents from the Buckingham Club" and a Mr. Donavan "holding the watch" as the cabman and the tailor were "running a hundred yards on a bet."

But I hesitated to identify the scene as American without more evidence. Conrad Aiken had been one of our Bollingen Prize jurors in 1949 and 1950 (he won the prize for 1955), and I had met him several times during that period. I ventured to telephone him Sunday evening in Brewster, Massachusetts, though I knew he was not well and, even if at home, might not be able to come to the phone. Mary Aiken answered and I explained why I was calling. Conrad did come to the phone, and I asked him about "Buckingham." But, alas!, he did not recall his own reference and could not confirm that the ex-pugilist's name was Donavan rather than O'Donnell.

In her edition of the manuscript three years later, Valerie Eliot wrote about this passage:

When Eliot was an undergraduate at Harvard, he attended melodrama at the Grand Opera House in Washington Street, Boston, and after a performance he would visit the Opera Exchange (as he recalled it in later life, although the name cannot be traced in records of the period) for a drink. The bartender, incidentally, was one of the prototypes of Sweeney.

In the *Waste Land* draft, the friends "Blew in to the Opera Exchange, /Sopped up some gin, sat in to the cork game,". Thus it seems that an American setting was indeed intended, though I did not have the courage to add that claim to my report when I telephoned Arthur Crook the next morning.

I put through the call at about 6:15 (11:15 London time) and got him almost at once. The transmission of my article by telex had only just been completed (at 10:25) and the copy was "a bit of a mess," but he had already decided to reverse the order of the two sections, placing *The Waste Land* first. I had dictated to him the new passage and had got down to the last two or three corrections, when he told me, much to our mutual relief, that my airmailed copy had just been placed upon his desk!

Crook asked me to reassure Mrs. Eliot that the photographs and the entire article were all being copyrighted in her name, and to tell her again how very deeply he and the *TLS* appreciated her great kindness and generosity. I wrote Valerie accordingly, enclosing a copy of my article with the last-minute corrections. (I was relieved to have her telegram in response: "YOU HAVE DONE A SPLENDID JOB VERY MANY THANKS.")

Later that morning at the Beinecke I found a letter from Dorothy Pound thanking me for the copy of the *New York Times* story that I had sent her and adding that she was glad the New York Public Library would not be allowing any quotations. I had given little thought to the few words of Ezra Pound that I had used in my report, and now began to worry about Mrs. Pound's reaction. I decided to mention her letter to Crook if he telephoned again the next day, and in the meantime sent her by airmail a copy of my article.

On Tuesday morning at about 6:30 Crook did telephone, with a few, mostly minor questions. I suggested that in view of Mrs. Pound's letter he might like to call her in Rapallo, but he felt that it would be best not to do this for, if she should refuse permission, the *TLS* would be in an impossible situation. They were having difficulties with the printers because the correction of each error seemed to result in the commission of new ones, but Crook thought they would eventually get the article right. The *Times* had advertised the feature and was already beginning to receive inquiries.

Still worrying about possible complications on the Pound front, I tried all day to reach James Laughlin (his publisher), but without success. I eventually wrote him, explaining that I had tried to telephone. On Friday he called me, kindly agreeing that so far as my article was concerned, it was pointless to raise the question of permission to use Pound's words. He was interested to hear of Mrs. Eliot's plans for a facsimile edition and would write Harcourt Brace Jovanovich to remind them that Pound should get some recognition for his contribution. On Monday I received from Mrs. Pound an acknowledgment of the copy of the article I had sent her. She wrote—much to my relief—that she found nothing to object to on Pound's behalf. I telephoned J. Laughlin to give him this information.

On Tuesday, I received from the *Times* "blanket" proofs of the issue of the paper, the original opening of the poem by itself on page one, with my article and the two additional illustrations—each printed actual size—on the following three pages. The leading (and only) editorial was devoted to "T. S. Eliot and the *TLS*." I read through the proof hurriedly and found just a few minor errors.

On Wednesday, the editor of the New York Public Library *Bulletin,* William Coakley, telephoned asking to reprint my article in his December issue. I gave permission, suggesting that he add acknowledgment for the Pound quotations to Dorothy Pound (as committée). Because I wanted to make some changes, I decided to go to the Berg Collection and add the corrections to the copy of my typescript I had left there, which could then be photographed for Coakley. When I got to New York, I telephoned him and explained that, if there was plenty of space in the December issue, I'd like to rearrange parts of the article relating to the notebook and its laid-in leaves in separate paragraphs rather than run-on as they had been printed in the *TLS,* thus making the listing of contents much easier to follow. He replied that space was no problem. I marked the Berg Collection copy appropriately and thought to myself that I could now get back to work on Eugene O'Neill.

In New York that Wednesday afternoon I found, just outside the library, a newsstand that carried foreign papers. There, prominently displayed, was the *TLS* for 7 November 1968—my first sight of the article as printed—and I bought the last three copies. My own copy, which I get through my subscription, did not arrive until 17 December, almost six weeks after it had been mailed from London.

III

I was not so blindly optimistic as to expect that readers of the *TLS* would not discover faults in a description of such complicated materials written under pressure in so little time. One of the very few typographical errors in the paper had made my transcription of Ezra Pound's comment on Eliot's use—in "A Game of Chess"—of the word "inviolable" read "too pretty." What I had written was "too perrty," and a *TLS* reader (having Pound's note before him in one of the illustrations) suggested "too penty," meaning "too much [iambic] pentameter," as more likely—and consistent with his marking of the first three lines as "too tum-pum at a stretch." Other, mostly minor points were called to my attention in due course, but in retrospect, I count myself fortunate to have come through this ordeal by fire relatively unscathed.

A parenthetical remark that seemed to me innocuous enough at the time had unexpected and—from my point of view—entirely unwarranted reverberations in England. In the *TLS* I had written that "T. S. Eliot himself, perhaps indulging in some wishful thinking, supposed that the manuscripts had been destroyed." I altered this in the NYPL *Bulletin* to "T. S. Eliot himself referred to the manuscripts as untraceable and presumably destroyed"; but the harm had been done. I wrote Peter du Sautoy, vice-chairman of Fabers, on 22 November:

Dick Ellmann tells me that you . . . were rather sorry that I had made reference to Tom's (probably) wishful thinking that the *Waste Land* manuscript had been destroyed. I was basing what I wrote solely on Tom's own reference to the manuscript in the essay . . . he contributed to the book . . . that Peter Russell edited for Pound's 65th birthday (reprinted from *Poetry*, 1946):

I should like to think that the manuscript, with the suppressed passages, had disappeared irrecoverably: yet, on the other hand, I should wish the blue pencilling on it to be preserved as irrefutable evidence of Pound's critical genius.

I sent more information the next day:

When I wrote you last night, I remembered another printed reference by Tom to the disappearance of the *Waste Land* manuscript, but I didn't have a copy of the magazine in which it was contained ... .
I have now found it. . . . It is . . . in "A Conversation with T. S. Eliot <by> Leslie Paul" printed in the *Kenyon Review* for Winter <1964/> 1965 ... . The reference appears on page 21:
"*Eliot:* You know, I'm in two minds about that search [for] the manuscript of *The Waste Land.* I should like it to be found as evidence of what Ezra himself called his maieutic abilities—evidence of what he did for me in criticizing my script. On the other hand, for my own reputation, and for that of *The Waste Land* itself, I'm rather glad that it has disappeared."

Peter replied on the 27th that he was perhaps wrong in feeling uneasy about my remark, but all the talks he and Eliot had had about *The Waste Land* had given him the impression that Tom would have been glad to know what had happened to the manuscript, with no suggestion that he hoped it would not eventually turn up. Peter added that he felt it was extremely odd that Tom had been kept in the dark about the location of the manuscript for so many years.

I wrote Peter again on 2 December:

Valerie also seems to be upset about my suggesting that it was wishful thinking that caused Tom to say that the *Waste Land* ms. had probably been destroyed. She tells me that *The Times* picked up that phrase from my article and the result is that the talk at Oxford is that Pound really wrote the poem—or words to that effect. The Oxford gossip comes apparently from Wystan Auden, with whom Valerie had lunched. Of course all this amazes me, because one has only to read my "report" to find out that all Pound did, basically, was to advise Tom to cut out a couple of long, rather prosaic passages and tighten the poem up; and I am sure that Tom would have eventually done the tightening in any case. I simply cannot understand why Valerie should be disturbed by such talk, since there is obviously no basis for it, but if my reference to "wishful thinking" stimulated such gossip, I am truly sorry. My only point was that there never was any real ground for supposing that the manuscript did not exist, somewhere: Quinn was an astute collector and knew its value and would certainly not have destroyed it. His heirs would also be quite aware of its importance and value. The Conroys were notorious in the '40s for not wanting to be bothered by scholars and the NYPL had strict orders to protect them by not giving their address etc., and it is certainly not surprising that they did not go out of their way to inform Tom that the manuscript existed. I am trying to clear up the mystery as to exactly who was responsible for not letting Tom know the manuscript had been sold to Berg. I had assumed that Mrs. Conroy was the one, but the Acting Curator of the Berg Collection [Lola Szladits] told me that it was John Gordan who was responsible, and asked me not to mention John in my *TLS* article for that reason. Now the NYPL has apparently told Valerie that it was Mrs. Conroy. Well, I shall find out eventually, and shall let you know when I do. I quite agree that it is most unfortunate that Tom wasn't allowed to see the manuscript because he could have answered so many questions about it that are now, I am afraid, unanswerable, *i.e.*, I doubt that Pound will remember.

As it happened, Dr. Conroy had written to me on the same day:

The decision not to announce the acquisition by the Berg Collection was not ours. We have to presume that Dr. Gordan was solely responsible. We were very disturbed by the delay but felt bound by a 'gentleman's agreement' altho actually never so expressed by us. Please recall that Mrs. Conroy did not say [in 1962] that 'she didn't know where the Waste Land was.' Rather she said that 'she couldn't help you' in your efforts to find it. What more could she say?!

I let both Peter and Valerie know of Dr. Conroy's letter.

IV

In my discussion of the proposed facsimile edition with Valerie and the representatives of Harcourt Brace Jovanovich, I had at first favored including only the earliest draft of each section, along with the three appended poems. This would have satisfied no one for long, and I came around to agreeing that all of the material must be reproduced, with facing transcripts. Although Valerie, in England, would have to work primarily with photographs, she had the enthusiasm, energy, and courage to take on the assignment as editor.

On her return to London she devoted herself full-time to the *Waste Land* edition. She wrote me on 5 February 1969 that she had asked the New York Public Library not to allow the manuscript to be shown to scholars until her edition was published "as it is not in Tom's interest to have slanted articles appearing before the reader can check them against the text." She reported the library's answer to me on 26 March:

Mr. Henderson writes that the Committee are of the opinion that it would be "extremely difficult and probably improper" for the Library to withhold the manuscript from qualified scholars, and so that's that. But no one will be allowed to do any copying, and the Library will inform all applicants that no lines may be quoted until after the work is published. Of course each scholar will want to be the exception to the rule and I shall be bombarded with requests. Oh, dear!

Valerie travelled to Venice to consult with Ezra Pound and Olga Rudge on 9 April 1969, but the results were not very satisfactory. She reported to me on 13 May:

I am sorry to say that Ezra cannot remember a thing about the manuscript, and as far as his own comments are concerned he does not know what he meant in several cases. The one thing he was positive about, however, was that he has never used the word "purty", and we can only think that he wrote "too penty", referring to the pentameter [in his comment on Tom's use of the word "inviolable"]. . . .

Some of Pound's more cryptic references in his annotations were characteristically obscure. Any other editor would probably have given up the attempt to discover his meaning, but Valerie's persistence was more often than not rewarded. She wrote me from London on 1 September:

After a long search I traced one of Ezra's quotations to a French periodical of 1918—and danced for joy among the stacks of the London Library!

She had already found, in Dickens's *Our Mutual Friend,* the source of "He Do the Police in Different Voices," the title her husband had given tentatively to the first section of his poem. Lines from songs popular in America in the early teens of the century, quoted in that same section ("Tease, squeeze, lovin' and warm" and "Meet me in the shadow of the water melon vine") were impossible to trace in England. She had returned briefly to New York in May to check these and various other points in the manuscript (and found the music at Harvard). I lunched with her at the River Club on the 19th and, at the Berg Collection, we went over some of the problems. Determining whether Eliot or Pound had been responsible for a particular cancellation was difficult, even with the manuscript before us. Fortunately, Pound had used a softer pencil and his slashes tended to be more emphatic than Eliot's, but there were instances where distinguishing between the two was just not possible. In the drafts, a veritable palimpsest of readings made it extremely difficult, from photographs, to puzzle out Eliot's intentions. But even with the originals, the solution was by no means immediately evident. Later, from England, Valerie asked me to recheck some of her readings. At the Berg Collection I puzzled over the phrase "doggerel deduction" for hours with a magnifying glass before finally deciding that Pound must have written "dogmatic deduction." Valerie accepted my suggestion as "an inspiration worthy of Sherlock Holmes!"

She wrote me on 2 October that Lola Szladits was allowing her to have a portable machine brought in to x-ray the undeciphered words. Valerie reported the result to me on 2 January 1970:

> Lola [Szladits] has had two indecipherable passages of THE WASTE LAND photographed in different ways—infra-red, ultra-violet and the masking method, but the one result I have seen does not amount to much, alas. When I dined with Kathleen Raine a little while ago, she mentioned that . . . [X] had used a process on . . . [a] Notebook which is in pencil. Szladits had a word with him about it, but instead of confining his attention to the technical matters, he examined the MS and wrote a rather pompous letter saying that he had solved all the problems. He was wide of the mark in every instance!

By dint of a great deal of hard work, Valerie did meet her deadline and handed in her manuscript as scheduled in the spring of 1970. But Fabers and Harcourt Brace Jovanovich had decided that the difficulties involved in achieving a clear presentation of the manuscripts and their transcripts were beyond the powers of their usual printers. The choice of the Oxford University Press meant that the master-printer Vivian Ridler would turn his mind to solving some formidable problems.

T. S. Eliot's annotations and corrections would be printed in black, Pound's in red, and Vivien Eliot's in black with a cancelled broken line. Directional lines would indicate words and passages to which marginal comments related. Such a complicated, but essential scheme demanded extraordinary care on the part of the press, and it is not surprising that publication had to be postponed more than once. Valerie had written me early in October 1969 of her disappointment that problems with the printing of the book were forcing both Fabers and Harcourt to put its appearance off until September 1970, and there were more postponements. *The Waste Land: A Facsimile and Transcript of the Original Drafts Including the Annotations of Ezra Pound* was not finally published until 8 November 1971. Eleven thousand copies of a regular trade edition were issued on that day in London by Fabers at five pounds. A limited edition of five hundred copies at twelve pounds contained a frontispiece photograph of Eliot, a facsimile of the mailing label addressed by Eliot to John Quinn, and facsimiles of three bills from the Albemarle Hotel, Cliftonville, Margate, where part of the poem was written. Two days later, a trade edition of four thousand copies was published in New York by Harcourt Brace Jovanovich at $22.50. Their limited issue, of two hundred fifty copies at $50.00, contained the same photograph and extra facsimiles as the Faber copies. The book was received in both countries with wide acclaim, with especial praise for Mrs. Eliot's expert editing. (Both American and English publishers later issued revised, paperbound editions: Harcourt Brace Jovanovich's in 1974 at $7.50; Fabers' in 1980 at £5.95.)

Although when Valerie had talked with him in May 1969, Ezra Pound had not been able to recall the details for which she had hoped, he bestowed his blessing upon her edition in a preface written 30 September 1969:

The more we know of Eliot, the better. I am thankful that the lost leaves have been unearthed.

The occultation of 'The Waste Land' manuscript (years of waste time, exasperating to its author) is pure Henry James.

'The mystery of the missing manuscript' is now solved. Valerie Eliot has done a scholarly job which would have delighted her husband. For this, and for her patience with my attempts to elucidate my own marginal notes, and for the kindness which distinguishes her, I express my thanks.

V

During part of this period, early in 1969, I was having to take more time off from Eugene O'Neill in order to read proofs for a new edition of my T. S. Eliot *Bibliography*. In this version of the book, I had for the first time attempted to confront the problem of the "F—

M—" contributions to the *Criterion*.

An article by Gwenn R. Boardman, "T. S. Eliot and the Mystery of Fanny Marlow," in *Modern Fiction Studies* (Summer 1961) had noted that the work of four contributors with the initials F. M., printed in six issues of the *Criterion* from February 1924 to July 1925, present "a general impression of work that fails to meet the *Criterion*'s otherwise high standards under the editorship of T. S. Eliot." She pointed out that the stories *do* resemble the prose experiment, "On the Eve," printed in the magazine for January 1925 as by T. S. Eliot himself.

He resolved part of the mystery by admitting to Kristian Smidt and other scholars that he was not the author of "On the Eve," but had merely revised it. (When I once mentioned the Boardman article to Tom, he commented: "They [the scholars] just won't leave your private affairs alone"—which struck me as being not quite fair, in that he, by signing "On the Eve," had opened himself up to some quite legitimate questions. Edmund Wilson told me that it was "assumed generally" in 1924 and 1925 that the F. M. contributions in the *Criterion* were by Vivien Eliot.)

Even at the time of publication of some of the pieces, T. S. Eliot had let a few of their friends know about his wife's authorship. On 8 April 1925, he had written to Richard Aldington:

[Vivien] . . . is doing a lot of the Criterion work, and also writing. She is very diffident, and . . . therefore writes only under assumed names; but she has an original mind, and I consider not at all a feminine one; and in my opinion a great deal of what she writes is quite good enough for the Criterion. . . . You are the only person, except two of her friends, who now knows of her writing. But I see no reason now for concealment.

And in the same month he had written to Ada Leverson (spelling his wife's first name in its longer, less usual form):

I am so glad you like the new Criterion. I think it *is* a particularly good one. I believe you must have guessed that all the contributions signed by F- M-★ are by Vivienne and although the secret is *not out* yet, I have no objection to *your* knowing—in confidence. . . .

★ These were "Necesse est perstare? By F. M.," "Night Club. By Feiron Morris," and "A Diary of the Rive Gauche, II [by Fanny Marlow]."

On 17 May 1925, Eliot had sent to Ellen Thayer a story by Vivien, "The Paralyzed Woman," for possible publication in the *Dial,* explaining that it was to appear in the July issue of the *Criterion:*

It seems to me amazingly brilliant and humorous and horrible, and I have never read anything in the least like it. It is likely to attract a good deal of notice here, and it is the longest story she has yet published.* You could publish it under her own name (V. H. Eliot), or "Vivien Eliot", as you think best.

And he added a postscript:

Vivien wrote "Night Club" and also the poem by "F. M," ["Necesse est perstare?"] in the last CRITERION. Did you read them?

Scofield Thayer himself replied to Eliot's letter, on 4 June, regretting that the *Dial* could not publish Vivien's story:

Your opinion, as you know, is held in the most profound esteem by the editors of The Dial, and we could not be insensible to the resilience and grace, of this story; yet, it has not for us, that finality which you feel it to have.

Armed with these references, I had ventured to include in the new edition of the *Bibliography,* a revised entry for Section C, "Contributions to Periodicals":

C161 On the Eve, A Dialogue. *Criterion,* III.10 (Jan.1925) 278–81.
    Actually written, at least in part, by Vivien (Mrs. T. S.) Eliot and extensively revised by T. S. Eliot. (Other contributions by Mrs. T. S. Eliot printed in the *Criterion* are the following: "Letters of the Moment—I[-II]," signed: F. M. (Feb.-Apr. 1924) 220–2, 360–4; "Thé dansant (A Fragment)," by Feiron Morris (Oct. 1924) 72–8; "Mrs. Pilkington," by Felix Morrison (Oct. 1924)103–6; "A Diary of the Rive Gauche [I-II]," by Fanny Marlow (Jan.-Apr. 1925) 290–7, 425–9; review of Virginia Woolf's *Mr. Bennett and Mrs. Brown* by Feiron Morris (Jan. 1925) 326–9; "NECESSE EST PERSTARE?," by F. M. (Apr. 1925) 364; "Night Club," by Feiron Morris (Apr. 1925) 401–4; and "Fête galante," by Fanny Marlow (July 1925) 557–63.)

On checking "Letters of the Moment—II" in my set of the periodical, I was astonished to discover, incorporated in the article,

---

*The July 1925 issue of the *Criterion* contains no story by this title. There is a story, "Fête galante," by Fanny Marlow [*i.e.,* Vivien Eliot], but it does not seem to fit T. S. Eliot's description of "The Paralyzed Woman."

twenty lines of verse which appeared to be a version of part of the original opening of Section III of *The Waste Land*. I made a special trip to the New York Public Library to compare the passages and found that the subject matter and form were the same, one line was identical, and four lines varied only slightly from the typescript in the Quinn manuscript in the Berg Collection. In considerable excitement I reported my findings to Valerie Eliot on 22 January, concluding:

So Vivien must have had a retained copy of this (earlier) version and Tom obviously allowed her to print it as, presumably, her own work. Well! I'll be interested to have your reaction to this.

Her answer, when it came on 16 March, was somewhat deflating:

Yes, I did know about those lines from "The Waste Land"* in Vivien's article, and by a curious coincidence her brother asked me not long ago if I could identify some miscellaneous pages in Tom's writing which he had taken over at his sister's death. In pencil in a black exercise book I read "it seems to me that in this island" (the beginning of the 1st paragraph after the quotation in her article) and continued, with variations to the end of the first paragraph on page 362. . . . You can imagine my excitement! . . . There is also a draft (many variants) of "Mr. Bennett and Mrs. Brown" which appeared in the January 1925 number as "reviewed by Feiron Morris", another pseudonym of Vivien's. . . .

She had begun her letter by telling me that Tom's reason for printing Vivien's "dialogue" as his own work was for amusement. I answered on the 20th:

Tom's idea of "amusement" in signing his own name to something that Vivien had written doesn't, I am afraid, send me into paroxysms of laughter. And I gather from your description of the black exercise book that Vivien's brother has that Tom also wrote part of "Letters of the Moment" and (all of?) "Mr. Bennett and Mrs. Brown." This doesn't surprise me, but I don't think I shall try to change my general note on Vivien's contributions.

---

*In the notes to her edition of *The Waste Land,* Valerie Eliot commented on these lines:

It probably amused Eliot to print 'these few poor verses' knowing that only two other people knew their source. In addition he drafted (pencil holograph in a black exercise book) the two paragraphs that follow, ending with a parody of *Prufrock*: ' . . . if one had said, yawning and settling a shawl, "O no, I did not like the *Sacre* [*du Printemps*] at all, not at all." '

The new edition of the *Bibliography* was eventually published on 24 November 1969. Fabers had sent a copy to the *TLS* for review, and on 1 January 1970, Arthur Crook wrote me that his reviewer wanted to know whether I was identifying Vivien Eliot's contributions to the *Criterion* for the first time; if so, he wished to make a special mention of that fact. Valerie had written me the very next day about my F.M. entry:

Are you sure about your attributions to Vivien as F. M. in C.161? These initials were shared by another woman too, and I notice on a copy of an undated postcard which Tom sent to Conrad Aiken, he wrote: "The FM who wrote the letters you liked is the author of 'Thé Dansant'—not the other."

In replying to Crook on 7 January, I quoted Valerie's letter, and continued:

This is by way of being a bombshell if indeed, as Valerie says, the initials "F.M." were "shared by another woman, too." I can only hope that Valerie is referring to other contributions in the *Criterion* signed "F.M." written by Frederic Manning. It would be too diabolical of Tom to countenance the use of "F.M." for three different contributors all at more or less the same time. . . . Could I ask you to ring her up and see whether she agrees that Tom's reference in the postcard to Aiken is to "the other <F.M., i.e. Frederic Manning>" and not to "the other <woman>?"

As to my authority for the attributions: there is a letter from Tom to Ellen Thayer <of the *Dial*>, 17 May 1925, in which he writes "Vivien wrote 'Night Club' and also the poem by 'F.M.' in the last Criterion." . . . (. . . so far as I know, the entry under C.161 in the new edition of the Eliot *Bibliography* is indeed the first published attribution.)

On the same day I wrote to Valerie:

this morning I have a letter from Arthur Crook saying that the reviewer of the new edition of the *Bibliography* for the *TLS* has asked whether the attributions to Vivien under my C.161 have ever been made publicly before. In view of what you say in your letter about F.M. being another woman too, I have suggested to Arthur Crook that he telephone you on this point. . . . I would have assumed that Tom in his postcard to Conrad by "the other" was referring to the other F.M. <i.e., Frederic Manning, who did indeed write some book reviews signed with those same initials, and who, incidentally, is credited with some of Vivien's work in the consolidated Index to the *Criterion* issued by Faber & Faber>. . . . If there is an error, possibly the *TLS* reviewer should be allowed to point it out (in the customary way in such reviews) and thus get the correct facts into print?

She answered on the 12th:

I will try to help Arthur Crook if he telephones, but I am not really clear about the position myself. I have seen the carbon of a letter written by Tom in response to an enquiry, in which he says that F.M. stood for two ladies, and I will trace it as soon as possible. There may be some clues in the Criterion files, but I rather doubt it. Anyway, I will *not* encourage the TLS reviewer to fault you in print! . . .

P.S. Crook has just telephoned. Would it be possible to have a copy of the letter you quoted in your letter to him as I have no carbon. If it is owned by the Library perhaps they will sell me a photostat?

I replied to Valerie on the 15th, enclosing a photocopy of Tom's letter to Ellen Thayer, and added a query:

I wonder if Tom by "two ladies" meant two different aspects of Vivien?

And I wrote again to her on the 24th:

I shall be eager to see the text of . . . Tom's letter about the F.M. contributions. Do you suppose this could possibly be his joking way of referring to the fact that he had helped Vivien? Certainly with the evidence of his manuscript of part of "Letters of the Moment" and its inclusion of the lines from the *Waste Land* draft, along with his signing as his own the "On the Eve, a dialogue," one could well say that the F.M. contributions were by Tom *and* Vivien. . . . Under the circumstances, I think you are right in steering the *TLS* away from the Vivien problem until we have all the evidence in hand.

Meanwhile, Crook had written me on 13 January that his reviewer realized that his planned reference to my C.161 was no longer valid. Crook had suggested to Valerie that the question of the F.M. contributions to the *Criterion* would be of great interest to readers of the *TLS* and an article on the subject from either or both of our pens could be fascinating. I had answered him on the 19th:

I certainly agree that, under the circumstances, it would be best for your reviewer not to mention my "solution" of the F.M. problem until Valerie's doubts are resolved. I have had a letter from her but she still has not given me the exact phrasing of Tom's letter stating that the F.M. contributions were by two women; until she does I can do nothing to defend my attributions.

. . . I think I have Tom pretty well pinned down as to Vivien's authorship of all save the one contribution "Mrs. Pilkington" by Felix Morrison in the issue for October 1924, and I myself do not seriously question that Feiron Morris, author of "Thé dansant" in that same issue, identified by

Tom as Vivien, and Felix Morrison are the same person, although the two pieces might be held to be in different veins. As soon as Valerie and I get to the bottom of the mystery, either she or I or both of us will let you know.

Meanwhile, I hope and trust that your reviewer's "projected references to C.161" are still valid, but, let us say, are in the process of being tested.

Still having had no word from Valerie, I wrote Arthur Crook again on 30 March:

Valerie hasn't yet located and sent to me a copy of Tom's letter about the "two women". . . . She has, I am sure, been attempting to answer all questions in connection with the *Waste Land* facsimile before copy . . . goes to press and I am not the least surprised at not having heard from her.

Unfortunately, so far as the F. M. question was concerned, Valerie Eliot had no sooner completed her exemplary editing of the *Waste Land* manuscripts than she embarked upon the even more time-consuming job of editing her late husband's *Letters*.* When that five-volume work is complete, it will doubtless provide at last the documentation for a final solution of the F— M— mystery.

VI

The *TLS* article had stirred up a good deal of interest in both Eliot and Pound. One of the first letters I received was from Robert Manning, the editor of the *Atlantic Monthly*, asking me to write a piece about their friendship. This was a request that I could not refuse, and I spent a good deal of time during the next months of my Guggenheim year working not on O'Neill but on the fascinating subject of the relationship over the years between "Old Possum" and his friend "Ez." The result of my research was published in the *Atlantic* for January 1970, with a brilliant cover illustration by Adrian Taylor, showing Eliot with Pound looming over his shoulder. Although both Manning and Peter Davison, of the Atlantic Monthly Press, professed themselves pleased (and paid me a fee a good deal larger than that originally proposed), the general readership of the magazine was not much impressed. But I had sent a copy

---

*In his will, T. S. Eliot had authorized her to publish his letters.

of the article to Thornton Wilder in Milan, and I was proud to receive his comment:

What a great story it is and how zestfully you tell it. This is just one more grand example of how well you write,—the economy, the objectivity. In fact the excitement and high comedy emerge precisely because D. G. effaces himself. Never a wasted word—never an overcharged word.

The *Atlantic* had had no space for the careful documentation that lay behind the account that I had written. I therefore welcomed the suggestion of Henry W. Wenning, who was undertaking a program of publishing in addition to his bookselling activities in New Haven, that he reprint the article as a separate pamphlet, including the annotations and acknowledgments that the magazine had had to omit. When *T. S. Eliot & Ezra Pound, Collaborators in Letters* appeared, on 5 November 1970, the 268 footnotes occupied almost half as much space as the text itself.

VII

In February 1972, I had done some research in the Berg Collection and had talked briefly with Lola Szladits, now the curator. She told me that, so far as she knew, no plans were afoot for the publication of the Quinn notebook of T. S. Eliot's early verse. I ventured to write Peter du Sautoy at Fabers:

Of course anyone interested in Tom's poetry would jump at the opportunity to work with these manuscripts with their . . . problems, especially of dating. Is there any chance, do you think, that Valerie would be willing for me to try my hand at editing them? . . . it seems to me that . . . [they] would make a fascinating book documenting Tom's early development as poet ... .

He replied on the 25th, explaining that Valerie continued to be mindful of the early poems, but she did not want them published separately. He thought that they would probably be printed first in "some vast complete" volume of Tom's poetry. I wrote him again on 1 March:

I agree with Valerie that as poems the unpublished ones belong only in a possible appendix (of early work) to the "vast complete volume." But the book I had in mind would be something else: a very scholarly (I'd hope) study of composition, dating, influences, drafts, which would be in effect an analysis of Tom's development as poet up to 1920. The unpublished poems would appear as documents embedded in that study and not really as publishable poems. And of course it would be necessary to do this kind of detailed study, thus establishing probable dates of composition, etc., before their inclusion in the "vast complete volume" would be possible.

Peter answered on the 9th that he would try to have a talk with Valerie about the poems, but he doubted that she would want to have a separate publication, even in such a scholarly study as I proposed. And that was the last word I had from Fabers or Valerie until she wrote me on 30 October 1989 that she had invited Christopher Ricks to edit the Berg Collection poems.

Three years and three months later, I had more information from Christopher Ricks himself. He wrote me on 1 February 1993:

> Mrs Valerie Eliot was so good as to invite me, two or three years ago, to edit *Inventions of the March Hare* and the allied poems in the Berg Collection. . . . [She asked] that I edit the poems much as I had edited Tennyson.★ I have already gathered a good deal of material, mostly bent upon where the poems came from (Symons as well as Tennyson, and the haunting Laforgue, of course), and where they went to (in the rest of Eliot's work). Your original account of the poems, in the *TLS* and in the *BNYPL,* has been . . . indispensable. ... I shall be grateful for any advice you may wish to give me ... .

I answered on 15 February:

> I rejoiced when Mrs. Eliot wrote me that she had decided to entrust to you the editorship of the "Inventions of the March Hare": first because of your impeccable credentials, and then because she had at last decided to abandon the fond hope of being herself the editor of *all* the Berg materials in addition to the Letters. . . .
>
> Of course I shall be happy to help in any way I can and look forward to meeting you when you come to New Haven. I suppose the most important Yale materials—indeed they are essential—for your project are the leaves cut from the Berg notebook and sent to Pound. . . . I daresay you know of these already; but in case you don't, the portions of the "Inventions" they involve are these:
>
> "Goldfish <IV, lines 18–37, with date Sept 1910>" (cancelled in ms.)

★*The Poems of Tennyson, Edited by Christopher Ricks.* 2d edition (3 vols. Harlow, Longmans, 1987).

"Suite Clownesque <III, last line, plus section IV, with date Oct. 1910>"
"Portrait of a Lady <I, last 4 lines, with 2 final lines unpublished, and unpublished epigraph for III>"
"Portrait of a Lady <III, last 11 lines>"

At least one of the other leaves bearing Bolo poems★ was removed from the Berg notebook; it contains "The Triumph of Bullshit," 2pp., with date Nov. 1910<?>. There is also a leaf . . . bearing a poem "To Helen," written, as poetry, in 9 unrhymed lines, very much in the manner of "Hysteria."

I'm sure you know that the Eliot letters to Pound are for the most part at Yale (some are at Indiana; and some . . . are known to have been destroyed . . .). Yale has other letters, notably those to Thayer and *The Dial.* . . .

I wonder whether Lawrence Rainey [at Yale] has been in touch with you? (He promised some time ago to write you.) He and one of his students have been pursuing indefatigably a study of the stationery Eliot used up to 1922, with a view to shedding light on the dating of the early poems. The results of their research would, I am certain, be useful for you in editing the "Inventions."

Christopher Ricks thanked me for my letter and wrote again at the end of March, asking me to suggest "a date or two, in May perhaps, which would he convenient to you, and which—please—would be possible for the Library?" We eventually fixed upon 17 May for his visit. He lunched with me at the Graduate Club and spent the better part of the day with the Beinecke Eliot materials. I was relieved that he had decided to include in his edition only the "Bolo" poems that had been actually part of the Quinn notebook and not all of those given to Pound. He later sent me his transcripts of the Beinecke leaves and I compared them with my own, finding only a few minor points where we disagreed in our readings.

In a letter of 28 May 1994, I had asked Ricks if he had noted (what I took to be) "the Oedipus echo in 'Goldfish, IV': 'At the four crossroads of the world'?" He added a postscript to his letter to me of 8 September:

Goldfish IV: "At the four crossroads of the world"—You suggested Oedipus, but I can't make that fit (the place where *3* roads meet, a fork in the road)—& what are "four crossroads" exactly, a crossroad being a foursome, no?

★The "Bolo" poems were scatological verses, some of them narrating the exploits of King Bolo, Chris Columbo of Genoa, and other worthies.

On the 30th of September, I replied:

In "Goldfish IV" it was "oracle" [*in the following line*] that made me
think of Oedipus. As for "four crossroads," serendipity★ has produced
these final two lines in Thomas Hood's "Faithless Nellie Gray":

> "And they buried Ben in four cross-roads,
>   With a *stake* in his inside!"

He answered on 5 October:

Yet once more, my heartfelt thanks. I'd insufficiently seen the salience
of "oracle"—& I'd missed entirely the Hood lines (my father's favourite
poet, so perhaps there's a touch of the parricidal, or OEdipus Ricks . . .)

I was surprised—and delighted—to hear from him in September
that he had handed his manuscript in to Faber & Faber "though
aware that there are i's to cross and t's to dot (it feels that way round,
I'm afraid), and aware that I shall be sending them corrections and
additions. But at least they can be vetting it." I had offered to read
the typescript and, sparing me the 150 pages of his notes, he sent the
preface, the body of the text, and the appendix. "Any corrections,
suggestions, queries, will be gratefully received ... ."

On 16 September, Ricks had asked me about the original manu-
scripts, given by Eliot to Conrad Aiken, of the poems "Suppressed
Complex" and "Afternoon" (both copied into the Berg notebook).
I answered on the 20th:

Aiken, "sometime in the thirties," sold the . . . [manuscripts] to Maurice
Firuski of the Housatonic Bookshop in Salisbury, Ct. Firuski sold them,
apparently quite promptly, to Urling S. (Mrs. O'Donnell) Iselin in New
York, NY. She died in the very early 1950s, and her husband followed her
a decade or so later. Part I of her library was sold by their heirs at Sotheby
Parke Bernet, New York, on 31 October 1972. It included . . . [three
Eliot] typescripts, some Eliot and Aiken letters about the poems (Eliot
thought them very bad and felt that they must be by Aiken!), and an Eliot
letter to [John] Rodker about *Ara Vos Prec,* but NOT the manuscripts. . . .
I have typed copies of . . . the Iselin poems . . . made for me by Jane
Quinby, Mrs. Iselin's librarian.

I had not yet examined Ricks's manuscript carefully when I wrote
him again. (I had found the notes I made in 1968 on the Eliot man-

---

★I had been "browsing" in *The Faber Book of Comic Verse, Edited by Michael Roberts* (revised
edition, 1974), which prints the Hood poem on pages 128–30.

uscripts at the New York Public Library, and had been reminded of my attempt to establish the order in which the poems had been copied into the notebook.)

I . . . don't find that you deal with this problem of the order in which the various poems were copied into the notebook—perhaps you do so in your Notes? I daresay it's just not feasible to try to print the poems thus, but I do find it unfortunate that "Fourth Caprice in Montparnasse" follows "First Caprice in North Cambridge" and precedes "Second Caprice," and that the "Interlude in London" [(April 1911)] interrupts the 1909–10 sequence.

A few days later, I called his attention to the Pierre Leyris translation of Eliot's poems, *Poèmes 1910–1930* (1947), of which he had not been aware:

Leyris, in his introduction, writes of the "exquise bienveillance de Mr. Eliot," and offers "les plus vifs remerciements à Mr. John Hayward ... ." All this preliminary to saying that the dates assigned have been taken as having Eliot's sanction. Should they not supersede—where they disagree with—dates given the poems in the Berg notebook? . . .

I apologize for having to raise this problem, but I daresay it's better dealt with now than after the presses begin to roll!

And I added a postscript:

Of course, one could argue that Eliot's memory was fresher when he assigned dates—probably in 1922—for the notebook than in 1946 or so when Hayward was insisting on correct dates for Leyris. But I suspect that TSE was no more punctilious about getting years correct in 1922 than he was for *Selected Essays* in 1932—see my note to A21 in the Eliot *Bibliography* (p. 48).

I sent him my copy of the Leyris translation.

Ricks was now once more teaching full-time at Boston University. He acknowledged receipt of my letter and the Leyris, and explained that he would write me "in a few weeks." He returned the Leyris promptly, thanking me, and telling me that he had still heard nothing from Valerie Eliot about his edition.

At last, on 27 May 1995, Ricks reported to me that he had heard from Valerie that she "is happy with my typescript" (he had heaved the traditional sigh of relief). He had considered my plea that the poems be printed in the probable order in which TSE had copied them into the notebook, but had found that he agreed with what I had written in an earlier letter: that to try to print them in that way was "just not feasible." He enclosed two pages on the subject that he had added to his preface, and hoped that "even if they don't meet with your concurrence, they aren't vexing or daft." A postscript to that letter explained that he had been unable to locate the manuscripts of "Afternoon" and "Suppressed Complex" and asked that I send him photocopies of the typed transcripts made for me by Jane Quinby. Of course I sent him the copies.

I was happy to have a final note from Boston, written on 6 September 1995, announcing that Mrs. Eliot had accepted the edition and that Fabers were planning, provisionally, to publish it in September 1996. *Inventions of the March Hare: Poems 1909–1919* was indeed issued in London on 9 September 1996. And so ends the long, long story of my involvement with the "lost" manuscripts of T. S. Eliot.

Acknowledgments

Acknowledgment is made to the following for permission to print indicated items:

Arts Club of Chicago: preface by Gertrude Stein to its *Paintings by Elie Lascaux* (Chicago, 1936).

Associated Press/World Wide Photos: photograph of Edith Wharton.

William H. Bond: excerpt from his "Jacob Blanck and *BAL*" in *Papers of the Bibliographical Society of America,* LXXXV (1992).

Robert Cowley: excerpt from Malcolm Cowley's review of *The Flowers of Friendship.*

E. Valerie Eliot: postcard of T. S. Eliot to John Rodker, 3 Oct. 1919, copyright © Set Copyrights Limited 1988; *Lines Written by T. S. Eliot to Accompany This Exhibition of Photographs* (London, 1940), copyright © 1963 by T. S. Eliot; excerpts from other letters of T. S. Eliot, copyright © 1989 Esmé Valerie Eliot.

Bruce Kellner: photographs by Carl Van Vechten of Virgil Thomson and of Elie Lascaux and Daniel-Henry Kahnweiler, both copyright © Carl Van Vechten; and excerpt from Carl Van Vechten's review of *The Flowers of Friendship.*

Edward Mendelson: "Edward Lear" by W. H. Auden; and excerpt from letter of W. H. Auden to Simon Nowell-Smith, both copyright © 1998 Estate of W. H. Auden.

New Directions Publishing Corporation: preface by Ezra Pound to T. S. Eliot's *The Waste Land, a Facsimile and Transcript of the Original Drafts,* copyright © 1971 Ezra Pound (permission given by New Directions as agent for Mary de Rachewiltz and Omar S. Pound).

Agent of Georgia O'Keeffe for the Stieglitz/O'Keeffe Archive in the Yale Collection of American Literature in the Beinecke Library: excerpt from letter of Alfred Stieglitz to Georgia O'Keeffe, 27 June 1929, copyright © 1998 Georgia O'Keeffe Foundation.

Eliot Osborn: "John, forward!" by Robert Osborn, copyright © 1998 Estate of Robert Osborn.

Mary de Rachewiltz: photograph of Olga Rudge.

Regnery Publishing, Inc. and Noel Stock: "The Search for Mrs. Wood's Program," by Donald Gallup, in *Ezra Pound Perspectives: Essays in Honor of His Eightieth Birthday,* ed. Noel Stock (Chicago, 1965), copyright © 1966 Regnery Publishing, Inc.

Yale University: letter of President Kingman Brewster to Jason Robards, Jr., 7 Nov. 1975; excerpts from letters from officials of the library and other staff members; and excerpts from documents owned by the library.

Yale University Press: excerpts from *The Bibliography of American Literature,* ed. Jacob Blanck, vols. 1 and 6, copyright © 1955 and 1973 Bibliographical Society of America; and photograph of Jacob Blanck used as frontispiece to volume 7 (1983).

Acknowledgment is made to the following for permission to print excerpts from letters to Donald Gallup: Frederick B. Adams; Rosamonde Blanck (letters of Jacob Blanck); Edward Burns (letter of Alice B. Toklas); Arthur Crook; Mollie du Sautoy (letters of Peter du Sautoy); Valerie Eliot; Paul Green; the Laura (Riding) Jackson Board of Literary Management (letters of Laura Riding Jackson, copyright © 1998 Laura (Riding) Jackson Board of Literary Management); James Earl Kendrick (letters of Virgil Thomson, copyright © 1998 Estate of Virgil Thomson); R. W. B. Lewis; Galérie Louise Leiris, Paris (letter of Maurice Jardot); Christopher Ricks; Frances Steloff; Gerald E. Stram (letters of Carlotta Monterey O'Neill); Xavier Vilató (letters of Elie Lascaux, copyright © 1998 Xavier Vilató); A. Tappan Wilder (letter of Thornton Wilder); Florence Derwent Wood. (*Apologies are offered to any person or estate overlooked in these acknowledgments. Information as to such omission will be gratefully received.*)

Acknowledgment is made to these periodicals in which parts of this book were first printed: the *Eugene O'Neill Newsletter* (by permission of the editor, Frederick C. Wilkins); the *Harvard Library Bulletin* (by permission of the editor, Kenneth E. Carpenter); the *Papers of the Bibliographical Society of America* (by permission of the society's executive secretary, Marjory Zaik); the *Times Literary Supplement,* London (by permission of the editor, Ferdinand Mount); the *Yale University Library Gazette* (by permission of the editor, Stephen R. Parks).

I record gratefully my appreciation for the concern shown for my book by Christa Sammons as its editor and Ralph Franklin as its publisher. For suggestions and corrections I am indebted to Ken Crilly, Bruce Kellner, Sue Davidson Lowe, Stephen Parks, Harold Samuel, Anthony Tommasini, Patricia Willis, and Marjorie Wynne. Whatever success I enjoyed during my thirty-three years as curator of the Yale Collection of American Literature was contributed to importantly by the librarians under whom I served (James Babb, Herman Liebert, Louis Martz, Rutherford Rogers, and James Tanis), and by many past and present colleagues, among them Matthew Blake, Lisa Browar, Peter Dzwonkoski, Richard Johnson, Stephen Jones, Karen Marinuzzi, Lori Misura, Kenneth Nesheim, Suzanne Rutter, Constance Tyson, Anne Whelpley, Althea Green Wilson, and Donald Wing. The memory of Norman Holmes Pearson, his friendship and counsel, and the enormous contribution he made to our university will always continue green.

D.C.G.

Index